VOICES
from the
GODS

VOICES
from the
GODS
Speaking with Tongues

David Christie-Murray

Routledge & Kegan Paul
London and Henley

First published in 1978
by Routledge & Kegan Paul Ltd
39 Store Street,
London WC1E 7DD and
Broadway House,
Newtown Road,
Henley-on-Thames,
Oxon RG9 1EN
Photoset in 11 on 13 Garamond by
Kelly and Wright, Bradford-on-Avon, Wiltshire
and printed in Great Britain by
Redwood Burn Ltd
Trowbridge and Esher
Plates printed by
Headley Brothers Ltd, Ashford, Kent

British Library Cataloguing in Publication Data

Christie-Murray, David

Voices from the gods.
1. Glossolalia
I. Title
291.4'2   BL54   78-40620

ISBN 0 7100 8810 8

Contents

Contents

Illustrations

Preface

My interest in speaking with tongues began when, some forty years ago, I heard an almost illiterate charwoman at a Pentecostalist meeting pour out a paean of fluent and ecstatic praise in what seemed a foreign language. Since then I have learned that glossolalia (paranormal speaking in tongues) and xenolalia (paranormal speaking in allegedly recognizable foreign languages) are features of many other sub-cultures, besides Pentecostalist Christian. Pentecostalism alone has grown so rapidly in the present century that something like one in every four or five hundred of the world's present inhabitants has spoken in Christian tongues at some time in his life; and if all the cultures which exhibit glossolalia, including Spiritualism, are included in the reckoning, the proportion is appreciably higher. It is true that in the latter cases tongues are more limited than with Pentecostalists; for whereas every Christian in many Pentecostalist denominations is expected to speak in tongues at least once, as a sign of his baptism with the Holy Spirit, the gift in the other cultures is limited to individuals, shamans and mediums.

The bibliography of glossolalia is far more extensive than might be expected. The books and articles deal, however, with limited aspects of the subject – Christian, anthropological, Spiritiualistic, linguistic or psychological – and there has been no survey which tries to give an introduction to the whole subject and discover the relationship, if any, between tongues spoken by different cultures. Psychological explanations, moreover, which seemed final in the 1920s have been overtaken by recent developments. Tongues are not necessarily motor-automata exhibited by illiterates worked up into pathological mental states by revivalist campaigns. They are practised by educated, intelligent worshippers in quietness and without emotionalism and are taken seriously by many in the older-established Churches.

Nor is there any reason why there should not be varieties of glossolalia. Psychologists and theologians are apt to assume that outbreaks of motor-automata and charismata are always to be ascribed to approximately similar conditions. But each case must be taken on its merits and the evidence, after being studied as objectively as possible, allowed to speak for itself.

Changes in the law and in the atmosphere of thought mean that phenomena once suspect can be studied objectively in the open. There is also widespread contemporary interest in the occult and anything connected with it, both on a popular level and among serious scholars trying to add an understanding of psychical phenomena to the body of human knowledge. It is hoped that this book may have something of interest for both these, as well as for the ordinary reader who is perhaps only slightly affected by the contemporary interest in strange phenomena. All these types of reader may like to have a general introduction in all its ramifications, and a one-volume alternative to the collecting of a not-inconsiderable library.

Any author owes a debt to more people than he can possibly name. My own obligation is not only to the many hundreds of books and articles written on speaking in tongues by theologians and Spiritualists but to many individuals who, hearing of my interest, communicated spontaneously with me. I am particularly indebted to the headquarters staff of the Society for Psychical Research, to Mr Nigel Buckmaster, a member of the Society, who, after a chance meeting in its Library, supplied me with a bibliography which otherwise might have taken me many months to collect, and to Dr W. J. Samarin, Professor of Linguistics at the University of Toronto who, unasked, sent me copies of some of his important articles on glossolalia containing the findings of linguistic scholarship. In naming these benefactors I acknowledge equally many others, recorded where possible in the Notes or in the Bibliography.

Acknowledgments

The author and publishers are grateful for permission to quote from the following works:

Morton Kelsey, *Tongue Speaking*, Doubleday, New York; J. Beattie and J. Middleton (eds), *Spirit Mediumship and Society in Africa*, Routledge & Kegan Paul, London; J. L. Sherrill, *They Speak with other Tongues*, Hodder & Stoughton, London; X. M. Twigg, private correspondence; New English Bible, 2nd edition © 1970, by permission of Oxford and Cambridge University Presses; the articles of W. J. Samarin.

Permission to use the illustrations has been courteously granted by: National Gallery (1); Mary Evans Picture Library (2–9); Keystone Press Agency (10).

1

Tongues in
Non-Christian Cultures

Glossolalia in the Bible is a specifically Christian phenomenon
and mentioned only in the New Testament. It is true that there
was substantially no fundamental difference between the
Hebrew doctrine of possession by spirits, especially the Spirit
of God, and the Christian; any supernormal ability or faculty
among his followers came to be attributed to the Spirit of
Jahweh, and the activity of false spirits in deceiving and
misleading men was equally recognized. It is also true that some
Biblical scholars see glossolalia under every Old Testament
prophet's tongue; but all passages thought to refer possibly to
tongues may be interpreted, usually with more justification, in
other ways. Isaiah's 'ghosts and familiar spirits who squeak and
gibber' (Isaiah 8:19) may simply have been producing artistic
preliminaries to intelligible utterances. The same prophet's
words, 'So it will be with barbarous speech and strange tongue
that this people will hear God speaking' (28:11), though
quoted by St Paul in I Corinthians 14:21 in his discourse about
tongues, in context plainly means, 'If God's people will not
learn from his prophet, then they will have to learn from foreign
invaders talking a strange language.' There is a continuity of
thought between the Old Testament and the New. The earliest
Christians were, after all, Jews, at first perfectly orthodox in
every way except that they were convinced that Jesus, rejected by

1

their Establishment, was the Messiah. There were charismata in both Testaments – 'I believe in the Holy Ghost . . . who spake by the prophets' is no mere Christian hindsight. But there is also an awareness of something entirely new. The gifts of the Spirit in Jerusalem at the first Whitsun and as manifested by the church at Corinth were unlike anything to be found in the old dispensation.

Greek culture probably had more influence on the Christian churches of Asia Minor than Hebrew. 'The Greek belief in mantic ecstasy and the Greek affection for the mysterious and eloquent explain the predominance of [tongues] in the [Corinthian] community.'[1] A language of ghosts is said to have been spoken in an old Corinthian religion. In the cult of Thracian Dionysus the god-possessed devotee spoke *glottys Baccheia*,[2] with the tongue (personality or language?) of Bacchus. The Homeric 'Hymn to Apollo', lines 162–4, suggests that 'the Delian singers reproduced the speech and the musical accompaniment of the various pilgrims: but there is no other reference to this curious mimicry of (apparently) different dialects',[3] a passage which will be seen to be relevant to the disciples' experience at the first Whitsun. Sophocles in his *Ajax* writes:

> Then two white-footed rams he found:
> Of one, beheaded first, the tongue
> He snipped, then far the carcase flung.
> The other, to a pillar lashed
> Erect, with double rein, he threshed,
> And as he plied the whistling thong
> He uttered imprecations strong
> Dread words a god, no man, had taught.[4]

Herodotus (c.480–425 BC) gives the one allegedly historical account of xenolalia in classical times when he describes how the diviner in the temple of Ptoan Apollo talked Carian to Mys of Europa who had come to consult him.[5] But Herodotus is not trustworthy in recounting events he did not personally witness, and the incident could have been stage-managed.

There are many references in classical literature to spirit-or god-inspired ecstasy – but few, if any, that mention tongues. Clement of Alexandria is quoted as saying, 'Plato attributes a peculiar dialect to the gods, inferring this from dreams and oracles, and especially from demoniacs who do not speak their own language or dialect, but that of the daemons who are entered into them',[6] but Clement may have read more into the philosopher's words than he intended.

Yet what Plato calls 'theomania' was to be widely found in the Greek world and it would have been strange if Greek converts to Christianity had not brought it with them. And there are strains in the Stoic concept of a divine world-spirit manifesting itself through human personalities which are not far from Pauline thought.

Quintilian (AD 40–c.100) in post-Christian times mentions the 'more unusual voices of the more secret language which the Greeks call "glossai"',[7] while Dio Chrysostom (AD c.40–120) in his 'Tenth Discourse on Servants' speaks of the language of the gods and hints at sham glossolalia in referring to 'persons who know two or three Persian, Median or Assyrian words and thus fool the ignorant'.[8] Lucian (AD c.120–90) mentions an Alexander of Abonutichius who utters 'unintelligible vocables which sound like Hebrew or Phoenician'.[9]

Besides the writings ascribed to individuals there are formulae and unintelligible lists of names and letters used in magical papyri for the invoking of gods and spirits and thought by some to derive from glossolalia. In these there are echoes of oriental languages mingled with gibberish, thought to have originated in allegedly supra-terrestrial tongues used by gods and spirits, each class being allocated its peculiar language or dialect. The ecstasies of oriental cults, common in the Roman Empire, are described by Lucretius, Catullus and Apuleius, and that associated with Hermes is known to have practised glossolalia. That something akin to tongues was known among pagans in the second century is shown in the reports of the Christian writer, Irenaeus,[10] about the Gnostic magician Marcus and his prophetesses, who indulged in unintelligible ecstatic speeches.

3

It is possible that one factor which later caused Christian leaders to look with disfavour on charismatic expression was the similarity of its ecstasies to those of contemporary heathen cults. Another is that in the general evolutionary pattern of religions certain stages and phenomena are usual and that advanced religions develop beyond these. There are, however, few advanced religions in the world and a great many primitive ones. To the ordinary Bible reader to whom the story of Pentecost appears as an experience never before undergone by any mortal, it comes as a shock to discover that glossolalia is a commonplace in human cultures from Asia to America and Siberia to Africa. The reasons for this are that animism is an early stage in the evolution of religions; that primitive peoples imbued with animistic beliefs commonly accept that human beings may be possessed by spirits and speak their languages when under possession; and that a very large number of religions, because of a lack of writing essential for progress, have not advanced beyond the animistic stage and may have remained in it for centuries.

Scientific anthropology is little more than a century old. Early reports of savage cultures came from men untrained and often incompetent to judge accurately. 'Command performances' may have drawn from natives what they thought was expected of them rather than their normal practices. Yet even with these caveats there is sufficient evidence from the past supported by scientific observation in recent times to sustain the surmise that glossolia may have existed throughout the world for hundreds of years.

For the most part, references in anthropological literature to the ecstatic vocalization arising from shamanistic ceremonies are brief, vague and mentioned in passing without definition. But L. Carlyle May has collected and collated reports from a number of authorities and classified the types of primitive glossolalia.[11] There are four: (1) languages of spirits; (2) sacerdotal languages; (3) languages of animals; (4) xenolalia. There are also *phonations frustes* (inarticulate sounds which sometimes precede glossolalia and are, as it were, its raw material) and

4

ermeneglossia (interpretation of tongues). Under (1) he lists the speaking of languages of supernatural beings which occurs frequently in divinatory and cursing ceremonies while the speakers are entranced or religiously exalted. The Hudson Bay Eskimos spoke to the spirits in their own language amid sounds of trickling water, rushing wind, snuffling of walrus and growling of bear. There are spirit tongues among the shamanistic complexes of the Chukchee; the north-west and south-east Koryak (Asiatic Eskimos); the Lapps, Yakuts and Tungus; and the Samoyeds. Among the peoples of Siberia, 'he who is to become a shaman begins to rage like a raving madman. He suddenly utters incoherent words, falls unconscious', etc. Many spirit language words of the Asiatic Eskimos are analogous to the spirit languages of the Eskimos in the Alaska and Atlantic areas. A Tungus shaman is supposed to learn the entire language of nature in his trance. In the Ainu religion, the self-hypnotized shaman becomes the mouthpiece of gods who speak through him. He neither knows nor remembers what he says. The Hala (shaman) of the Semang pigmies speak to celestial spirits in their language and, among the Papar, Putatam and Tuaran groups of North Borneo cult, priestesses offer incantations to a *gusi* (sacred jar) in a language known only to the spirits and themselves. In the Mortlock Islands of Micronesia, spirits act upon the priest, causing him to twitch, nod and speak in a language very different from his ordinary speech. In the Solomon Islands, the medium talks with the voice of a ghost. Trhi-speaking priests of the Gold Coast (Ghana) mutter words or sentences in croaking, guttural voices, both vocabulary and voices being those of gods.

To May's collection may be added examples of god, spirit or demon tongues culled from other authorities. Davenport writes that in primitive China, when a supposed spirit entered a man, his 'eyes close tightly, his whole body trembles, his hands and feet continually move, his hair loosens from the braid – then he begins to speak, and is able to talk not only in his own dialect, but in others as well.'[12] This spirit-inspired human language is almost comparable with the Christian gift of 'prophecy' mentioned in Corinthians. Oesterreich mentions the possession of a young man under the auspices of the priesthood of the Wu, in his day 'still . . . the repository of possession'.

> [He] begins to moan; some incoherent talk follows, mingled with cries; but all this is oracular language which reveals unknown things. . . . An association of men . . . is now quickly formed. . . . Henceforth they are frequently seen in this temple to conjure the spirit into him and interpret the strange sounds he utters; and in the end it is they alone who, by dint of experience and exercise, can understand those inspired sounds and translate them into human language. . . . The symptoms of the descent of the spirit into the medium shortly appear. . . . This is the proper moment for the consultant or the interpreter to put his questions. Incoherent shrill sounds are the answer; but the interpreter translates this divine language with the greatest fluency into the intelligible human tongue, while another brother writes these revelations down on paper.[13]

Van der Goltz records that members of the religious sect of the Shang-ti-hui in a state of ecstasy utter exhortations, reproaches and predictions in often unintelligible but generally rhythmical phrases. He also mentions 'spirit-hopping', when someone is ill. An old witch is summoned who, doing a hopping dance on one leg, 'mutters without intermission unintelligible words which seem to be now song and now rhythm. The words are not consecutive, but are subject to a certain rhythm.'[14]

A collection of essays, *Spirit Mediumship and Society in Africa*,[15] contains several allusions to spirit language. In Kalabari religion an 'Oru' (spirit) manifests its presence not by frenetic behaviour but by the speaking of an alien tongue. Samples of the 'fairly standard water-people's language' spoken by such spirits suggest that many words are formed by substitution of syllables in ordinary Kalabari words, lengthened forms from the drum-language, or a stuttering form of ordinary Kalabari. Some spirits speak in the tongues of neighbouring tribes, professedly not understood by those possessed, and require an interpreter.

Tonga mediums claim a knowledge of all languages, and spirit-possessed 'foreign dancers speak in the language of their spirit's homeland'.

The Zulu Amandiki and Amandawu cults possess their own languages, usually a distorted form of Zulu. Amandawe doctors cure their patients by inducing one of their ancestral spirits to enter an initiate; following days of exhausting dancing, the spirit expresses itself in a so-called foreign tongue, Indian or Thongan. The languages may be only a series of meaningless sounds. Sometimes as many as seven ancestral spirits can enter the possessed person, speaking different languages, and modern tongues such as 'English' tend to supplant the more traditional. Another Zulu treatment of some psychological illnesses is the smoking of a certain mixture which induces possession and results in the patient's speaking in a 'foreign' language appropriate to the medicine administered.

Like the Zulus, the Segeju of Tanzania use dancing (which lasts for a week) in the Shetani cult for the healing of spirit-possessed women. One of the symptoms of possession is speaking in tongues. During the dance the medicine man (*mganga*) and drummers sometimes chant 'in an esoteric tongue not understood by ordinary people'. The climax comes when the *shetani* is to reveal its name. The patient is enclosed in a 'tent' of cloths held round her by women dancers, from which comes the squeaky voice of the *shetani*. The *mganga* feeds a mixture of sacrificial goat's blood and honey to the women, several of whom behave wildly and speak with tongues.

When Bunzoro doctor diviners persuade a 'destructible' ghost to leave its victim, it often uses the patient as a medium, protesting energetically in a falsetto voice and in a special 'ghost' vocabulary; and Bunzoro mediums have to acquire an unfamiliar vocabulary said to be used by ghosts and spirits.

Among the Alur, Jok Riba, a nature deity, speaks *dhuthugi* – 'the language of their own country', that is, that of Jok – which sounds like meaningless groans.

Alur séances are lacking in formal elaboration and especially in the ritually induced terror which is used to ensure secrecy in the nyoro and sumbwa rites. All employ garbled speech but in alur again, it is not formalized into a secret 'language' as in the other two areas.

In the practice of Sukuma, a magician, curing a patient,

hiccoughs a little and mutters to himself in a rising crescendo, often accompanied by piercing whistling resembling the Masai cattle-calls. The muttering then becomes clearer and resolves itself into a jumble of words and sounds uttered in falsetto voice. . . . Informants state that the language of this delirium is *kinaturu*, which is regarded as the tongue of the ancestors of all magicians, since they are all thought to have descended from the Naturu tribe. This, however, is unlikely, as the sounds seem to be merely a repetitious jumble of monosyllables, used because of their phonetic simplicity rather than because they might make connected phrases, and indeed no one was able to interpret any of the words or phrases used. The connection with Naturu, a small hunting tribe to the south-east, seems to be mythical; there is certainly no present connection between mediums and this tribe. There does not seem to be a distinct vocabulary as with the Buchwezi cult in Usukuma, possibly because mediumship no longer involves any group activities or initiation in which such a vocabulary could have been learnt and passed on.

In Ankole glossolalia entered through western Pentecostalist missions. 'An independent group, known as Lisanga, is remembered as "making horrible noises to show their closeness to God".' 'In Nkore there is a secret language used only within the society; and [African] Israel [a title used to mean 'set apart as the people of God'] uses theological terminology which makes no sense outside the context of Christian Spirit-possession.'

Every king of Uganda had a *mandwa* (medium) to represent him after his death. Once, when Canon Roscoe was hearing the history of the kings from a *mandwa*, the man suddenly began to talk allegedly in the obsolete form of Luganda spoken three centuries before in the lifetime of the dead king whom he represented. Nor was the *mandwa's* personality his own. To Roscoe the phenomenon seemed like a genuine case of possession by the dead, until the rational explanation was presented to him that each clan in Uganda responsible for providing the *mandwas* of the dead kings had to transmit orally and mimetically the characteristics of their masters at the time of their decease. 'In the clan to whom Roscoe's *mandwa* belonged the obsolete dialect was preserved – how much of it we do not know – as a part of the mantic technique.'[16]

Zar, or Sar, spirits, usually troubling women, are to be found in Africa and the near East. The *shechah* (exorcist) does not question the patient herself but the spirit possessing her, frequently using the Zar language which cannot be understood without the *shechah's* interpretation. Among the Somalis the Zars demand through the lips of women luxurious clothes, perfume and exotic dainties from their menfolk in their own language, translated, for a suitable fee, by female shamans who know how to handle them. External or 'peripheral' spirits of neighbouring peoples and of Europeans regularly plague the Kamba women of East Africa who speak in the supposed languages of the invading spirits. A similar invasion developed about 1914 when spirits from the Shona peoples of Southern Rhodesia caused Venda women of southern Africa to speak in the Shona dialect.

Status rather than possessions seems to be the object of spirits in Mafia Island, off the coast of Tanzania. There the Muslim population consists of tribal elements arranged in a clear order of precedence with the Pakomo, the most African and least Arabian in ethnic affiliation, occupying the lowest rung. Parallel to a Pakomo shamanistic cult is a separate possession-cult among the higher Pakomo status groups that is restricted to women. These are prone to possession by spirits coming over the sea from Arabia who cause those they possess to speak in Arabic. Also in East Africa the Mpepo possession sickness can descend, epidemic-like, on whole regions, causing

9

its victims to speak in strange voices, the women in a deep bass, or in a foreign tongue such as Swahili or English which they neither speak normally nor understand.[17]

Spirit language is spoken in many parts of the world. In Malaya, for example, possessing spirits are said to use a language which strikingly recalls ancient Batak, expressed partly in cautious circumlocutions, partly in quite strange words. It is unlikely that mediums could have practised the language previously. A woman possessed by the spirit of a *datu* or *dato* (wizard), though normally unable to read, will read a magic book fluently in a singing voice, such as the wizard used in his lifetime. A sick Malay after exorcism speaks in spirit-language. The god Oru, of the Sandwich Islands, throws his priest into a frenzy in which the latter reveals Oru's will in shrill cries and violent indistinct sounds which other priests interpret. In Tahiti, men normally lacking eloquence, under possession declare the will of the gods and prophesy future events with all the fire and skill of accomplished orators, an experience paralleled, as will be seen, in Christianity.

In earlier times, the Sufi of Islam continued a tradition of God's unintelligible speech. This had originated from the prophet Mohammed's telling that he had heard sounds and confused speech which he understood only after they had ceased, and that it was a great effort for him to pass to the state of logical and intelligible language. The later writers described such speech, and it is possible that their descriptions relate to a practice comparable to tongues, although they specify hearing and translating a speech beyond comprehension, not uttering one. Islam also has a tradition of the names of God which are numberless; for each name there is a tongue and for each tongue a word.[18] Among Muslims in India, individuals are said to have recited portions of the Koran in its original language, Arabic, without having previously learned them.

Examples of spirit-possession of the type exhibited by some western trance-mediums can be found all over the world, often accompanied by faculties which are dormant in the normal state. Unmusical people sing, unliterary individuals write

10

poetry. When their trance is over, they are unaware of what they have done.

Sacerdotal language is not attributed to supernatural agencies. It may be completely unknown to any but the priest, or it may be full of obsolete words. Red Indian priests, for example, may invoke the Great Turtle in articulate but unknown language and afterwards interpret their own speech, giving, it is claimed, correct information. When South Sea Island priests proclaim the will of the gods, they achieve a religious enthusiasm in which their language becomes weighty and imposing. Again Christian experience is paralleled in that people without natural eloquence under enthusiasm speak in majestic language very different from that in common use and employed only by chieftains and orators. Eskimo shamans of East Greenland speak a mystic language identical for all who practise in that area.

The Dyak *manang* (medicine man) intones a *timong*, a monotonous chant which is a mixture of prayer, invocation and imprecation, with archaic forms and disused words, sense giving way to the demands of rhyme with jingling endings. The Macassarese and Buginese priests of southern Celebes speak in a language like old Buginese preserved in an ancient epic. The Olo-ngadju Dyaks of Borneo, during exorcism rites, chant language containing words either obsolete or of Malayan origin. Balinese priests use an oracular speech which is probably an archaic form of their language and may include words of Pali and Sanskrit. In Haitian ritual the special language used by religiously excited priests may contain vestiges of African with some Spanish and Indian words, or it may be oriental in origin. Only the god is supposed to understand it – it is doubtful if the priest does. All these languages are learned, like the Latin and other archaic languages used by some Christian churches, and are said to be stereotyped argots used by shamans through many centuries.

Peruvian priests uttering oracles worked themselves into a frenzy of dancing and leaping by the drinking of *chicha* and the inhalation of narcotic smoke until they fell into trances. On recovering from these they gave forth the oracles in a language incomprehensible to the uninitiated. In Siberia shamans speak *khorro*, 'shaman's language', during their fits of inspiration. *Khorro* is usually the language of a neighbouring people which the shaman himself does not understand. A Tungus shaman will, when inspired, sometimes talk Koryak, though normally quite ignorant of the language. One such shaman was heard making a speech in a drawling chant in which the Tungus who were present joined, but this chant's language was unknown.

Xenolalia recorded by anthropologists is attributed to the same psychological causes as western xenolalia. Possessed persons in Ghana, for example, often speak and understand languages of which they have no normal knowledge, but investigation of their life-histories always reveals that at some time in childhood they were exposed to the languages and had forgotten them. Chinese in Fukien, a southern province, can, when possessed by demons, speak Mandarin, a northern dialect – but, presumably, they will have heard Mandarin spoken at some time in their lives. Among the people of Anadirsk near the Behring Strait, some, usually women, have spasmodic outbreaks of second-sight during which they speak languages which they are said never to have heard, particularly Yakut, but the accounts may be garbled and misunderstood. The practice is paralleled by that of the lamas and Bön priests of Tibet who in their incantations use corrupt Sanskrit formulae which they do not understand.

The practice of xenolalia is claimed in some cases where it is doubtful. Among the Singpho of south-east Asia a *natzo* (conjurer of spirits) heals the sick by calling on his *nat* or demon to possess him and give the cure. The *nat* is the soul of a dead *foreign* prince, and it can be assumed that the attribution of the answer to a foreign spirit is a rationalized explanation of glossolalia being spoken. In the more sophisticated religion of Islam, devotees attempting to achieve mantic dreams by practising with strict intention the ritual acts of Muslim prayer (which can be extremely strenuous) repeated gibberish which seemed Hebrew or Aramaic in origin.

A strange case of possession is known, though only by hearsay (for Europeans are not allowed to see the phenomenon) among the Bantu. The possessed woman disappears from her home at night and is found the next morning tied to a branch at the top of a high tree by lianas. Upon being freed she glides like a snake down the trunk and hangs for several moments suspended above the ground, speaking fluently a language of which she previously knew not a single word. It cannot be known whether this is xenolalia or intended to be 'snake-language', or some incubated and artificial tongue.

Even if it is accepted that natives have put on acts for the benefit of missionaries and other investigators of what they thought was expected of them, or that professional sorcerers work themselves up artificially or wholly feign their phenomena, there seem to be enough examples of genuine glossolalia, such as the above, culled from incidental reading, to prove that speaking in tongues is, indeed, a very widespread practice in human culture. It may be asked why natives should have assumed that those interested in their customs required glossolalia if they did not normally practise it – it is not the kind of activity which would spring universally to mind unless it already existed. As for exaggeration or pretence, the capacity of human beings to attain expected charismatic gifts by psychological means will be sufficiently exemplified in subsequent chapters for such explanations to be unnecessary, though they may apply in individual cases. It can be stated with some confidence that if an anthropologist were to work systematically through the literature of his subject, he would find glossolalia in one form or another to be almost universal.

2

The First Whitsun

So many are the theories put forward by scholars about what happened at the Feast of Pentecost after Jesus's death that a complete study of the account in Acts 2 would fill a volume by itself. At one extreme, radical critics, basing their contentions on textual analysis or a rejection of anything savouring of the miraculous, maintain that nothing out of the ordinary happened. They allege that the story is based on accounts exaggerated by gullible contemporaries into the marvellous and is written in its present form by an editor with no first-hand knowledge of the phenomena he was describing. Conservative critics like the *Catholic Encyclopedia*, on the other hand, write that 'faithful adherence to the text of Sacred Scripture makes it obligatory to reject those opinions which turn the charism of tongues into little more than infantile babbling, incoherent exclamation, pythonic utterances or prophetic demonstration of the archaic kind'.[1]

The radicals base their views on the fact that the account is clearly not that of an eye-witness. An examination of the New English Bible version of the relevant passage[2] will show how vague its details are.

> While the Day of Pentecost was running its course they were all [the twelve apostles? or the 120 followers of Christ

14

mentioned in Acts 1:15?] in one place [where? the upper
room of the Last Supper would have been small for 120
members; a room in the precincts of the Temple is likely],
when suddenly there came from the sky a noise like that of a
strong driving wind, which filled the whole house [the Greek
can mean a private house, a room in a house, the Temple or a
part of the Temple] where they were sitting. And there
appeared to them tongues like flames of fire, dispersed
among them and resting on each one. And they were all
[again, the twelve or the 120?] filled with the Holy Spirit and
began to talk in other tongues, as the Spirit gave them power
of utterance.

Now there were living in Jerusalem devout Jews drawn
from every nation under heaven; and at this sound [the wind?
the tongues? or both?] the crowd gathered, all bewildered
because each heard his own language spoken [were the
speakers still inside the building with their hearers crowding
round the door and windows? Were they all shouting
together, in which case how could any of them have been
heard distinctly? Did they pour out, shouting in ecstasy, into
the street or Temple courtyard?]. They were amazed and in
their astonishment exclaimed, 'Why, they are all Galileans,
are they not, these men who are speaking? How is it that we
hear them, each of us in his own native language? . . . we
hear them telling in our own tongues the great things God
has done.' [No individual made this speech, which is
obviously a composite utterance designed to inform the
reader.] And they were all amazed and perplexed, saying to
one another, 'What can this mean?' Others said
contemptuously, 'They have been drinking.'

Peter, with the eleven apostles round him, their ecstasy
apparently sobered into quietness, then explains in the
vernacular that his companions could not be drunk, seeing that
it was only nine in the morning. (No Jew worthy of the name
would have touched food or drink until the religious services
were over.) The ecstasy, Peter continues, is a fulfilment of the

15

prophecy that in the last days God's spirit will be poured out on everyone, accompanied by portents and signs occurring before the day of the Lord comes. (A general outpouring of the Spirit of God was part of Israel's eschatological hope.) He concludes by references to Jesus of Nazareth, crucified but raised to life again, who received the Holy Spirit from the Father and 'all that you now see and hear flows from him'.[3] God has made him Lord and Messiah.

Most of the radical critics show an unawareness of the cognate phenomena to be found so widely in human culture. Some of their theories smell too much of the study and reflect minds closed not only to the miraculous but even to the psychologically abnormal. Lack of a considered treatment here of their arguments does not mean ignorance nor a cavalier treatment of them. But the events at Pentecost could have happened as stated without outraging the susceptibilities of any critic with an anti-miracle bias; while Christian believers can see miracle in its literal sense of 'something to be wondered at' in the timing of the event and its place and purpose in the economy of God.

Once an event has passed into history, no one can be certain that any account of it is at best more than approximately accurate. So to say that the following reconstruction could have happened is not to state dogmatically that it did happen but only that it is a possible occurrence, fits the recorded facts and does not outrage probability. The facts can be accepted by both radicals and conservatives, although they will differ in their interpretation of them.

The first followers of Jesus were orthodox Jews who differed from their co-religionists only in that they claimed to have discovered and recognized the Messiah. They were in Jerusalem partly to keep the feast, which all male Jews were required to attend, partly to obey the command of Jesus to await the fulfilment of a promise of the coming of the Holy Spirit. They did not know the way in which the gift would come, but only that it would.

On the Day of Pentecost the priests opened the gates of the Temple to worshippers at midnight. It is probable that Jesus's male followers would have entered the Temple together early as a community of like-minded men and would have occupied one of the large rooms affixed to the interior of the Temple courtyard wall. If the number 120 included women who, if they had gone to worship, would have been confined to the Court of the Women, the maximum would have been perhaps a hundred, possibly half that number (there could easily have been more women than men among Jesus's followers). Even if Peter and his friends had not gone early to the Temple in order to get a room to themselves, it seems certain that, as loyal Jews for whom the feast might have an added significance they would have been there before nine o'clock, the hour of public prayer on one of the most important feast-days in the Jewish calendar. This is a strong argument that the speaking with tongues happened in the Temple, for it is unlikely that the disciples, all faithful Jews, would have segregated themselves from the worship of their fellows on that day. The 'all in one place' is a semi-liturgical expression meaning almost 'in church'.

The disciples, then, can be pictured worshipping together in a large room within the Temple precincts shortly before the official hour of prayer. They hear the sound of the 'strong driving wind' which fills the room and see, perhaps in the centre of the room under the ceiling a body of flames of fire, maybe like the petals of a flower, which separate from each other and linger, one over the head of each disciple. The wind and flames may very well have been collective hallucinations, heard and seen only by those in the room. They were followed by a mass ecstasy in which the praises of God, shouted aloud in foreign languages, was the noise which drew the other worshippers in the Temple to the room in which the disciples were.

The ecstatics, like the early Old Testament bands of prophets and the modern Dervishes, unable to remain still, emerged from the doorway one by one, each speaking a different tongue and attracting to himself, as he came out, speakers of the language in which he was crying the praises of God. So, for a time, we can imagine little knots of men, each surrounding an individual talking their own language. Some of those in the Temple on the fringes of the crowds, not understanding any language they heard spoken and seeing only the ecstasy, in its effects not unlike intoxication, accused the disciples of being drunk. In time the ecstasy died down, and Peter took the opportunity to preach Jesus, crucified and raised, as the Messiah.

It should be noted that the Acts account says only that the disciples told in tongues 'the great things God has done'. They praised, not preached. There is no suggestion that the gift of tongues outlasted the ecstasy, that their content was Christian, or that the speakers understood what they were saying. Christians, as well as others, have misunderstood the record and thought that tongues were given miraculously so that the first missionaries could preach to all nations in their own languages. There are sad instances of men who have gone to foreign lands in the faith that the Holy Spirit would give them the language to speak the moment they disembarked; and who, unable to express their simplest wants, have almost starved and returned disillusioned at least with their interpretation of Scripture.

This suggested reconstruction will seem at first sight too extraordinary for acceptance by a twentieth-century reader living in a sceptical age. Let us examine the argument in more detail.

First, the disciples formed a 'psychological crowd'. They had been together constantly, as commanded by Jesus, waiting for and expecting the coming with power of the Holy Spirit that had been promised them. They were living in a spiritual limbo between the departure of Jesus and the coming of the Comforter, united in their expectancy of and longing for the fulfilment of Christ's word to them. The tense emotional atmosphere engendered by these conditions, heightened by their awareness that the promise was likely to be fulfilled that very day, brought them to a pitch of mass receptivity which prepared them for almost anything. On a less intense level something of the same kind can be seen in the 'waiting meetings' of Pentecostalist churches where believers pray for the

18

baptism with the Spirit in the expectancy that some of those present will receive it and show it by speaking with tongues.

Pentecostalists know what form the baptism should take. The first disciples did not know what to expect. Yet they knew that Pentecost was likely to be the day on which the gift would come. It was the first major feast after the Passover at which Jesus had been crucified and therefore logically a day on which the next step forward for the members of the Messiah's kingdom might be revealed. Second, Jesus had promised his disciples that, after staying in the city, they would be 'armed with power from above', and Pentecost was a feast which accentuated the power of God. Third, the feast was associated with the giving of the Law and might therefore be connected in the disciples' minds with the new gift that had been promised.

There were hints as to the vehicles of the expected power in the readings from the Law and Prophets and in the Psalms appointed for the feast, probably established by the time of Christ. All but the first of these – Deuteronomy 19:3 or Exodus 19; Habbukuk 3 or Ezekiel 1; and Psalms 29 and 68 – have certain features in common. Fire blazes from Sinai in Exodus 19; whirlwind, with other manifestations, attends the Lord in his work in Habbukuk 3; wind and flashes of fire are seen in Ezekiel; fire and power are ascribed to the Lord in Psalm 29; wind driving smoke and fire melting wax symbolize God's scattering of his enemies in Psalm 68. Isolated phrases emphasize detailed similarities. 'I saw a storm wind . . . with flashes of fire and brilliant light about it,'[4] writes Ezekiel. Acts records 'suddenly there came from the sky a noise like that of a strong driving wind . . . and there appeared to them tongues like flames of fire'.[5] Psalm 29:7, 'The voice of the Lord makes flames of fire burst forth' ('divideth the flames of fire' is the Authorized Version translation) corresponds to Acts 2:3, 'flames of fire dispersed among them'. The same Psalm uses the phrase, 'the voice of the Lord', no fewer than seven times, and in verse 9 asserts that 'in his temple doth every one speak of his glory' (AV). The exultation of Psalm 68 with its 'But the righteous are joyful, they exult before God, they are jubilant

19

and shout for joy. Sing the praises of God, raise a psalm to his name, extol him',[6] suggest the ecstasy the power of the Spirit was to bring.

Part of Jewish lore is the Rabbinic tradition that, when the voice of God uttered the Law from Sinai, the one sound was divided into the seventy-two languages that were then believed to comprise all the tongues of earth. A Midrash on Psalm 68:11 says, 'When the Word went forth from Sinai, it became seven voices, and from the seven voices was divided into seventy tongues. As sparks leap from the anvil, there came a great host of proclaiming voices.'[7] Philo, a Jewish philosopher born about 20 BC, describes a stream of fire out of which a voice spoke to each hearer in his own language at Sinai. 'I should suppose,' he writes,

> that God wrought on this occasion a miracle of a truly holy kind by bidding an invisible sound to be created . . . which giving shape and tension to the air and changing it to flaming fire, sounded forth like a breath, a trumpet, an articulate voice so loud that it appeared to be equally audible to the farthest as well as to the nearest . . . the new miraculous voice was set in action and kept in flame by the power of God which breathed upon it and spread it abroad on every side. . . . For from the midst of the fire (on Sinai) that streamed from heaven there sounded forth to their utter amazement a voice, for the flame became articulate speech in the language familiar to the audience.[8]

The disciples might have heard the Midrash read mere hours before their Pentecostal experience. They were almost certainly unacquainted with Philo, but the association of tongues of fire with speech was 'in the air' and was enough to suggest to them the form that the power from on high should take. In Jewish thought any unusual appearance of fire was an emblem of the presence of God. The divine presence or Shekinah was said to rest on the pious Jew studying the Law, and there were stories of rabbis encircled with fire as they discussed holy writings. In pagan circles, flames were said to be seen round the heads of ecstatics in the Dionysian cult, while in modern Spiritualistic séances there are alleged spontaneous appearances of flame-like lights. The wind was a symbol of the Spirit and connected closely with him both in the Old Testament and in the thought of Christ – 'The wind blows where it wills; you hear the sound of it, but you do not know where it comes from, or where it is going. So with everyone who is born of the Spirit'.[9]

There are cases of mass hallucination in history where the creation by one person of an appearance for himself of something which a number of people have been ardently longing to see has almost instantaneously communicated the same vision to them. The wind and fire may have seemed objective to the disciples and, even if hallucinations, may have symbolized a real spiritual experience. There is, however, no need to doubt the objectivity of the tongues they spoke nor the fact that they were heard by all within earshot, for all the conditions were right for such an outburst.

There are literally hundreds of cases known to students of medicine and abnormal psychology in which patients in trance, ecstasy or delirium have spoken with astonishing fluency languages of which they were ignorant in their normal state. Acts nowhere suggests that the *speakers* in tongues understood what they were saying or that they were given a supernatural knowledge of foreign languages. They praised God in other tongues apparently with a wonderful fluency and freedom from provincial accent – another common feature of speakers in ecstasy down the ages. All that need be demonstrated is that they could have heard the languages they spoke under ecstasy in conditions in which these could have been recognized by them as praise of God and entered into their subconscious minds.

There were several such sources for the tongues. A census made during Nero's reign showed that two and a half million Jews attended Jerusalem for the Passover; there could have been more at Pentecost, from all over the world. These pilgrims often travelled to Jerusalem in national groups, chanting in their vernaculars their own choruses and possibly some of the Davidic psalms of praise. These choruses and psalms, chanted as the marchers processed through the streets of Jerusalem, could well have been one source of the disciples' tongues.

There was, second, the polyglot condition of Jerusalem. There were many opportunities for the disciples to have overheard religious addresses in foreign languages in the city. There were also the acclamations, prayers and hymns absorbed during the special week that preceded the Day of Pentecost itself or from attendance at past feasts in which the disciples worshipped side by side with strangers from afar, praising and blessing God in their own vernaculars. Jewish religious rules allowed the Shema, the Eighteen Benedictions and grace at meals to be repeated in any language. When the ecstasy came upon them, the praises they had heard and subconsciously absorbed flowed from their lips.

Various surmises have been made as to the spark which fired their ecstasy. One suggestion is that there burst upon them the full realization of the significance of Christ's resurrection (*they* believed in the empty tomb and the rising again of the physical body of Jesus, whatever doubts modern churchmen may have). This, incubating in their minds since the events of Easter, suddenly culminated in the removal of the fear of death and the conviction of eternal life with God. Another suggestion is that the whole plan of salvation flashed upon their minds in its completeness with a burst of enlightenment which raised them to ecstasy. The association of Pentecost with the coming of God in power may have been enough. At this distance in time no more than guesses can be made.

It has been objected by a number of scholars that the miracle of Pentecost was unnecessary. Greek and Aramaic were spoken and understood throughout·the civilized world, and all Jews and proselytes returning to Jerusalem would have understood the disciples, had they spoken only these languages. But just as in the British Isles Welshmen, Scots and Irish carry on their relationships with their fellow-Britons of other races in the common language of English yet, in certain districts, speak and often worship in their native tongues, so it must have been in the Roman Empire in the first century. There was a great variety of languages in the ancient world mentioned by contemporary writers; and the astonishment aroused in the multitude of foreign Jews (whether visitors or, as the Greek suggests, permanent residents who had returned to Jerusalem to live after residing abroad) by the praising of God by Galileans fluently in their own language gave Peter an opportunity he would not otherwise have had. He then preached Christ crucified and raised from the dead in a vernacular which they understood equally. Given the local conditions and the nature of human beings, whereby languages subconsciously absorbed can be reproduced in ecstasy, nothing could be more natural than the events of Pentecost.

Explanations of the story which demand an other-than-obvious interpretation of the facts as they are given are unnecessary. Some writers maintain that the miracle was one of hearing – the disciples spoke but one language which was translated into the native tongue of each listener as he heard it. A more sophisticated version of the same explanation is that there was some kind of telepathic communication. Scholarly erudition has been brought to bear on the list of nations, it being pointed out that their source is more likely to be found in an eastern than a western writer and that they are drawn from an astrological grouping of countries arranged according to the signs of the Zodiac. What this proves, or what its relevance is, is difficult to say. It is the business of scholars to accumulate every scrap of knowledge they can. But if an account of an event which has passed into history can be given which corresponds to the facts recorded without going beyond the bounds of credibility on the one hand or altering them more than is necessary on the other, it is more likely to be closer to the truth than one which necessitated some twisting of the story to fit a theory or a prejudice. There is no reason to doubt that the disciples were moved to ecstasy, that in that state they praised God in foreign languages absorbed by their subconscious minds, that this caught the amazed attention of those around them and gave Peter the chance to preach his gospel of Christ crucified and resurrected.

3

From Jerusalem to Corinth

The certain authorities for tongues in the New Testament are four passages in Acts (including chapter 2) and I Corinthians, chapters 12 to 14. Ten other extracts[1] may refer to glossolalia but all are capable of different interpretations and, if Paul had not written the Corinthian passage, it is unlikely that they would ever have been thought possibly to refer to tongues.

Acts may have been written in the 60s or 70s AD, I Corinthians in the mid- to late 50s. But whereas Paul's letter and possible references in other epistles deal with a contemporary phenomenon, the Acts account of Pentecost is a historian's relation of an event that had happened at least twenty-five years earlier. It is implicit and sometimes explicit in the writings of many commentators that the glossolalia of Jerusalem and Corinth must have been similar and that Paul's account must therefore be regarded as more accurate than Luke's. According to this view, Luke's discrepancies were due to inaccurate source material edited by a historian who had not had first-hand experience of tongues himself and did not know what he was talking about.

In the twenty years, however, that elapsed between Pentecost and the tongues of the Corinthian church there was time for an entirely different kind of glossolalia to develop. The tongues at Jerusalem can be adequately explained by the cryptomnesia of the first disciples. Acts records two more certain examples of tongues and one probable one. In chapter 8 Philip converts some Samaritans, among them Simon, who had previously swept them off their feet with his magical arts. Seeing that the Spirit was bestowed through the laying-on of the apostles' hands, he tried to buy the gift. It is argued that what Simon saw included glossolalia, though there is no certainty that this occurred. If it did, it could be called a second breakthrough of the Holy Spirit; following the revelation to the orthodox worshippers of Jahweh at Pentecost was one to men who were 'heretical' worshippers, half-way between Jew and Gentile.

The third glossolalic experience was that of Cornelius, a Roman centurion and a 'God-fearer' – that is, a man who, while attracted to Judaism and an attendant at synagogue worship, was not a full proselyte. The experience of Cornelius and his friends is described as 'speaking in tongues of ecstasy and acclaiming the greatness of God',[2] and Peter later reported that 'the Holy Spirit came upon them just as upon us at the beginning'.[3] The statement can be interpreted as 'The Holy Spirit came upon them as he came to us at Pentecost' or it can mean 'Both we and they produced the same kind of phenomena as the result of the Spirit's coming, that is, the praising of God in recognizable foreign languages normally unknown to the speakers'.

The second interpretation is possible. Caesarea was a polyglot garrison town. Cornelius would have absorbed the Hebrew prayers heard Sabbath by Sabbath in the synagogue, to him expressed in a foreign language. He would probably have spoken Aramaic and Greek in his daily life, for both were *linguae francae* of the Roman Empire. His native tongue was Latin. These would have been sufficient to impress Peter with his ability to speak in tongues. Or his tongues could have been of the modern Pentecostalist type, incubated in the sub-conscious mind and produced when sufficient emotional or spiritual impetus had been built up to achieve the breakthrough which Pentacostalists recognize as the baptism with the Holy Spirit.

25

The fourth outpouring of the Holy Spirit was upon Ephesian Gentiles who had become Christians probably without having been first God-fearers or proselytes.[4]

There are two views as to what happened in the years immediately following. The orthodox view is that while tongues manifested themselves in certain churches, such as that of Corinth, these were eccentric communities affected by local conditions, and glossolalia formed no part of regular Christian worship. Even where it did, it was an immature form of adoration and passed away naturally and quickly when the church settled down into routine and organization. If the Corinthians had not happened to ask Paul which were the most important spiritual gifts, no tongues would have been known outside the three or four instances in Acts, and all Bible scholars would then have regarded them either as legendary or as unique instances of an introductory outpouring of the Holy Spirit once and for all upon different classes of believers.

The Pentecostalist view is that tongues were so much a part of ordinary Christian worship in the primitive Church that there would have been no more need to mention them than to record the fact that their speakers breathed. It was fortunate that Paul was questioned by the Corinthians, for his answers revealed to Christians of later ages valuable forms of worship neglected by the developed Church. Had the question not been asked, the practice of tongues would have been lost owing to the increased falling away, hardness of heart and worldliness of the Church in post-apostolic times. Now that the faithful remnant is aware of their importance and significance, they have been recovered with much else of the early purity of worship and doctrine; we can see this process of recovery gathering impetus in modern times.

If the Corinthian church was unique or one of a few churches which practised glossolalia, there were good reasons for this. The pagan Greek belief in mantic ecstasy must have been prominent in the thought of many of the Greek converts. The Delphic oracle was not far away, and the idea of a worshipper becoming *enthusiasmos* – filled with god – was a common one

26

in Greek thought. In this state his personality was temporarily expelled and his body taken over by the god who spoke through him, very often in words which, although in the vernacular, were so opaque in meaning that they needed an interpreter to translate them. Such 'enthusiasm' was recognized as legitimate and respectable by the Socratic–Platonic and Stoic philosophies which aimed to use it to improve the enthusiast's character permanently. There were marked differences between these ideas and those of Paul, to whom the Lord was *the* Spirit, but they were current and could have influenced the Corinthians, especially as a number of contemporary Greek sects are said to have practised glossolalia. There were also similarities in the external appearance of the ecstatics. Not the manner but the content of ecstatic speech determined its authenticity.

For Paul, Christian glossolalia was not derived but a uniquely new experience. Its novelty lay in that, whereas in pagan worship ecstasy was sought, in Christianity it came spontaneously, followed by the tongues. But although this may be true of the experience in Acts, it is not necessarily true of Corinth. By the time that church was flourishing it could have been the custom of those churches which practised tongues, especially if they believed that these were evidence of the Spirit's presence, to seek baptism with the Spirit as Pentecostalists do today. The novelty of the Christian experience would then be not in its practice but in its quality, the difference between human personalities opening themselves to the influence of pagan gods and spirits – who were devils – and to that of the Holy Spirit of God himself. Another difference was that, whereas once under the influence the pagan could neither control nor shake off the god, in Christianity it was for 'the prophets to control prophetic inspiration',[5] and control was always possible. Even Christians, however, might be influenced by wrong spirits. In mentioning the cry 'a curse on Jesus',[6] Paul may have been referring to the resistance of Christian ecstatics to the power coming upon them as did the Sybil and as did Cassandra who curses Apollo in Aeschylus' *Agamemnon*.

When asked about tongues Paul showed no surprise and

accepted the phenomenon as a normal part of worship. His view of them may be deduced from the key passage, I Corinthians, chapters 12 to 14. Tongues, he said, when interpreted or understood, are to be judged by their content. In order of importance in a list of gifts of the Spirit, tongues and the interpretation of tongues occupy the last two places. The Corinthians should seek the higher gifts, above all the gift of Christian love. Prophecy, that is, inspired preaching, the forth-telling of the mind of God, was better than tongues, for the prophet built up the church in the faith whereas the glossolalic, although inspired, talked only with God, unless he could also interpret. Let him therefore pray for the gift of interpretation too. Paul spoke in tongues more than any Corinthian Christian, yet he would rather speak five intelligible words in church than thousands of unintelligible tongues. The function of glossolalia was to be a judgment on unbelievers in so far as it was a sign of God's presence which the unbeliever who heard it would reject.

In worship each individual should contribute a hymn, some teaching, some glimpse of enlightenment he has had, a tongue or its interpretation. There should never be more than two or three speakers in tongues and they should not speak publicly if there were no interpreter present but keep their tongues for private worship at home. Glossolalia was not to be forbidden, but let everything be done decently and in order.

In summary, Paul accepted tongues as a part of normal worship, inspired by the Spirit and their use appointed by God. He used them himself. They were not expected to be understood without an interpreter, were a form of prayer especially associated with praise and thanksgiving and some of them ('tongues of angels') were languages unknown to men. Tongues may be inspired by evil spirits and even the rightly inspired gift is not for everyone. In the polyglot port city of Corinth recognizable foreign languages might emerge in glossolalia, and Jewish worshippers might share the belief of some of their countrymen that a language existed by which angels might be invoked, abjured, collected and dispersed and by which many secrets might be discovered and curious arts and sciences known. A famous rabbi, Jochanan ben Zaccai, was said to understand the languages of devils, angels and trees, and a principal object of Dr Dee, the Elizabethan magus, was to obtain from the spirits a complete vocabulary of the angelic tongue.

The origin of tongues as a normal element in worship may have arisen from their association with the coming of the Holy Spirit upon new converts as recorded in Acts. This could have inspired a doctrine that glossolalia was one of the signs, even an essential one, proving that the believer had been genuinely baptized with the Spirit; and the fact that certain ecstatics continued to speak in tongues whenever the spirit (or Spirit) moved them led to the teaching that glossolalia was one of his gifts. The notion of the interpretation of tongues as a further gift is something that would follow naturally. The bursting into tongues proved clearly that something was happening – though the primitive Church wisely recognized the need for the gift of the 'discernment of spirits' to distinguish between faculties divinely and demoniacally inspired.

In all his discussion about tongues, Paul never says what they are, for he and the Corinthians knew what they were talking about. The Greek word *glossa* is used much as the English word *tongue*. It can be the physical organ, a language, a flame of fire, and an antiquated, foreign, high-flown, mysterious or unintelligible language. Christian commentators in the second and third centuries assumed that the Corinthians spoke foreign languages and some modern scholars have argued with considerable erudition that Paul used 'tongues' in this sense. Languages produced by cryptomnesia would be recognized, and once there had been verifiable instances of foreign languages, it would be relatively easy to accept the idea that tongues not recognizable by anyone present might be non-human – angelic or, if wrongly inspired, demonic.

Equally erudite scholars have argued that Paul uses *phonai* to mean foreign languages and reserves *glossai* for a different context. His description rather requires the conception of an altogether uncommon use of the vernacular or an entirely new spiritual language which differed from *all* common speech. If the vernacular, the believer, caught up into ecstasy, expressed himself in fragments of psalmody, hymnody and prayer which conveyed to the speaker an irresistible sense of communion with God and to the bystander an impression of an extraordinary manifestation of power. Such fragments would, however, scarcely need interpreting. The new spiritual language could have been an involuntary psalm-like prayer or song, a heavenly melody played by the Holy Spirit on an almost passive human instrument. Or *glossa* may mean only that language of the Spirit, used between God and his angels, to which men can be raised in worship if seized by the Spirit and caught up into heaven as Paul on one occasion claims to have been.

These divergent views can be largely reconciled if Paul's phrase, 'kinds of tongues' is taken to mean different types of language rather than praying, singing, praising and blessing. If it is, then he could have known snatches of foreign languages, recognized and translated by other worshippers, and also languages unknown to everyone present which would have been considered supernatural tongues which needed interpretation in the sense of paraphrasing in earthly terms. Anyone who has heard a really fervent glossolalic praising God in tongues will readily understand how such an expression of ecstasy could be taken as the language of angels.

There is no reason why Corinthian theory and practice should not have closely resembled those of modern Pentecostalism. The experiences of glossolia recorded in Acts might well have led some Christian communities to emphasize the charismatic aspects of their faith (where did Paul learn to speak in tongues?). It can be further assumed that some genuine converts of a more phlegmatic or intellectual nature did not immediately exhibit any of the gifts; and believers of longer standing might ask, if there were no signs following, how the genuineness of their conversion could be recognized. It is easy to see that in some churches a doctrine of a 'second blessing', 'the baptism with the Holy Spirit', would emerge, especially as

Christ himself had talked of two baptisms, by water and the Spirit. The water-baptized but uncharismatic believer would be instructed to work for, pray for and expect in due course the baptism with the Spirit; and his 'gifted' brethren would teach him that he would not become a Christian in the fullest sense until this happened.

One can imagine a crowd of earnest believers praying for the second blessing over a period of time and fulfilling all the conditions of a psychological crowd. In time, one would 'break through', then another, then another, each adding his psychic impetus to the spiritual snowball until it became an avalanche overwhelming the most (though unwillingly) obdurate.

Nor, in a charismatic community, would the signs following be a once-and-for-all matter. Congregational fervour of adoration would soon so overcome some illiterate member that he could not find words in his own limited vocabulary to express the strength of his feelings but would give vent to them in exalted pseudo-language such as can be recorded and analysed today. This would happen whenever he and others like him reached a certain threshold of worship, and so they would come to be recognized as having the gift of tongues, which would come to be accepted as something different from the once-and-for-all sign of tongues following Spirit-baptism. So impressive and spectacular a gift, too, would be regarded as desirable, and those who achieved it might regard themselves and be regarded by others as more spiritual than the average; and thus there would be a considerable impetus given to seeking the gift with that yearning for it which would eventually be fulfilled in the contagion of charismatic excitement.

No doubt genuine foreign languages were sometimes spoken, too, owing either to cryptomnesia of the first Whitsun type or to the resurrection of languages known in childhood but forgotten, in conditions of ecstatic trance. There could also have been hymns, psalms and prayers sung or said in ecstasy as one hears articulate and inarticulate cries of joy or groans of repentance at some charismatic services today.

The gift of interpretation follows naturally upon that of

tongues and may have descended from those officials in the synagogues who interpreted the classical Hebrew of the Scriptures and services for proselytes, God-fearers and even some Jews. But there is a more basic reason for the gift of interpretation than this. If a fervent flow of inspired and beautiful language were heard in a service, the question would naturally arise, 'What does it mean?' Equally natural would be the expectation that the Holy Spirit would vouchsafe the meaning as he had granted the tongue. Prayer for the meaning would be made, in response to which would come to another member of the church the charismatic conviction that he had been given the answer. The best tongues have the rhythm, flow and exaltation of poetry or music – in fact, though analysis of modern Pentecostalist tongues has proved them to be usually pseudo-languages (a term not used in any pejorative sense), they may be regarded as a species of mouth-music expressing worship, praise, repentance and rebuke. They can be interpreted into thought by someone in tune with them as one who appreciates music can be in tune with a composer.

It may be noticed in passing that theology follows practice, experience coming first and the explanation of it later. So tongues happened spontaneously, their appearance inspiring the questions 'Why?' and 'How?' and the answers influencing later behaviour, modified by changing circumstances as time passed.

There is one other apparently clear reference to tongue-speaking in the New Testament, St Mark's Gospel 16:17, 'Believers will cast out devils in my name and speak in strange tongues.' This is said by many critics to be an ending, substituted perhaps as late as 130 AD, for the original ending, which was lost, torn off the end of the roll. But the reference may not be to glossolalia at all. It may mean simply that the Holy Spirit would give a new energy and power to the tongue, or that the words mean 'languages newly acquired by them'; a third view is that an entirely new language, never before spoken and prompted by the Holy Spirit, is indicated. If the late date of composition is accepted and if the passage does refer to glossolalia, then it can be concluded that speaking in tongues survived well into the second century.

4

Tongues before the Reformation

If glossolalia were ever a regular practice of the Christian Church, it soon disappeared. It may have survived under the name 'prophecy' which seems sometimes to have included speaking in tongues. There were, however, good reasons for its disappearance. First, its practice in some mystery religions probably made it suspect. Second, in days of persecution the Church would not want to draw attention to itself by noisy and extravagant behaviour. Third, an ethical rather than charismatic emphasis came to be given to Christianity. Fourth, in most religions, decorous worship, conducted 'decently and in order', by sober priests, succeeds initial enthusiasm. Fifth, tongues came generally to be attributed to devil-possession and, later, to witchcraft. Finally, solitude, humility and self-control came to be valued and, in spite of a continuing belief in miracles, there was a steady underlying movement towards a healthy scepticism. Extravagant behaviour was also more likely to attract accusations of heresy than praise for godliness.

Yet, although glossolalia became rare and insignificant, disappearing for decades, almost for centuries, it never died permanently. It was accepted as a divine gift of some saints, whose holy lives proved their faculty to be God-given. For ordinary Christians, speaking in tongues, together with other psychic manifestations, was condemned as a devilish imitation of the divine gift, and the *Rituale Romanum* explicitly states this.[1]

Passages in certain early non-canonical writings may suggest the existence of glossolalic practice but may equally be flights of imagination. In the *Acta Perpetuae et Felicitatis*, the Spirit overpowers Perpetua and constrains her to the utterance of a name she had not known before.[2] *The Book of Enoch* portrays the patriarch in heaven as shouting 'with a loud and unusual voice' and 'with the spirit of power'.[3] In this strange tongue he magnifies God. *The Apocalypse of Abraham* and *The Ascension of Isaiah* both describe an ecstasy in which a person is able to speak, sing and understand the language of the angels, of which every order has its special voice.[4][5] In *The Testament of Job*, Job's three daughters are provided with a miraculous girdle which enables them to live in heaven, receive a new heart and speak in superhuman languages.[6] The first speaks in the tongue of an angel, the second in the tongue of principalities and the third in that of the cherubim. Lucian (125–c.181) designates Jesus 'that Syrian of Palestine who cured the rich man', saying, 'The man is silent but the demon answers in the language . . . of whatever country he be,'[7] and after his description of a false prophet, already mentioned (page 3) he describes exorcists who hear the devils within their patients talking in Greek or a barbarian tongue saying who they are, whence they come, and how they have entered into the possesseds' bodies.[8]

Irenaeus (130–202), Bishop of Lyons, referred in his *Against Heresies*, to 'perfect' persons who through the Spirit of God spoke in all languages as the Apostle (Paul) used himself to do. 'In like manner,' Irenaeus continues, 'we have heard [of?] many brethren who . . . through the Spirit speak all kinds of languages.'[9] The word translated 'all kinds of' is obscure, capable of meaning either foreign languages or glossolalia, and, although commentators slightly incline to Irenaeus' having heard glossolalia himself, he could be referring to past phenomena. Justin Martyr, a contemporary of Irenaeus, says that in his time spiritual gifts were active in the Church, but nowhere specifically mentions tongues.

In 157, Montanus, from Phrygia, a land which in times past had been associated with the orgiastic worship of Dionysus and Cybele, claimed to be a prophet with authority from God to proclaim a fresh influx of the Holy Spirit and called for a reform of the Church. His was an attempt, against increasing secularization and organization, to recapture the practices, enthusiasm and purity of the primitive Church. He demanded asceticism and a holy life which should distinguish the devoted Christian from the non-believer outside the Church and the wordly Christian within it. He gave tongues a position of great importance, his two female lieutenants, Maximilla and Priscilla, perhaps speaking in tongues and Montanus himself raving in ecstatic trance and babbling in a jargon. Describing the action of God, Montanus is quoted as saying, 'Behold the man is as a lyre and I play over him like a plectrum; the man sleeps and I wake; behold it is the Lord who takes away the hearts of men, and gives to me [another] heart.'[10] Because Montanism was regarded as heretical it is meagrely documented and information about it comes mainly from its opponents. The movement was widespread and came to an end only in 381 when the Council of Constantinople refused to recognize the validity of Montanist baptism.

Montanus's notable disciple, Tertullian (160–220), writing against the Gnostic, Marcion, challenged him to produce from among his followers any who had prophesied in tongues or manifested other gifts of the Spirit, all of which were 'forthcoming from my side without any difficulty'.[11] In his *Concerning the Resurrection of the Flesh* Tertullian mentions a kind of utterance which no one can know without interpretation and in *Concerning the Soul* describes a glossolalic woman who 'converses with angels and sometimes with the Lord; she both sees and hears mysterious communications.[12]

Origen (185–254) erroneously interpreted Paul's claim, 'I speak in tongues more than you all', as the Spirit-given ability to talk in the languages of all nations.[13] Celsus, an opponent quoted by Origen, possibily referred to glossolalia when he described beggars and soothsayers pronouncing threatenings of doom followed by unintelligible, obscure, half-crazy words. Origen, however, seemed to deny the existence of tongues in his day when he said that Christians did not utter unintelligible prophecies beyond their ability to put into rational speech.

Eusebius (c.264–340), a principal source of information about Montanism, quoted another authority who maintained the impropriety of a prophet's speaking in ecstasy and himself made a psychologically interesting comment: 'The false prophet speaks in a trance, which induces irresponsibility and freedom from restraint; he begins by deliberate suppression of conscious thought, and ends in a delirium over which he has no control.'[14]

St Pachomius (292–c.348), an Egyptian abbot, 'was frequently admitted to intercourse with the holy angels'[15] and wrote letters to his bishop in a mystic alphabet only manifest to those of special grace or desert (it is to be hoped that the bishop cracked the code). He is reported to have spoken 'Roman' after three hours' prayer and Greek and Latin, languages he had never studied, after special prayer to meet immediate needs. Although Pachomius' exploits, recorded a hundred years later, were probably legendary, the account of them proves the acceptability of tongues in the fourth century.

Gregory Nazianzen (325–403) suggested that the tongues of Pentecost could have been a gift of hearing (each auditor *hearing* the language spoken by the disciples as his own), not of speaking[16] – a view repeated by several writers up to the present day.

St Chrysostom (345–407) believed that the whole 120 spoke with tongues at Pentecost and that each individual spoke several languages. At baptism, believers spoke in recognizable languages that proved the presence of the Spirit. The gift became a source of division among Christians 'from the perversity of them that received it' and Chrysostom reported– presumably because of these rifts – that tongues no longer happened.[17]

St Augustine of Hippo (354–430) seems to have believed that each of the apostles was able to speak all languages. Tongues had been a sign that the Gospel was to run through the whole earth. But in his time the *Church* spoke all languages, since it contained believers of every race. The sign of tongues for the individual believer had been replaced by the presence in him of Christian love. Even Simon Magus received the sacrament and even Saul had the gift of prophecy; whatever might be received by heretics and schismatics, 'the charity which covereth the multitude of sins is the especial gift of Catholic unity and peace'.[18]

Some notable Pentecostalists claim that Augustine wrote, 'We still do what the apostles did when they laid hands on the Samaritans and called down the Holy Spirit on them by the laying on of hands. It is expected that converts should speak with new tongues.' But no source for this quotation is given, and Augustine is not likely to have contradicted himself so blatantly.

In the same century as Augustine's a hagiographer (writer of lives of saints) reported that there was a church near Bethlehem where the *daimonizomenai* or *energumenoi* prayed 'in their own language'.[19] During the next six hundred years, however, no Christian glossolalia seem to have occurred. This is understandable in the light of the already-mentioned con-demnation of the practice as a sign of devil-possession by the *Rituale Romanum*, which reached its present form in about the year 1000. Then individual glossolalics appeared, safeguarded by their reputations for saintliness. The German abbess, St Hildegard (1098–1179), claimed to be able to understand the Holy Scriptures without a grammatical knowledge of Latin. She also spoke and wrote in an unknown alphabet of twenty-three letters an entirely strange language which she interpreted into German. Fortunately, specimens of the tongue, which developed after powerful mystical experiences, were preserved in a manuscript printed later under the title *The Unknown Tongue* and were shown by analysis to be a jumble of German, Latin and misunderstood Hebrew.

Some saintly glossolalia is mentioned almost in passing. St Dominic (1170–1221) prayed for a knowledge of their language so as to be able to converse with some German fellow-travellers and immediately spoke German for four days. He had a second similar experience later. Ange Clarenus received a knowledge of Greek during the night of Christmas 1300. Two preachers, St Anthony of Padua (1195–1231) and St Vincent Ferrier (1357–1419) repeated the miracle of hearing. The former was understood in their own languages by Europeans who heard him preach at Rome. The latter, though speaking naturally only Limousin, reached and converted people all over Europe, many in isolated areas such as the Alps. He was understood by Greeks, Germans, Sardes, Hungarians and Bretons and allegedly preached in Latin, French, Spanish and Italian, none of which he understood.

Some thirteenth-century mendicant monks are said to have talked in tongues. Another movement which allegedly contained glossolalics was that of the Dancers or Chorizantes. This cult, whose members danced in honour of St John, emanated from Flanders in 1374 and spread to other countries, notably Germany. Protestants before Protestantism, some of the Waldenses, founded by Peter Waldo in 1170, are also said to have spoken in tongues. This is not unlikely, for they were mercilessly persecuted; and men hunted and harried among mountains and forests may be psychologically conditioned by their sufferings and the strain of living one step ahead of their persecutors to find relief in visions and ecstatic experiences.

St Thomas Aquinas (c.1226–74) held what may be regarded as a typically orthodox doctrine of tongues. They had been given for a purpose, as they had been needed. Since God is perfectly able to give supernaturally, to bypass 'second causes' and still produce their effect, a natural ability to acquire other languages does not stand in the way, any more than the talents given the physician prevent some people from having perfect health without a doctor. Tongues were given for a particular purpose which no longer existed; to claim the gift now meant that it came from demons. 'Tongues of angels' meant 'pure reason', since angels are purely intellectual beings and their speech must be pure reason.

St Francis Xavier (1506–52), though contemporary with Luther, was little affected by the Reformation because he spent most of his life evangelizing the East. It is recorded that at first he could baptize or help the sick only by signs. His letters emphasized the difficulties his ignorance of languages imposed upon him. His practice was: to learn just enough of a language to translate into it some of the principal Church formulae; to get others to help him patch together pious teachings to be learned by heart; to mix various dialects eked out by signs; and to use interpreters. His voyage to China was held up because a hired interpreter failed to meet him. Turesellinus, an early biographer, describes the laughter caused by his efforts to speak Japanese. Xavier's own statements favouring the study of languages by missionaries, his descriptions of his linguistic difficulties, similar assertions in the letters of his associates and a companion's declaration that he laboured hard in the study of languages, all emphasize the normality of Xavier's learning to communicate with the inhabitants of Asia. Another companion, however, a Portuguese named Vaz, claimed for Xavier the gift of tongues, asserting that he spoke Chinese without having learned it. He often preached to men of different nations, each simultaneously understanding him in his own language. At his canonization in 1622, Xavier's gift of tongues was stressed as fact, and Father Bohorus, writing a century after his death, claimed that he preached to the Japanese with the ease of a native and spoke other 'barbarian' tongues without having learned them. Father Coleridge, SJ, wrote in 1872 that he spoke Japanese as if he had lived in Japan all his life. Such are the records; the reader will draw his own conclusions according to his predilections.

Catholic teaching that tongues were normally a sign of devil-possession limited their appearance before the Reformation. Since they were largely ignorant of Scripture, the common people did not know there was a gift of tongues and neither sought nor expected it. Any fortuitous appearance of glossolalia would have disconcerted the orthodox and been suppressed. It is surprising that when the Reformation opened the Scriptures to the public and movements began to try to recapture the purity of doctrine and practice of the primitive Church, tongue-speaking was not encouraged more. But it seems to have been generally accepted by the Reformers that tongues were a temporary gift of the Spirit, needed to spread the Gospel in the first days but no longer an essential in times when the Bible and enlightened preaching were available to all as the media through which the good news could be spread. But after the Reformation Catholic tongues continued sporadically and considerable Protestant glossolalic sects were to spring up from time to time.

5

From the Reformation
to 1800

Catholic tongues after the Reformation were either a gift of saintly individuals or the product of communities and movements allegedly devil-possessed or heretical. St Louis Bertrand (1526–81), as his bull of canonization (1651) claims, had the gifts of tongues, prophecy and miracles, and is said to have converted in South America Indians of various tribes and dialects numbering, according to different authorities, from 30,000 to 300,000. The gift of tongues was also ascribed to Dominick of Neisse (died 1650), librarian of the Escurial, who knew most European languages and Tartar, Indian, Chaldean, Hebrew, Syriac, Chinese, Japanese and Persian. Like Cardinal Mezzofanti, later famous for his linguistic abilities, Dominick seems to have been one of those who learn languages with such speed and facility that the faculty appears supernatural, whereas it is but supernormal and not to be taken as a paranormal facility.

Julien Maunier (1606–83), a Jesuit, after prayer to the Virgin Mary, spoke and understood Breton, 'one of the most difficult [languages] in the world', and preached as easily in it as in French. St Claire of Monte Falcone, although she had never learned the language, is said to have talked French with a Frenchwoman for a long time. Saint Colette (the later of the two of that name) had the gift of tongues, including Latin and

German. The Abbess Elizabeth had a religious experience similar to St Hildegard's and developed the gift. Jean (John) of St Francis prayed for the ability to speak Mexican and at once preached in it, to the astonishment of his hearers. The same was said of Martin-Valentin as of Bertrand and Xavier. St Jeanne of the Cross had the gift of tongues when she was in ecstasy and was able to communicate in different languages according to her listeners' needs. She converted and instructed two Mohammedan Arabs in divinely-given Arabic. In the missions to Georgia, St Stephen spoke Greek, Turkish and Armenian without having learned them.

The story of the devil-possessed Ursuline nuns of Loudun is widely known through the film *The Devils*. A feature of their mania, which lasted from 1632 to 1634, when Urbain Grandier, a curé of Loudun, was burned for bewitching them, was the ability to speak in foreign languages of which they were ignorant. The anonymous author of the earliest history of the outbreak did not doubt the genuineness of the tongues. He cited the testimony of a doctor of the Sorbonne and other prominent personages to the effect that the devils answered questions put to them in Latin, Greek, Spanish, Turkish and a Red Indian language, often in the same tongues as those in which the questions were asked.[1] But he did not write from first-hand knowledge and gave no authorities for his statements; and his testimony is vitiated by his theological bias. Other sources, such as a Protestant *Histoire des Diables de Loudun*, published at Amsterdam in 1693, give further details. The nuns replied in very bad Latin to the priests who catechized them, and the Mother Superior, while answering in Latin questions on the Ritual put to her in that language, excused herself from replying in Greek on the ground that there was a pact between the demon and Grandier not to talk it. Some Normandy gentlemen certified in writing that one sister had replied correctly to questions put in Turkish, Spanish and Italian. Monsieur de Nismes, Doctor of the Sorbonne, received satisfactory replies in Greek and German, certain sisters obeyed a string of orders given them in Greek, and others, questioned by doctors as to the meaning of some extremely difficult Greek technical terms, explained them clearly.

In the atmosphere of salaciousness and intense neurosis arising from sexual frustration, the records of the alleged happenings at Loudun are not to be trusted. Most of the phenomena were probably inaccurately observed, and imagination, no doubt, exaggerated the resemblances to foreign tongues that emerged from the hysterical utterances of the nuns. If any languages were spoken supernormally, cryptomnesia is an adequate explanation. In such an atmosphere clairvoyant faculties normally latent *may* have been awakened. If the testimony of Monsieur de Razilli, who alleged that the nuns had not only replied to him in a Red Indian language but had revealed to him events that had taken place in America, was true, extra-sensory perception of some kind could have played a part.

In 1652, a papal formulary condemned as heretical five theses in the *Augustinus*, a work by a Dutch theologian, Cornelius Jansen (1585–1638), published posthumously. A controversy, originally religious but soon bitterly political, broke out in France between Jansen's supporters and the government-backed Jesuits and continued for nearly a hundred years. In 1727 the tomb of François, Jansenist Archdeacon of Paris, in St Médard's Cemetery, became a centre of pilgrimage and the scene of excesses by the Convulsionnaires, as the more violent of his followers were called. Among their activities was glossolalia which they believed was controlled by a power outside themselves. Sometimes they uttered unintelligible expressions in an unconscious state, producing senseless combinations of sounds which they regarded as words from foreign languages, remembering nothing when they returned to consciousness. At other times, some of them, though not knowing what their words would be until they actually spoke them, retained consciousness and memory and could correct speeches taken down by their friends.

Often the tongues were in public, sometimes in private or semi-private, such as those spoken by the Chevalier Folard who had convulsions every day when he began the Magnificat at Vespers and talked monosyllabic gibberish alleged by some hearers to be Slavonic. A widow Thévenet likewise spoke rapidly in an unintelligible vocabulary. There were the usual examples of the release of people of little talent into abnormal fluency and the usual unsubstantiated claims that they spoke Arabic and other languages they had never learned. Mademoiselle Lordelot, for example, reported as having had great difficulty in expressing herself from her birth, discoursed in an unknown tongue with all possible grace and facility, and another young lady who had never had any voice sang canticles admirably in a strange language.

Jansenists discerned three degrees of inspiration. Ideas first take hold of the speaker in a manner he feels to be supernatural; then, though at first using his own language to express them, the expressions come to be internally dictated; finally, he speaks involuntarily and without previous thought.

St Médard's Cemetery was closed in 1733 because of the excesses, but the Convulsionnaires continued their activities privately. The more responsible Jansenists condemned and eventually disowned their practices, and the movement became increasingly political and in due course petered out. Its glossolalia had no theological basis beyond being miraculous evidence of the truth of the Jansenist position and seems to have been only gobbledygook.

Accounts of tongues in the Orthodox Church seem not to exist, at least in any language accessible to the average Westerner. The mystical other-worldly tradition of the Eastern Church may accept glossolalia as too normal to need mentioning; a Patriarch of Constantinople has been quoted as saying that tongues were a continuing experience among the Orthodox throughout the ages and that there were provisions in their Church to govern the practice.[2] There is, however, no apparent record of its use in ordinary Orthodox worship, either public or private. Certain Eastern practices, such as constant repetition of the name of Jesus, result in strange experiences, a sense of being prayed through and unknown words coming to

45

the tongue (this 'Jesus-prayer' is used as a technique by western seekers to lead them into tongues). But the repetition of any word, such as one's own name, can so lull the consciousness into a somnambulistic state that either the subliminal or the lower brain centres (if they are not the same thing) take over and control the subject's behaviour. A devotionally-directed 'take-over' of the personality may be valuable in a sense that a mere experiment in self-hypnosis is not. But it has dangers, especially for neurotics.

In the West, at the Reformation, not one rediscoverer of New Testament doctrine and practice found tongues to be a normal gift bestowed by God on his Church; although, surprisingly, one biographer[3] ascribes tongues to Luther. If the reformer did have the gift, he regarded it as merely personal. Isolated examples outside the main stream of religious controversy are to be found in post-Reformation times. In 1566, seventy children at an Amsterdam orphanage climbed on walls and roofs like cats, made horrible faces, related events happening at the same time in other places and talked in languages they had never learned. In 1639 a woman called Lücken, racked at Helmstädt for being a witch, was seized with dreadful convulsions, spoke High German followed by a strange language, and then fell asleep on the rack. In 1673, a young soldier became possessed. 'His language was unintelligible; but by intervals he knew how to express himself in a clear and precise manner, and . . . was able to respond to each in his own language, whether in French, or in Latin or otherwise.'[4]

Glossolalia is said to have been practised in Cromwell's time among the Quakers (Society of Friends), founded about 1650 by George Fox. Some modern American Friends who use tongues believe that Fox himself did, and there are records of individual Quakers speaking in tongues. One pathetic story describes two Friends found in Paris in January, 1657, half-dead with cold and hunger. They said they were ambassadors from the Lord to the Duke of Savoy and despaired not of the gift of tongues, and the Lord had told them they should be successful.

Protestants, like Catholics, tended to regard tongues as a sign of devil-possession. In 1697, it was said of 'The Surrey Demoniack' in 'an Account of Satan's strange and dreadful Actings in and about the Body of Richard Dugdale, of Surrey, near Whalley, in Lancashire', that he, a youth of nineteen, 'spoke in foreign languages, of which at other times he was ignorant'. Unlearned in English and of very ordinary ability, when the fit seized him, he spoke Latin, Greek and other languages.

The first Protestants to use tongues widely were the Camisards. When the Edict of Nantes which had given French Protestants freedom of worship was revoked in 1685, Huguenots in the Cevennes, known as Camisards from the white shirts (*camis*) which they wore as a uniform, rose in revolt. In a resistance worthy of Judas Maccabaeus, 3,000 Camisards held out against 60,000 royalist troops until 1705. Their importance to the history of glossolalia arises from the remarkable, though limited, talking in tongues which accompanied their struggle, inspired, perhaps, with other mystical experiences they had, by the strain imposed by constant hunting and harrying and the threat of torture and hideous execution if they were caught. Some of the 'French Prophets' later went to England and Germany and became the spiritual ancestors of later glossolalic movements.

The first Camisard glossolalic was Isabel Vincent, a Dauphiny shepherdess, daughter of a weaver who had been bribed to turn Roman Catholic. Fleeing from her father's blows to her godfather's house, on 12 February 1688, she passed into a stupor from which she emerged after several hours, then into a somnambulistic state from which she could not be awakened. In this state, insensible to her surroundings, her lips moving only slightly, her pulse normal, she preached that all, especially apostates, should repent. During subsequent ecstasies she composed admirable prayers, sang psalms beautifully and accurately, preached on the controversial points which separated Huguenots from Catholics and repeated clearly and correctly portions of the Mass in Latin which she then refuted. Sometimes she spoke for five hours in a single night and went unfatigued to her work next day. At first she spoke only in the Cevennes patois, which is quite unlike French, but later addressed French-speaking visitors in the most correct and purest Parisian French. Her preaching, beautifully adorned by ecstatically lively gestures, was individual, full of good sense and outside the usual rules of sermonizing. When she emerged from her abnormal state, she remembered nothing of what had happened in it.

Isabel's phenomena fired the ecstatic movement of 'The Little Prophets of the Cevennes'. Within a year there were an estimated thousand prophets in Languedoc, the fever spreading from Dauphiny and Vivarais, where five or six hundred appeared between June 1688, and February 1689. The ecstasy fell mainly upon the young, the poor and the simple – pastors, labourers, nubile girls and children, and childish adults – never upon the wealthy and learned. Some ecstatics swooned as if poleaxed and experienced anaesthesia, others remained standing, gasping for breath. Some broke out into exhortations in eloquent French, a language known to them through their Bible and religious services. Others allegedly talked in unknown languages, though a surviving specimen of these (*'tring, trang, swing, swang, hing hang'*) is scarcely impressive.

Contemporaries were, however, astonished by the fluency and correctness of the French spoken for, as one commented, it was as difficult for a Cevennois to speak French as for a Frenchman, newly arrived in England, to speak English. Isabel was illiterate. Jeanne, a 'poor idiot of a peasant woman . . . the simplest and most ignorant creature', produced elevated discourses in such good French that it was said of her. 'This ass of Balaam has a mouth of gold.'[5] Instances of such adults could be multiplied.

More astonishing was the extreme youth of the Little Prophets, a feature both of the 1688 epidemic and of another in 1700. An illiterate, shy girl, twelve years old, prayed and exhorted boldly for forty-five minutes in good French. The youngest preacher seen by one contemporary witness was five. A boy of three preached in adult style in French woe unto

Babylon, blessings upon the Church and repentance to his hearers. In his normal state he could not pronounce 'Babylon'. A child of fifteen months spoke clearly in a loud voice. Another, two months younger, exhorted his hearers to repentance. Neither of these could talk at all when normal.

The reports of these wonders were mostly made by Camisards or their sympathizers, and perhaps some of the phenomena were not as spontaneous as they would have had men believe. A Monsieur de Serre, for example, trained fifteen children of either sex from the peasantry of the Vivarais in prophecy. Doubtless, too, there was exaggeration, probably considerable. But a movement of such proportions cannot be entirely dismissed. The speaking of good French can be accepted and explained by cryptomnesia triggered off by almost intolerable stress. There is a parallel between the Camisards speaking their patois and the Galileans speaking their dialect who both, under the influence of inspiration, spoke fluently and correctly other languages which they had heard. There could also have been pseudo-languages, such as may be heard in some charismatic communities today, and these may have contained actual words, picked up from some quoting pastor a trifle more learned than the average. A surviving specimen, somewhat reminiscent of Hebrew, contains two Hebrew words: '*Schetekero olahamanu alasch schemene takera rischema schetebirekora . . . ruach Adonai* [the Spirit of the Lord] . . . *alla, Jesus, alla.*'

There was nothing extraordinary about the ecstatic sermons, which contained material common to many fundamentalist Protestant sects – the immediate Second Coming of Christ, the establishment of his personal reign on earth, the call to repentance, the claim that they were returning to the purity of the untainted primitive Church. What is extraordinary – if true – is the absorption of enough of this material, to be later produced in sermons, by the subliminal minds of infants still at the breast or scarcely older. The explanation of some authorities that the sermons arose from racial memories of countless sermons heard by the children's ancestors, even if not rejected

49

out of hand, seems to be belied by the fact that those sermons would have been delivered in patois, not French.

The contention that some Protestants might make, that the Camisards were in truth inspired by the Holy Spirit, seems invalidated by the partisan nature of the communications and, in some instances, by the lack of fulfilment of predictions made under inspiration. They are not what are to be expected from the Spirit, part of whose function is to lead believers into all truth.

A number of Camisards emigrated to London in 1706. Further claims were made for them that by the Holy Spirit several spoke languages which they were otherwise unable to speak and that dialogues were carried on between people who did not understand each other's language. Their enemies acknowledged the existence of the gifts but attributed them to the devil. Although declared imposters by the French Church in the Savoy (London), the Camisards won some English adherents, notably Sir Richard Bulkeley and his friend John Lacey who, under the influence of the Spirit, spoke Latin fluently though he had not read a Latin book for twenty years. Another friend, an attorney named Dutton, was heard by Sir Richard to utter 'compleat discourses in Hebrew for near a quarter of an hour together, and sometimes much longer'. Sir Richard honestly but ingenuously confessed that he could not speak Hebrew but 'catched at several words here and there'. These he knew to be Hebrew, and he had a mental impression that the discourse was a hymn of praise to God for the calling of Israel. The words Sir Richard 'catched at' were 'panis gnal haerets col lamma ruach shalom Ishrael bajom velo Adonai'.

Lord Shaftesbury, contemporary with Sir Richard, in his *Essay on Enthusiasm* was reminded by the sight of a gentleman under 'an Agitation' (perhaps Sir Richard himself) of Virgil's description of the frenzied Sibyl in *Aeneid*, Book VI. He reports that the inspired undergo a probation 'wherein the Spirit, by frequent Agitation, forms the Organs, ordinarily for a month or two before Utterance', an interesting comment in that it indicates, at least in some instances, a gradual development and preparation of the glossolalic.

Mr Lacey, described as construing Cicero, Horace, Juvenal, Lucretius, Martial, Ovid, Pliny and Virgil in an hour's coach drive, might have heard them taught to others at his school (in some schools of his day all the pupils were taught in a single large room) and been able to reproduce them by cryptomnesia under the influence of the ecstatic 'Gift'. Mr Dutton likewise might have produced an apparent language containing some recognizable Hebrew words leading to the assumption that the whole was Hebrew.

There are few examples of tongues among the followers of Wesley (1703–91). He himself did not disbelieve in their possibility, as is shown by the fact that he referred to Camisard glossolalia to rebut a certain Dr Middleton's assertion that since New Testament times there had not been a single instance of speaking in tongues. Methodist 'enthusiasm' was not charismatic and lasted continuously into serene old age. One certain example only of glossolalia appears, in the diary entry of Thomas Walsh for 8 March 1750: 'This morning the Lord gave me language that I know not of, raising my soul to Him in a wonderful manner.'[6]

The American revival called the Great Awakening in the 1730s likewise produced no certain glossolalia. Jonathan Edwards, its principal instigator, came to despise the charismata as childish. 'The glory of the approaching happy state of the church,' he said, 'does not at all require these extraordinary gifts.'[7]

The Camisards found spiritual descendants in the United Society of Believers in Christ's Second Appearing, popularly known as the Shakers. This was founded about 1747 by ex-Quaker tailors, James and Jane Wardley, living near Manchester. Their worship, which included tongues, drew persecution. Ann Lee (1736–84) was converted to the Society's beliefs in 1758 and, although illiterate, became so prominent in it that she is frequently called its founder.

Accused of blasphemy and threatened with branding and

tongue-boring because of her claim to speak in tongues, Ann was examined by four erudite Anglican divines. She addressed them in seventy-two languages (the same number used, according to rabbinic tradition, to broadcast the Law from Sinai throughout the world), and the Anglicans, allegedly recognizing that she was truly inspired, advised she be left alone. Further persecution, however, drove her in 1774 to America where she founded the first American Shaker settlement two years later. There the charismatic, psychical and spiritualist aspects of the faith developed, expressing themselves in clairvoyance, telepathy, prophecies, glossolalic singing, dancing and possession by departed spirits. The Shakers regarded it as part of their mission to preach to the 'lower spirits', and one of their elders described how 'a whole tribe of Indian spirits would troop into the house . . . everybody in the house would be possessed . . . they would sing songs entirely unknown to our people and sometimes they would sing in a foreign language that none of us knew'.[8] A certain Sister Sally, encouraged by the elders and the drinking of native spirits, danced to the following:

> *Te he, te haw, to hoot, te te hoot,*
> *Me be mother's pretty papoose,*
> *Me ting, me dant, te I diddle um,*
> *Because me here to whites come.*
> *He ti diddy, ti diddle O;*
> *Round, around, and round me go,*
> *Me leap, me jump, e up and down,*
> *On good whitey, shiny ground.*[9]

There were the claims, usual in such sects, to an ability to speak recognizable languages and the stories of conversions through messages in tongues. William Lee, Ann's brother, was understood by Indians in their own language, though he was entirely ignorant of it. Seth Y. Wells, Principal of Hudson Academy, was converted because he heard one Shaker sister talk in an unnamed language he recognized and another who did not understand it interpreted it correctly as referring to a journey he intended to make of which only he knew.

Critics found the tongues unimpressive – 'a succession of unmeaning sounds, frequently repeated, half-articulated, and plainly gotten by heart, for they all uttered the same sounds in succession'. The Shakers suggested this might be 'the Hotmatot language' but when challenged to speak Greek or Latin or French, were silent.[10] Haskett, a Shaker apostate, in his *Shakerism Unmasked*, describes the 'quick meeting' or 'Shaker high'. An elder shouts, 'Shake off the flesh!', stamps violently, and shakes. All the members then shout and stamp and after a slight pause the sisters talk in tongues. They 'gently gestured their language, waved themselves backward and forward like a ship in the billows of a ceased storm, shook their heads, seized their garments, and then violently stamped on the floor'.[11]

In mountain meetings, the Shakers, exhorted by their ministers, laboured for days, even weeks, until they broke out into unknown tongues. Two specimens of these have survived:

> *O calivin Christe I no vole,*
> *Calivin Christe liste um,*
> *I no vole vinim ne viste*
> *I no vole viste vum.*

> *Selera vane van vo canera van re lava*
> *Oilera van se lane cinera van so vo.*
> *'Tis Mother's holy love, love, she sent it by his*
> *dove, dove, dove,*
> *'Twas vene van se vane, 'twill ever more endure.*[12]

Other observers denied that the tongues were 'gotten by heart'. During their shaking one member would begin to sing some old tune; another, then another, joined in until all were contributing, some singing without words, some in unknown tongues, some in a mixture of English and glossolalia, some repeating inarticulate and unintelligible sounds. Observations of hostile critics are balanced by those of sympathetic ones who observed, apparently accurately, that the Shakers showed marked moral earnestness and passion, a rare acuteness of conscience and a unique purity of life.

From August 1837 there was an intense revival of charistmatic expression in the Shaker Church. This seems to have been caused by the doctrine of 'Mother Ann's Work' or 'Mother Ann's Second Appearing'. Shakers lost their native speech for hours or days, talking either in an unknown tongue or mongrel English, or sang but could not talk in English. The gift came unexpectedly, usually during worship but sometimes in ordinary everyday activities. The tongues carried messages from Jesus, Mother Ann, the apostles and great personalities of the Old Testament and history. But the Shaker view of glossolalia then altered. Believed originally to be a special sign from God to be utilized by all true believers, tongues were belittled by a directive of the Church elders in about 1841 as useless unless interpreted: 'We find no unknown words in the Scriptures.' The Shakers disappeared as a sect in 1866 at the death of their last leader, Mrs Girling.

From the Camisards tongues came to England, influenced individuals in society and found renewed expression among the Shakers. The latter overlapped though they did not influence the early nineteenth-century Church of the Irvingites. From 1685 to 1800 there was a tradition of glossolalia among minorities in the Christian Church, not continuous but becoming so. From 1800 to the present day, there probably has not been a year when some Christian sect or collection of individuals somewhere in the world has not spoken in tongues.

6

The Nineteenth Century

Whereas speaking in tongues in previous centuries had been comparatively rare and sporadic, from the beginning of the nineteenth century there is an almost unbroken continuity and a new development in that Christian tongues of the first half of the century are matched and reinforced by Spiritualist tongues during the second. Irvingites, Mormons, revivals in Europe, movements in the Orthodox Church and among Armenians, all produced glossalalia, overlapping and coming on stage one after the other like actors pat upon their cues.

Edward Irving (1792–1834), appointed Presbyterian Minister of Cross Street Chapel, London, in 1822, drew extraordinary crowds by his fiery eloquence and athletic and dignified physique. He became associated with the Albury Circle, a group founded in 1826 to study the Scriptures, whose members were inspired by happenings in Clydesdale to resolve 'that it is our duty to pray for the revival of the gifts manifested in the primitive Church – healing, miracles, prophecy, kinds of tongues and interpretations of tongues'.

The Clydesdale manifestations concerned a Greenock woman, Mary Campbell, dying of consumption in March 1830. Prayer, with special emphasis on the restoration of the gifts of the Holy Spirit, being made in her bedroom, the sick woman spoke out at great length (one account says for more than an

55

hour) with superhuman strength in an unknown tongue. Meanwhile, across the Clyde from Greenock, at Port Glasgow, Margaret MacDonald, sister of James and George, also lay dangerously ill. An unnamed lady was inspired by the Spirit to a two- to three-hour session of mingled praise, prayer and exhortation, culminating in a request that James be filled immediately with the Holy Ghost. Exclaiming, 'I have got it,' James then twice commanded Margaret, 'Arise and stand upright,' and took her by the hand, whereupon she arose. He next wrote to Mary Campbell, commanding her in the name of the Lord Jesus to rise, whereupon she did and from that time had good health.

Mary seems to have been a natural sensitive who, in other circumstances, would have made a successful medium. Following the example of the MacDonald brothers, who had added the gift of tongues to that of healing, she spoke in at least two distinguishable tongues, some utterances being musical, others harsh. She claimed that these were Turkish, Chinese or the language of the Pelew Islanders, thus, as Knox remarks, taking 'fewer risks than Mr Lacy, the adherent of the French prophets, who discoursed at large in Latin, and is reproved by Nathaniel Spinkes for crediting the Holy Spirit with a large number of solecisms in that language, duly set out in a footnote'.[1] Later, believers came to regard the glossolalia as an attestation of the intelligible prophecy which came presumably in a given interpretation rather than as an actual language.

Mary also developed automatic writing in strange characters which she wrote very rapidly apparently unaware of the energy expended. According to experts to whom it was subjected, the writing represented no language under the sun, being like characters on Chinese tea-chests, memory of which might have been subconsciously retained by the writer. Such memories, however, usually bear some resemblance to the originals, and one would expect individual ideograms to be the same.

Irving gradually came to believe that the apostolic charismata belonged to all ages and had been in abeyance through want of faith alone. A deputation of five members from London, led by

Cardale, a solicitor, heard nine people, not fanatics but of pious character and sound common sense, speak in tongues distinct in themselves and from each other. James MacDonald spoke two; he spoke more frequently than the others, sometimes for twenty minutes at a time.

The result of Cardale's report was that prayer meetings were held in private houses in London 'for the outpouring of the Holy Ghost'. On 30 April 1831, the first case of glossolalia in the Irving circle occurred when Mrs Cardale uttered three sentences in a tongue and three in an English interpretation: 'The Lord will speak to His people; the Lord hasteneth his coming; the Lord cometh.' Later a Miss Hall (governess in the family of Spencer Perceval) sang in the Spirit, in July two members of Irving's congregation received the gift of tongues and prophecy, and in November Miss Hall brought matters to a head by interrupting one of Irving's sermons with an outburst of glossolalia. The 'sudden, doleful and unintelligible sounds' bewildered the congregation, but on Irving's explanation that these were tongues, a sign of God's will and to be restrained by him at his peril, the contagion spread. Tongues and prophecies were heard at every service. An epidemic of cholera raging at the time encouraged the fanaticism.

Such excesses were not allowed to go unchecked. In 1832 Irving was summoned before the Presbytery of London and was expelled from the ministry in 1833. He became a moving spirit in a new sect, the Catholic Apostolic Church, but died in 1834, partly, perhaps, of a broken heart, for, however mistaken his views and policy, he was a deeply sincere and devout Christian. He did not even have the satisfaction of the gift of tongues for himself, though he sought it.

Irving accepted the possibility that some tongues might be entirely unknown, viewed merely as signs of the Holy Spirit. He regarded attempts at interpretation without being in the Spirit as impious, reproving a Mr Pilkington for ingenious interpretation of certain glossolalic phrases. *Gthis dil emma sumo* he translated as 'I will undertake this dilemma'; *Hozequin alta stare* as 'Hosanna in the highest'; *Hozehamenanostra* as 'Jesus in the highest will take care of this house'; *Holimoth holif awthan* as 'Holy, most holy Father'; and *Casa sera hastma cara* as 'The house will be in my care', thus reducing the tongues to the level of spiritual Esperanto or the language of James Joyce's *Ulysses*. At first a follower of Irving's, Pilkington wrote his conclusions in a tract entitled, 'The Unknown Tongues, Discovered to be English, Spanish and Latin' (1831).

Irving also asserted that Hebrew, Greek, Spanish, Italian and other unidentified languages were spoken by persons who did not know them, but his claim is entirely unsupported by evidence. He denied that glossolalia was a short cut to the speaking of foreign languages but surmised that tongues could be a means towards the evangelization of the world in readiness for the imminent Second Coming. Impressed by the power and majesty of some tongues, Irving commented that

> when the speech utters itself in the way of a spiritual song, it is the likest to some of the most simple and ancient chants in the Cathedral service, insomuch that I have often been led to think that those chants of which some can be traced upon as high as the days of Ambrose, are recollections and translations of the inspired utterances in the primitive church.[2]

Others have suggested that plainsong may be formalized glossolalic chanting.

Beauty of sound seems to be just as much in the ear of the beholder as visual beauty in his eye. Thomas Carlyle, a friend of Irving's, describes the scene in his congregation as 'foul uproar . . . more like a Bedlam than a Christian Church'. Pilkington and Baxter, both Irvingite apostates, describe motor-automata of an extreme type and 'the crash of tongues' while other observers call them gibberish, outpourings of hysteria and shrieking from stentorian lungs. But even Baxter wrote at length of the impression made upon him by his first contact with the Irvingites and their powerful and commanding utterances. Erskine of Linlathan, a believer, was favourably impressed by the loudness of the voices which repelled other listeners and maintained that the tongues were true languages, recognizable as such by their inflections, natural variety and different lengths of words. Other listeners heard the tongues as 'imposing and awful' or 'of thrilling power, march and majesty' and were impressed by 'the beauty and regularity . . . of some of the sounds'. Even hostile critics admitted that Irvingites sometimes spoke with extraordinary fluency in languages with which they were, at best, but very imperfectly acquainted. One observer mentions an individual whose natural voice was inharmonious and who had no sense of time. When singing in the Spirit, the person poured forth a rich strain of melody of which each note was musical and uttered with a truly astonishing sweetness and power of expression. He accelerated into a rapidity which neither detracted from the distinctness of his utterance nor appeared to agitate body or mind. Sometimes the voice became loud enough to fill the house and be heard a considerable distance outside it; yet in spite of the great mental and muscular energy involved, the singer showed a tranquillity and composure the very opposite of excitement.

Recorded examples of Irvingite glossolalia are unimpressive in cold print. Besides fragments and isolated words verses of two hymns have survived:

(1) *Hippo gerasto niparos* (2) *Hey amei hassan alla do*
    Boorastin farini   *Hoc alore loore*
    O fastor sungor boorinos   *Has hoo massan amor ho*
    Epoongos menati   *To prov his aso ore*

While 'the inspired brethren of Port-Glasgow [were] holding religious conversaziones in language which nobody understood' (Voltaire) the Church of Jesus Christ of Latter Day Saints (the Mormons) was coming into existence in America. Founded by Joseph Smith (1805-44) and built up by Brigham Young (1801-77), the Church, which in 1830 had six members, now has hundreds of thousands throughout the western world. Smith himself spoke in tongues in 1833, and Article 7 of his summary of doctrine, issued in 1842, states, 'We believe in the gifts of tongues . . . [and] . . . the interpretation of tongues.'

The practice of glossolalia among the Mormons was an organized affair. Prior to a meeting it would be announced that someone would speak in tongues. Every believer knew that he might be chosen as 'the mouthpiece of the Most High' and was prepared for a call to speak. The Mormon leaders would then call upon some brother, 'Father So-and-so, rise in the name of Jesus Christ. Make some sound without thought, continue to make sounds and the Lord will make a language from them.' The individual would stand, pray silently, lean in faith upon Christ, open his lips and utter the first sounds which came. The Spirit would make it a language and give an interpreter (any kind of gibberish was declared a language, and critics declared that the glossolalics were generally the most illiterate among the saints).

The tongues were believed to be equally foreign to speaker and listeners, known only to the Lord. When one ended, a different brother interpreted, for among the Mormons no person had both the gifts of tongues and interpretation. The written examples of Mormon tongues are not inspiring, but they were recorded by hostile observers probably unskilled in shorthand and only averagely trustworthy in memory. Hawthornthwaite, writing for the Anti-Mormon Committee, gives an example of a tongue and interpretation in which the length of the latter contrasts with the brevity of the former.

O me, contra von te, par las a te se, ter mon re ke: ran passan par du mon te! O me, sentrate kursh kramma palassate Mount Zion kron coe che and America pa palassate pa pau pupe! Santro von teli tarattata tow!

This was interpreted,

Yea, beloved sister, thus saith the Lord unto thee, be thou humble and obedient to the priesthood that is placed over thee, and thou shalt be gathered unto the land of Zion, and see the Temple of the Lord, yea, thou shalt have thy washings and thine anointings, and thou shalt receive thy blessings! Yea, beloved sister, be thou faithful and obedient, and thou shalt have the desire of thy heart; yea, beloved sister, thou shalt be a mother in Israel, and thou shalt be great, yea, if thou art only humble and faithful, thou shalt be a saviour in Mount Zion, and receive the exaltation in the kingdom of God! Be humble and obedient, dear sister, and these are thy blessings in the name of Jesus Christ.[3]

Two further examples show the alliteration which is a common feature of tongues: '*O me, terrei te te-te-te! O me, terrei te! terrei, terrei, te, te-te-te! O me, terrei te!*' and '*Pa, pepepe pa pa! Pa, pa, pepepe pa! Pa pepepe pa, pa pa!*' while rubbish appears even more plainly in '*Ah, man, oh, son of man, ak ne commene en halle gaste en esak milkea, Jeremiah, Ezekiel, Nephi, Lahi, St John.*'

Nor do some stories of interpretations give much credit to the honesty or intelligence of the early Mormons. A Welsh girl who spoke in Welsh had an interpretation given by a brother quite different from the original. A young man recited a passage from Caesar's *Gallic Wars* and received an interpretation about latter-day glory. An apostate Mormon stated that a talk he gave in the Choctaw language about hunting was rendered into a florid account of the glories that would result from the completion of the great Temple then being built.

Early Mormon enthusiasts exhibited all the usual extravagant motor-automata of charismatic sects and whole days of 'speaking meetings' were devoted to glossolalia. At the dedication of the Temple in Salt Lake City, hundreds of elders spoke in tongues. By 1870, however, the practice was rare, and the modern Mormons, while recognizing tongues as a spiritual phenomenon, do not regard them as of practical value and discourage them as laying the faith open to ridicule from opponents. Their attitude may well give a clue as to why the practice of glossolalia apparently ceased after the apostolic age.

The tradition of saintly tongues in the Roman Catholic Church was carried on in the early nineteenth century by Katherine Emerick, 'the Nun of Dulmer' (Dulmen), an ecstatic, who often spoke in trance in a strange and beautiful language; later the experience of Bernadette at Lourdes in 1858 was followed by an outburst of visions and trances. Nearly all the visionaries also spoke in tongues and instances are recorded in the late nineteenth and early twentieth centuries. Not all these were accepted as God-inspired – two German boys who spoke in various classical languages had to be 'released from possession' in 1869.

Born in 1801 was Frederica Hauffe, the 'Seeress of Prevorst'. The vocabulary of her time described her as speaking and writing an 'inner language' in a half-waking state – the third of four degrees of a 'magnetic condition'. The language appeared 'when her spirit was in intimate conjunction with her soul' – whatever that may mean. She exhibited no mantic fury and always remained calm, although a shrillness of voice, followed by an impulse to speak High German, heralded the advent of her inner language. When she wished to return to normal speech, she made 'magnetic passes' over herself.

Listeners claimed that the language Frau Hauffe spoke resembled an Eastern tongue, and she claimed that it was a remnant of the early language of mankind, the tongue that Jacob spoke, natural to her and to all men. She used it with perfect consistency so that her close acquaintances grew to understand it, and she had a perfect memory for it. When a lithograph of a script written by her a year before, of which she had no copy, was brought to her, she objected that there was a dot too many on one of the signs and was found to be right. Philologists discovered in her language resemblances to Coptic, Arabic and Hebrew; for example, *Elschaddai*, her word for God, is Hebrew for the self-sufficient or all-powerful One, *bianachli* is the Hebrew for 'I am sighing' and the word *dalmachan* appears to be Arabic. Other words given with their meanings were: *handacani*, physician; *alentana*, lady; *chlann*, glass; *schmade*, moon; *nohen*, no; *nochiane*, nightingale; *bianna fina*, many-coloured flowers; *moy*, how; *toë*, what; *optini paga*, thou must sleep; *me li erato*, I rest.

Frau Hauffe said that only in her inner language could she fully express her innermost feelings, and when she wished to express them in German she translated them from that language, which proceeded not from her head but from the epigastric region. (This is reminiscent of the Greek term 'belly-talker', used to describe a certain type of supernormal speech, better known in its Latin form which gives the English 'ventriloquism'.) Every sensation and perception had its proper figure or sign, which fallen man had lost, though it still existed in him and could be recovered if sought for. One word of the language often expressed more than whole lines of ordinary speech and, after death, a man could read his whole life in a single symbol or character of it. The written characters were always connected with numbers, for words with numbers had a much deeper and more comprehensive signification than those without. In her somnambulistic state, Frau Hauffe often said that the ghosts spoke the language, for although spirits could read thoughts, the soul, to whom this speech belonged, took it with it when it went above, because the soul formed an ethereal body for the spirit. The phrase is reminiscent of the theory of the astral body which is not the inner core of human personality but its shell, fitted for at least temporary existence in a non-physical environment, while numerology is also closely connected with the occult.

It is worth including here for comparison a single paragraph of the original language spoken by Adam before the fall, taken from a page of it printed at the end of the very rare 'A True and Faithful Relation of What Passed for Many Years between Dr John Dee and Some Spirits' (London, 1659) and communicated to Dr Dee by an even rarer personality, the Archangel Gabriel himself. No translation is given but, like Frau Hauffe's specimens, it seems vaguely Hebrew. An analysis of it by a modern linguist would probably show it to be a meaningless verbiage possibly echoing the abracadabra type of formula used in magical spells.

Arney vah nol gadeth adney ox vals, nath gemseh ah orza vall gemma, oh gedvam on zembah hohhad vomfah oldru ampha note admancha nonsah vamfas orned, alphol andax, orzadah vos ausch hansab von adma wha notma goth vamsed adges ouseple oudemax orzan, unfa onmah undabra gouseh gole nahad na.

Between 1841 and 1843, following a Christian revivalist campaign, 'sermon-sickness' broke out in Sweden and Norway. This began with a young girl, Lisa Andersdocter, who sang and preached under the influence of the Spirit. Worshippers, who ordinarily had no power of utterance and were mostly youthful, even children, were suddenly irresistibly moved to sing hyms and preach sermons summoning to repentance. Some fell into deep trance, producing speech of 'great eloquence, lively declamation, and the command of much purer language than was usual, or apparently possible for them in their natural state'. Their words, the speakers said, seemed to be given them by someone else. Some of the seizures began with horrible oaths, a fact which suggests that this may have happened to some members of the Corinthian church, since Paul taught that no one in the Spirit could say, 'Jesus is anathema'. When the tongues ended, the speakers had little or no memory of their experience.

On the whole, the Swedish revival seems to have been beneficial. A child impressed the Bishop of Skara as 'characterized by a most beautiful calmness and quietness'. With arms meekly folded and with something saintlike in her appearance, she preached a sermon suited to an unsophisticated audience, yet conformable to the pure spirit of the Gospel. Her voice, normally hoarse, had softness, brilliance and clarity. Her tones were earnest and solemn, her spiritual vocabulary far beyond her waking capabilities.

There were, however, obvious dangers in the movement and doctors and clergy united in 1843 to end it.[4]

A volume could be written cataloguing minor instances of glossolalia during the nineteenth century, of which the following half-dozen are typical. A small girl with convulsions having been cured by means of a relic at Morzin, Haute-Savoie, soon after 1850, other girls were similarly affected. They had hallucinations, uttered terrible blasphemies and spoke in Latin, German and 'Arabic'. They could have picked up the Latin in church, there were German-speaking districts near Morzin and no witness knew a word of Arabic himself.

In Germany, the Rev John Christopher Blumhardt (1805–80), famous for prayer cures, healed Gottlieben Dittus, possessed by 1,067 devils (qualifying her, surely, for *The Guinness Book of Records*) at Möttlengen. He talked to several of the demons who spoke 'in all the different European languages' as well as others not recognized. It is fortunate that Blumhardt was linguist enough to recognize all the European languages and he may, perhaps, be forgiven for ignorance of the others. But would that he had kept records of the conversations.

In 1855 a great revival accompanied by tongue-speaking in the Russian Orthodox Church spilled over into Armenia, with far-reaching results. A boy in the village of Kara Kala, Armenia, had a series of prophetic visions and produced a number of scripts, pictures, maps and charts. In about 1880 many in the area began to speak in tongues and small groups, mainly Presbyterians, banded together in Pentecostal worship, among them a family called Shakarian. Among these 'Pentecostallers' was a prophet who foretold that the Turks would turn against the Christians, and all Pentecostal families began to leave Kara Kala in 1900, the exodus continuing until 1912. In 1906 Domos Shakarian and two other Armenians came across one of the fountainheads of the modern Pentecostalist movement in the Azuza Street glossolalia in Los Angeles, thus combining two strains of charismatic tradition in the United States.

In England in 1873, after a campaign by the American evangelist, Moody, who did not himself speak in tongues, a YMCA worker reported, 'I found the meeting on fire. The young men were speaking in tongues and prophesying.' There were also wholly independent manifestations. In the Unicois mountains in North Carolina, for instance, members of the Camp Creek Baptist Church spoke in tongues without knowing that such a phenomenon existed elsewhere.

In 1880 a Swiss, Maria Gerber, reported that in moments of

special joy, she sang spiritual songs in a language she had never learned. Later she went to America, unable to speak English. One day, while praying for a sick friend, her words, to their common astonishment, emerged as 'flawless English'. Living and worshipping among English-speaking people would have given her all the English she needed, subconsciously absorbed.

Dr F. S. Mayer, writing in *The London Christian* of peasant Baptist congregations in Esthonia, said,

> The gift of tongues is heard quite often in the meetings. . . . They are most uttered by young women, less frequently by men. When they are interpreted they are found to mean, 'Jesus is coming soon. Jesus is near. Be ready, be not idle'. When they are heard, unbelievers who may be in the audience are greatly awed. A gentleman who was present on one occasion was deeply impressed by the fact that those who spoke were quite ordinary people until they were uplifted as it were by a trance and then they spoke with so much fluency and refinement.

In 1885, Mrs Michael Baxter, though unable to speak or understand German, was inspired to preach in the language for thirty-five minutes. She was well understood, and one conversion resulted from her sermon. 'After that,' she claimed, 'God led me to speak almost every day, and often twice a day to hundreds of people.' This experience is contrary to that of other faithful Christians who have been disappointed in their expectation that the Holy Spirit would give them tongues for evangelization as they needed them. An explanation could be that Mrs Baxter, worshipping as she would have done with Germans of her own denomination, heard sermons in German which she was enabled by cryptomnesia to repeat.

A testimony to the continuous existence of tongues during the latter half of the nineteenth century is given by D. P. Simmons, of Frost Proof, Florida. Writing in 1909 he stated,

> While I have been a church member for sixty-two years, I have associated with those who talk in tongues for fifty-two years.

In Southern New England, among the Second Adventists, A.D. 1875, I learned that some had for three years previously in their religious worship spoken in what is termed as 'the unknown tongues'. From 1824 down to the present time, from Maine to Connecticut, quite a goodly number of the Adventist people (known as Gift Adventists) have had more or less talking in tongues, and also the interpretation of tongues.

Christianity, however, ceased to have a monopoly of tongues in the western world during this period. Modern Spiritualism came into existence at about the same time and made claims to xenolalia (paranormal communication in recognized foreign languages) by spirits, which by comparison reduced Christian wonders to triviality.

7
Nineteenth-century Spiritualism

Modern spiritualism is often dated from 1851 when communication with spirits was allegedly established by rappings made at the home of the Fox sisters at Hydesville, New York State. The movement spread rapidly through America, England, Europe and elsewhere, and was followed by scientific enquiry into its phenomena by such bodies as the English and American Societies for Psychical Research. The quantity of communication by xenolalia claimed in Spiritualist literature is enormous, its quality varying from the remarkable to the absurd.

Methods of communication may be classified under eleven heads:

1 Foreign languages, unknown to the medium and nearly all the sitters (sometimes originally to all the sitters, necessitating the introduction into the circle of expert linguists), spoken by or through the medium in trance or waking state. The communicating entity may directly influence the brain centres of language when the medium is possessed – communication of this kind may be coloured by the medium's knowledge and personality, which can affect the quality of the message. A 'Foreign' entity may transmit its *thought* to the sensitive who then translates it into his own language; so xenolalia need not be used by such entities. Some mediums claim that

they consciously interpret thoughts originally communicated in a language unknown to them.

2 'Direct Voice'. In this method the medium does not speak himself but acts as a power-focus which enables spirit-voices to talk from the air surrounding him. (One theory is that the spirits form ectoplasmic voice-boxes through which they speak.) This process can lend itself particularly to xenolalia, for the communicating intelligence remains sufficiently independent of the medium's personality to be able to express itself in a language unknown to him.

3 Languages overheard by clairaudience and repeated phonetically by the medium without understanding but comprehended by his sitter.

4 Languages spoken directly by materialized spirits.

5 Writing of unknown languages by sensitives in trance.

6 Automatic writing in a normal state. The technique is to place a pencil between the fingers, rest it on paper and allow it to move of its own accord. The ordinary experimenter will produce meaningless squiggles, but the gifted and developed automatist may produce pages of script written in other handwritings and containing intelligible messages, sometimes in foreign languages.

7 Writing by apparatus, such as ouija or planchette board.

8 Language communicated by physical means, such as raps.

9 Writing on cards, slates, photographic plates or other objects.

10 Writing by spirits materialized wholly or in part.

11 Xenolalia 'seen' by clairvoyance and copied down.

The number of cases of Spiritist xenolalia may be estimated at many thousands. I have in my files about five hundred instances, many of them single examples of the work of mediums who claim to have communicated in foreign languages dozens of times in their lives. The five hundred could probably be multiplied by a hundred when bulked up with such statements as 'Mrs Faye has written in ten different languages, including even the Sanskrit, Kanaka and Chinese characters' and 'Mrs Hollis wrote hundreds of communications in Latin, Greek, Hebrew, German, Italian, French, Welsh and English'. If an estimated fifty thousand occasions be accepted as reasonable, he would be a bold man who would say that these were all smoke and no fire, whatever their explanation. Yet no evidence remains to convince a determined sceptic; for even if a hundred Hollis scripts in the eight languages claimed survived, there could be no evidence that they had not been forged.

The variety of languages and communication codes claimed is also considerable, including Arabic, Armenian, Austrian German, Assyrian, Basque, Chaldean, Chinese (ancient and modern, in various dialects), Coptic, Croatian, Danish, deaf-mute sign language, Dutch, Egyptian (ancient and modern), Hawaiian, Hebrew, hieratic script, Hindi, Hungarian, Italian (Genoese, Neapolitan, Piedmontese, Sicilian, Venetian), Japanese, Javanese, Kaffir, Latin, Maly, Marathi, Mexican, Morse code (old and new styles), Norwegian, Old Castilian, Persian, Phoenician, Polish, Portuguese, Red Indian languages (at least six), Russian (ancient and modern), Sandwich Island tongues, Sanskrit, Serbian, shorthand, Sicilian, Sikh, South Sea tongues, Spanish, Swedish, Syrian, Turkish, Urdu and Welsh. A wide variety of regional dialects could be included – American, Cockney, Irish, Scottish, Welsh, etc. – and, if one wished to be 'way out' in every sense of the words, Martian, Saturnian and other tongues claimed to come from outer space. Xenolalia in some ancient tongues is incapable of proof in that no one knows how they were pronounced.

The beginnings of modern Spiritualism are more amorphous than those of Christianity. A convenient way to deal with its xenolalia is to present a number of selected cases, arranged chronologically, each numbered according to the heading under which it falls.

(3) Grotius (1583–1645) records[1] that a man who knew no Greek brought Monsieur de Saumaire, a counsellor of the Dijon

parlement, a paper on which some Greek words were written phonetically. He said that a voice had uttered them to him during the night and that he had written their sound down as best he could. M. de Saumaire translated the script, 'Begone! Do you not see that death impends?' The man left his house which collapsed the following night. It is suggested that the man might have received subconscious impressions of the house's dangerous state. But why Greek?

A possibly telepathic case is that of a little girl, reputed to be a witch, who could instantly interpret the words of Dr Cotton Mather (1663–1728), the notorious witch-hunter, when he recited Hebrew, Latin or Greek to her, but could not understand a Red Indian language. It is suggested that her mind took the meaning from his. Mather explained her inability to understand the Indian by the fact that the Devil was a good Hebrew, Greek and Latin scholar but could not understand Indian.[2]

(6) Baron Guldenstubbe (1828–73), a Scandinavian nobleman of the highest character and erudition, wrote a book, *La Réalité des esprits et le phénomène merveilleux de leur écriture directe* illustrated by sixty-seven facsimiles of actual 'psychographs' in twenty different languages, selected from hundreds of examples.[3]

(6) James Wingard, of New Orleans, a former Mississipi boatman, a simple and almost wholly uneducated man, wrote under spirit influence in Greek, Hebrew, Arabic and other classical and oriental languages, 'in the purest styles of diction'. Before the American Civil War, these writings were preserved and occasionally exhibited by a Dr Hyde. An article in *The Spiritualist Messenger* dealing with some of Mr Wingard's 'wonderful spirit-writings and drawings' states that they were executed in almost total darkness, and consisted of three verses in Greek, five lines of Latin poetry, seven lines of French Poetry, two sentences in Spanish, and an inscription in Hebrew.[4]

(1) The case of Laura Edmonds, daughter of Judge Worth

Edmonds of the New York bar, is one of the oft-discussed early ones.[5] From 1851 Laura developed as an excellent medium for speaking in and out of trance, the discernment of spirits and the gift of tongues, conversing fluently, sometimes for an hour at a time, in Spanish, French, Greek, Latin, Italian, Portuguese, Polish, Hungarian and several Red Indian dialects, although she had learned only a few words of French at school. She is described – strangely, when one considers the hostility between Roman Catholicism and Spiritualism – as having been a fervent, extremely pious Roman Catholic of high intelligence and irreproachable honesty. Her father, in his *Spiritual Tracts*, claimed that 'it is not infrequent, that foreigners converse with their spirit-friends through her, in their own language'. He gives the following examples of her gifts.

A Miss Dowd, of common country education and a medium, was troubled by the spirit of a Frenchman who spoke through her only in French. Laura conversed with her in rapid French for more than an hour, Miss Dowd's being a southern provincial patois and Laura's pure Parisian. There were 'five or six' people present at this conversation.

Two Polish gentlemen, entire strangers, talked Polish to Laura to which she sometimes replied in English, sometimes Polish, which they appeared to understand while she did not.

There were 'a hundred instances' in which Laura sang Italian, unknown entirely to her, improvising both words and tune. Her mother said that

> One day my daughter and niece came into my library, and
> began a conversation with me in Spanish, one speaking a part
> of a sentence and the other the residue. They were
> influenced, as I found, by the spirit of a person whom I had
> known when in Central America, and reference was made to
> many things which had occurred to me there, of which I knew
> they were as ignorant as they were of Spanish.
> Laura has spoken to me in Indian, in the Chippewa, and
> Menominic tongues. I know the language because I had
> been two years in the Indian country.

The most remarkable story of Laura's mediumship concerns her conversation with a Greek, Mr Evangelides, who met her at her home in 1854 in the presence of from eight to fifteen people (accounts differ). Neither the judge nor his daughter had met Evangelides before. The Greek spoke only broken English, but soon a spirit spoke to him through Laura whom he identified as a Monsieur Botzeris who had died at Evangelides's house a few years before. The conversation began in English, but as Laura now and again spoke a word or sentence in Greek, Evangelides asked if he would be understood in Greek. The dialogue continued for over an hour, entirely in Greek on the man's side and on the girl's sometimes in Greek, sometimes in English. At times Laura did not understand the idea conveyed either by her own words or his. At others she understood both his and her own Greek. He was once so grieved that those present wondered what was the matter. He refused to say at the time, but it was learned later that Laura had informed him of the death of his son in Greece, a fact afterwards found to be true. Not understanding her own xenolalia was a common feature of Laura's tongues, though they were understood by those to whom they were spoken.

Evangelides added

> that he had never before witnessed any spirit manifestations, and that he had during the conversation tried experiments, to test that which was so novel to him. Those experiments were in speaking of subjects which he knew Laura must be ignorant of and in frequently changing the topic, from domestic to political affairs, from philosophy to theology, and so on. In answer to our enquiries – *for none of us knew Greek* – he answered us that his Greek must have been understood, and her Greek was correct. He afterward had many other interviews, in which Greek conversation occurred [my italic].

Various explanations of Laura's gift have been suggested. Bozzano, a Spiritualist, put forward the unadulterated hypothesis that 'an independent spiritual entity made use of her larynx for his own ends'.[6] Fairfield claims that Judge Edmonds was of a 'cephalic temperament'. The failure of his health in 1851 led to persistent mental depression and an almost monomaniac persistency in discussing the subject of death and future destiny. He affirms that Laura presented physically

> one of the most pronounced examples I have ever glanced at, of the congeries of symptoms associated with active neurosis of this type. . . . In certain abnormal and highly excited states of the nervous system, as is proven by abundant facts, matters impressed deep on the memory of a father present themselves to the consciousness of his posterity. I have no doubt, for instance, that the daughter of Judge Edmonds derives her capacity to speak . . . in languages unfamiliar to her in the ordinary moods of consciousness, from her father's studies in that direction, or, rather, from the nervous habit engendered by those studies – for investigation has left no question that memory is an organic record, and that every event and idea of a man's life is distinctly recorded in his nervous system and hence transferable.[7]

But, as Cutten drily comments, 'The transference of acquired characteristics presents no difficulty to a writer of this kind'[8] and does not explain how Laura spoke so well in so many languages, some of them and the facts they recounted completely unknown to her father. De Verne, accepting the facts of the Evangelides encounter as reported, writes,

> Let us make an effort of metaphysical acrobatics; let us suppose that Evangelides had received the news of the death of his son telepathically, and that this knowledge had remained latent in his brain until the moment came for Miss Laura Edmonds' clairvoyance to dislodge it. . . . Only it would not be logical to attribute the gift of speaking Greek to the medium and her knowledge of the child's death to two distinct causes. Now, *how did Miss Laura speak Greek*? No hypothesis has yet been wrought to explain that phenomenon.[9]

Warcollier wrought such an hypothesis in reply, suggesting that Evangelides's subconscious mind communicated the idea of his son's death together with the Greek in which to express it telepathically to Laura, who spoke the man's subconscious thought. His thought was transmitted in a graphic form or, in this case, in the shape of Greek words heard in his mind's ear which Laura was able to express more easily even than she could have done in English.[10]

Others point out how very generalized Judge Edmonds's accounts are. He does not say how far his own acquaintance with Spanish and Indian went. He gives no examples of sentences actually spoken, no proof that his young ladies knew nothing of the languages they used (though to prove a negative of this kind is all but impossible) and no dates of incidents beyond the fact that the conversation with Evangelides took place in 1854, three years before its written record. A sceptic could believe that the recorded incidents never happened or were at best wonder-stories exaggerated out of all proportion from insignificant happenings.

Another explanation which might satisfy a sceptic is that of auditory hallucination. If a telepathic impact can clothe itself in audible words, it could have been that Evangelides, receiving the medium's message telepathically, clothed it himself in hallucinatory Greek words. No one present knew Greek, and such clues as to whether Laura spoke with a native or foreign accent are not given.

Bozzano also examines telepathic explanations. He mentions that the early mesmerists could not explain how their somnambulistic subjects, when interrogated in Latin, Greek or Hebrew, both understood and replied correctly – in their vernaculars – while they were not only incapable of formulating an answer to the language in question, but were quite ignorant of the meaning of the words composing the questions to which they replied. This is now explained by their reading the question in the mind of the hypnotist. It was the opposite with Laura. Her speaking in languages she did not understand, since the faculty of knowing what has never been learned does not exist in the subconscious, proved that they were spirits who spoke through her.[11]

Two theories remain, one of ancestral memory, the other of cosmic memory. But a medium speaking in ten languages would need the blood of ten nations in her veins, including, in Laura's case, several Red Indian tribes. The theory of cosmic memory, that there exists (though where or how is unknown) a repository of all the experience and knowledge of all mankind throughout all the ages, on which certain individuals with psychic talents can draw, is too far-fetched for most people. It is not, however, impossible, especially for some Theists who might be prepared to accept that everything past, present and future exists in what can be called the I-AM-NOW of God. Such a concept would also explain precognition. But how and why some individuals should be able to draw upon this source, and what the nature of the faith or psychic gifts involved is, is not apparent in our present state of knowledge.

Judge Edmonds, with a fellow-Spiritualist, Dr George T. Dexter, collected literally dozens of examples of Spiritualist tongues. He wrote to *The New York Tribune* that 'It is enough now to say that these letters give names, dates, and places so that the statements can be verified . . . and I hold the evidence subject to the inspection of any who may desire it.' For a lawyer Judge Edmonds had a lax view of evidence, and experienced psychical researchers may be forgiven for dismissing most of his material as hearsay, some of it at third hand. Many of his correspondents were semi-literate while much of the paraphernalia of sealed envelopes and similar conjuring tricks invites suspicion.

Podmore, one of the earliest investigators, a scholarly and cautious psychical researcher, points out that the cases sent to Edmonds were all over a year old and that in only two of them was a *recognized* foreign language *written*. The evidence in these two cases was unimpeachable except in the vital point of the medium's complete ignorance of the language written. It can be added that even the most honest of mediums might not know that he had been exposed to a language absorbed subconsciously. For the rest, the languages were vouched for by people ignorant of them, by the speakers themselves or by other mediums present. The kind of evidence which could mislead sincere but ignorant witnesses was of the type supplied by a lady who wrote a Latin sonnet by John Milton which was neither Latin nor a sonnet. It had a Latin sound and the word-terminations were Latin – but the lady had heard her father for years preparing boys in Latin for College.[12]

There may be mentioned in passing a number of examples of most beautiful singing in tongues, far beyond the normal capacity of the singers, quoted among Judge Edmonds's cases. These are reminiscent of the similar skills recorded by the Camisards and others.

Similarly numerous and equally lacking in evidence are multitudinous stores of Spiritualist glossolalia and xenolalia recorded by Mrs Emma Hardinge in her *American Spiritualism*. A strange story she tells cannot be classified under any of the usual headings. It concerns a Miss Mary Camstock upon whose arm there appeared beautiful and legible characters. No one could interpret these until a certain gentleman affirmed that it was the name of a masonic brother who had died twenty years before, given in the masonic alphabet. Other communications appeared on Miss Camstock's arm on many other occasions.[13]

(9) An example of spirit-writing on photographic plates is given by Campbell Holms. On 12 August 1910, Archdeacon Colley asked 'Segaski' (a spirit-control) to oblige him with a communication suitable for a lecture he had to give the next day and requested that some of it be in a foreign language. He held a packet of plates with Harold Bailey, a photographer, and Dr D'Aute-Hooper, an amateur psychic. Extreme vibration and heat were felt. The plates were immediately developed. Five were covered in minute, very neat writing in English and one entirely in Latin, which no one present knew. The writings were evidential in their references to individuals. The Latin was later found to be an ode of Horace, with some inaccuracies. The script was black on a transparent ground, a positive instead of a

negative. The smallness of the copperplate writing made it impossible to be reproduced by any engraving, and it was so microscopic that a high-powered lens was necessary to read it. Archaic Greek, Latin, Hebrew, French, Italian and Arabic allegedly appeared on plates on other occasions.[14]

(5) Just as Christians have their miracles of the dumb producing xenolalia, so the Spiritualists have theirs of the illiterate writing in languages not their own. An American boy aged thirteen, unable to write the alphabet, was controlled by a female German spirit who requested him to write a letter in German to her son. The recipient stated that it was German, purported to come from his mother, who had lived and died in Germany, and gave correctly her name, place of residence and place of death. These details were unknown in America where the incident happened. The story, itself second-hand, is quoted fourth-hand by Mrs Hardinge from *The Spiritual Telegraph*, November 1855.[15] Mrs Hardinge also reports several sermons by juveniles of the Camisard type but heard none of them in person. Her completely uncritical attitude is reflected in accounts of a number of cases of Spiritualist xenolalia written in the late 1800s which, though fascinating to read, are nearly all hearsay and completely lacking in evidence.

(8) An amusing variation on a theme is the experience of Mrs Hollis, an American medium mentioned earlier. On 12 November 1872 she received a communication in raps, recognized as Morse code. They were translated, 'We will do our best to give you telegraphing. It may take time, as all things do. F. Stevens' (a dead telegraphist).[16] There may be compared with this a message sent through another medium, Mr Eglinton, ignorant of telegraphy. He was 'given' a variety of Morse code used twenty years earlier by a spirit who had passed over at that time.[17]

(9) J. C. F. Zöllner records slate-writing exploits of the medium Slade, who recorded up to six languages in different scripts on a single plate. On one occasion, Slade placed a piece of pencil

between the folds of a double slate which he held over a table in view of all. Three sentences were written in English, French and German, each in a different hand.[18] On another he was handed a plate which he had never had in his hands before, laid a pencil on the table and over it the clean slate. This was done in bright daylight. Writing was at once heard and three raps given as a sign of completion. The whole underside of the plate was covered by an address from Slade's wife written in English and by a message in German from a spirit-relative, in their hands.[19] A Herr Kleeberg of Berlin accompanied by a 'thoroughly sceptical' friend took two slates to Slade who, beyond putting a piece of pencil between them, never touched them at all. The visitors held the slates above the table in broad daylight. Writing at once began, and when the plates were separated, the lower one was covered in writing in English, French, Dutch, Greek and Chinese. The foreign languages appeared one below the other in the centre with the English written round them in a circle.[20]

All these stories savour too much of the conjuring trick, leaving the reader with the feeling that, even if they were accurately observed and reported, 'they were tricks though I don't know how they were done'. If spirits can write on closed slates in broad daylight, why should they not write on open ones before the eyes of the observers?

(6) In 1881 J. L. O'Sullivan, at one time American minister at Lisbon, described a séance which he and Professor Buchanan had with another American medium, called Phillips. They were seated round a small table. Phillips, opposite and within two or three feet of them,

> snatched a sheet of paper and pencil and began to write
> backwards and upwards. . . . But he seemed to be drawing
> only straight lines backwards, nor had they any idea of
> finding them to contain anything legible. . . . When he got
> to the north-west corner of the sheet, the medium threw it
> from him. They both concurred in estimating the time
> consumed as under two minutes. On examining the paper

closely it proved to contain the last chapter of the Book of Revelations, in Spanish, with about half of the long, old, monkish, Latin hymn, the 'Dies Irae', interpolated in about the middle of it. The letters were small, upright, and perfectly legible, proving that the pencil in the medium's fingers had really traced all the successive up and down strokes, though to the closely observant eyes of the watchers it had seemed to be making only straight lines backwards. On his return home Mr O'Sullivan . . . ascertained that if the contents of the paper had been written forward in the ordinary way, without an instant's pause, and with the utmost possible rapidity, it would have required about twenty minutes. . . . The whole writing fitted exactly into the foolscap page. The last word (first in the writing) being Amen, it began at the tail of the 'n', and the initial capital letter at the beginning of the chapter proved to fall exactly into its proper place at the north-west corner of the page.

No conclusion about an interpretation of this remarkable *tour de force* is given. The incident could be explained by the common conjuring trick of substitution. The features of great speed and inverted, sometimes 'looking-glass' writing appear in other incidents, as will be seen.[21]

(1), (3), (5), (11) Hélène Smith, the pseudonym of a French-speaking Swiss woman born in 1864 of a Hungarian father, who was acquainted with some eight languages, and a mediumistic mother, produced some of the most sophisticated glossolalic phenomena on record. In spite of certain psychic phenomena during her girlhood, she grew up to be normal and capable, holding a responsible business position.

In 1892 she became a medium, performing at first consciously but after two years passing into total somnambulism. In this state she experienced three increasingly significant cycles of existence. In the first she claimed to be a reincarnation of Marie Antoinette. In the second she was Simandini, daughter of an Arab sheik who had lived at the end of the fourteenth century, and in the third the eleventh wife of the Hindu prince, Sivrouka Nayaka. During this phase she allegedly spoke Hindu (Sanskrit) but no Arabic, her mother tongue in her previous existence until she married at the age of eighteen. Thomas Flournoy, Professor of Psychology at the University of Geneva, who investigated Hélène with great thoroughness and published the results in *Des Indes à la planète Mars* (later translated into English), was handicapped by an ignorance of Indian languages and by the medium's rapid and indistinct pronunciation. He stated, however, that Sanskrit was not spoken at all in Nayaka's country, Kanara, at that period, but a Dravidian dialect, that women spoke Pracrit, not Sanskrit, and that Simandini's idiom was not Pracrit. Oriental scholars to whom Hélène's language was submitted, thought that it was a medley of Sanskrit and invented words, or that there were eight or ten Sanskrit syllables constituting a fragment of a sentence which had some meaning. It was suggested that Hélène possessed part at least of the Davangari alphabet, picked up subconsciously from a rapid glance through a Sanskrit grammar, or that the authentic fragments could have come from something overheard, such as an Indian student reciting aloud Sanskrit texts and their French translation. Her poor pronunciation could indicate a visual origin – the reading of texts printed in French characters.

Had Hélène's mediumistic career ended with the oriental episode, she would have been worth no more than a passing reference. But on 28 October 1894, Alexis Mirbel, the dead seventeen-year-old son of a widow attending Hélène's séances, 'came through'. He subsequently arrived on the planet Mars and in February 1896 spoke Martian, addressing his mother through Hélène in the new language which, naturally, meant nothing to her.

Hélène's first 'Martian' was analogous to the gibberish children use in their games, but after a further seven months' incubation she produced a genuine language-type formed of precise words and with a definite signification. Eighteen months later there appeared the Martian alphabet, of all the letters in the French except 'q', 'w', 'x' and 'y', but with no accents or capitals (indicated by a point above the letter) and including signs for 'ch', initial 's', double 's', the full stop and plurals. The second of double letters was replaced by a point placed at the right of the first.

Hélène used four methods of communicating her psychic information:

(a) *Verbo-auditive automatism*, that is, hallucination of hearing, accompanying visions in the waking state. She wrote during her visions or immediately after them as many of the unintelligible words as she could remember. Esenale (Alexis Mirbel in his Martian incarnation) translated them by clearly articulating each Martian word before giving it its French equivalent, but the translation did not necessarily happen at the same sitting. Sometimes, during her séance visions, Hélène repeated words she heard without understanding them and the sitters wrote them.

(b) *Vocal automatisms*. Sitters gathered what they could from Hélène while she talked with great volubility. Distinction had to be made between relatively clear phrases translated later by Esenale and rapid confused gibberish which was only a pseudo-language.

(c) *Verbo-visual automatisms*. Writing in strange unknown letters appeared before Hélène's eyes which she copied without knowing its meaning.

(d) *Graphic automatisms*. Hélène wrote while completely entranced and incarnating a Martian personality.

Some forty scripts were noted down, five given orally, two vocally – auditively, twenty-one auditively, three auditively–graphically, four visually and five graphically.

Flournoy inferred from the stages by which the Martian writing was achieved that it was the result of a slow auto-suggestion culminating in a vision in which its characters appeared on cylinders presented to Hélène by three Martians clearly enough for her to be able to copy them. Once established, words and characters were used with complete consistency over a period of years. Flournoy was able to analyse the syntax and trace much of the vocabulary to its origins. Martian was simply French with sounds and letters changed, each French word being replaced by another. Word order was identical. Personal pronouns, articles and possessive adjectives were analogous to French; the vowels corresponded exactly with the same shades of pronunciation; Martian 'c' and 's' behaved like the same French letters and, most convincing evidence of all that Martian was French new writ was the use of an unnecessary letter 'm' in Martian corresponding to the French euphonic 't'. For example, the Martian for '*Quand reviendra-t-il?*' was '*Keri berimir-m-hed?*' These are but some of the exact correspondences between the languages.

A further analysis of Hélène's Martian made by Victor Henri, Professor of Sanskrit at the University of Paris, confirmed Flournoy's findings. He further showed that of 248 words, 110 were French, disguised and altered not arbitrarily but according to a logical, uniform system applied by the medium's subconscious mind. Twenty-five were German in origin, 55 Magyar, 3 English, 5 Oriental, chiefly Sanskrit – only 5 defeated his efforts. Henri discovered at least 40 genuine words and a rudimentary knowledge of grammar in Hélène's Sanskrit. An interesting feature is that she never used the letter 'f', which is lacking in Sanskrit.

Martian was, however, a language, albeit a bastard one. It possessed a clear, consistent vocabulary conveying definite ideas, an acoustic quality and an intonation peculiar to it.

Hélène, whose auditory and visual hallucinations were immensely vivid and real to her, as is obvious from her drawings of the Martian landscapes she saw, did not accept Flournoy's explanations. Three views held of her phenomena were (1) that they derived wholly from spirits; (2) that they came partly from 'joking' spirits, partly from her subconscious; (3) that they were produced entirely by her subconscious. Hélène held the first, and Flournoy's acceptance of the third had two results. First, he was not admitted to observe her further in a mediumship to which, through a beneficiary, she could devote her whole time.

Second, she produced other languages in a subconscious attempt (said psychologists) to produce tongues which could not be linked with French. Ultramartian, Uranian and Lunar languages with their own scripts were produced, revealing the kind of life and civilization enjoyed on some heavenly bodies of which the Moon, Hélène stated, was only partially inhabited.

The three languages followed the same order of development as the Martian. Strange words were first heard and repeated phonetically, then seen, and finally written by automatic handwriting. The fact that all the languages were an incomplete extraction of French, owing nothing to the Hungarian and Italian Hélène's father spoke nor to the English and German she had learned herself (except for the vocabulary sources already noted), confirms the view that they were formed in an infantile part of her subconscious. She 'learned' her tongues as a child does – hearing, saying, seeing, writing – incubating each for from several months to eighteen. Ultramartian was a more puerile language than Martian and Uranian even more of an eeny-meeny-miny-mo type.

An interesting comment on Hélène's scripts was given by a prominent graphologist, Madame d'Ungern-Sternberg. Graphology indicated that Hélène's controls were only facets of her divided personality, and this was confirmed by the way she moved from type to type of handwriting in some of her ordinary letters. Readers who do not take graphology seriously may find the comment valueless; others may see in it one more ounce in the weight of evidence which suggests that Hélèn's otherworldly experiences were the product only of her subliminal activity.

An objective study of her case gives small grounds for any other explanation, and increased knowledge makes life on Mars and Uranus more unlikely than it might have seemed in Hélène's day. Man has even visited the Moon – though possibly only that part of it which she stated was uninhabited.

The interest of the case is the light it throws on the process of possible subliminal activity over a period of time. One can, for example, postulate a religious man attending 'waiting' meetings for a considerable time, expecting the Holy Spirit to enable him to speak in tongues. The longer he had to wait before the breakthrough came, the more opportunity his subliminal consciousness would have to incubate a language like Hélène's Martian and produce it fully matured when the time was ripe. This is a possible explanation of *some* religious glossolalia.

The protests of believers against such a possibility may be answered by the contention that it is no more blameworthy for a man to praise God in language which has been incubated in his subconscious than it is for him consciously to use his mother-tongue. It is the fact and quality of the praise that matter. Nor need the agency of the Spirit be denied because a mental mechanism that he can use has come to be better understood. Christians claim that he can speak through their conscious preaching and praying – why not, then, through their subconscious?

(10) There were other remarkable cases of xenolalia in the 1890s. An oft-published story, given for example, by Dr Bozzano,[22] concerns thirty Norwegians, fifteen of either sex, including University professors, men of letters, doctors, magistrates and Lutheran pastors (no women's professions are given). They agreed to abstain from tobacco, alcohol and other stimulants for six months to see if such preparation would favour the production of psychical phenomena. A series of twelve séances began after the third month. Very early on, Nepenthes, an ancient Greek spirit, materialized and wrote some Greek in a sitter's notebook. No one present understood the language. On a second occasion, Nepenthes wrote in 'Herr E.'s' notebook Greek which was found to mean, 'I am Nepenthes, thy friend. When sorrows or trouble shall hold thee fast, call upon me, Nepenthes, and I will bring thee help.'

There are several questionable details in this story. Did no one in that learned band of professors and pastors know Greek (a required subject in almost all theological colleges)? 'Names of all who were present at the séances are given' – then why is anonymous Herr E. so bashful? And where is the original report of investigators who set out to prove a point?

(1) In 1894 Mr Albert Le Baron (a pseudonym), a literary man aged 39, attended an open-air séance with a group of mystics while summering at a spot on the American coast.[23] A 'psycho-somatic force' laid him flat on his back, then produced a motor-disturbance of his head and jaws resulting, after a few seconds, in another's voice, 'unearthly, awful, loud and weird', bursting from his lips with the despairing words, 'Oh, My People!' Prophetic mutterings followed.

Later Le Baron spoke with a woman's voice, identified by his hostess, a medium, as her dead mother's and also recognized by the mother's dog. The Medium's deceased father's voice followed, uttering further 'prophetic' statements such as 'He shall be a leader of the hosts of the Lord!' The effect on the speaker was one of holy awe and euphoria, 'the most wonderful feelings' he had ever enjoyed. One night Le Baron slept in the father's bed (he had been lame, a fact unknown to the visitor) and next day limped painfully for hours.

Le Baron's psycho-automatism guided him to travel to Stowe in Vermont where he received an 'injection of verbiage'.

> I shall be glorified in the work of the people, for thou hast proved thyself to be the man whose voice is the voice of Him who sent thee. Thou hast obeyed the command of the Holy One, and the valleys shall rejoice in the hope and the joy of the Lord. I shall be in thy heart, and thou shalt answer to my voice.

The speaker had no 'idea of any deific object answering to such a communicatory style'. When not in ecstasy, however, he experienced depression, vibrating 'like a pendulum between the new world of psychic phenomena on the one hand, and the old world of physical phenomena on the other'.

Le Baron was then guided to visit 'the most occult man in the west' at St Louis. The man in semi-trance 'made a lengthy foreign speech which purported to come from the princely priest of the house of the Egyptian king . . . I have every reason to believe that the gentleman believed he was uttering a genuine foreign tongue'. The translation given concerned incarnation and inspiration.

Automatic writing, clairaudience and glossolalia all developed in Le Baron. The last occurred on a Sunday morning when the psycho-automatism suddenly broke abruptly from English into unintelligible sounds resembling a foreign tongue. Too taken aback to try to write down the sounds, Le Baron asked for a translation and received about 450 words of Egyptian mystical material. The writer realized, however, that this was another stratagem of his *alter ego* to keep him worked up, to be added to its repeated urging of him to make long journeys to China and Spain for the same purpose. For a time Le Baron believed that he was speaking a language known to him in a previous incarnation.

He analysed his experience thus.

From [clairaudience and seeing sentences in dreams] it is evident that, in its incipiency, the phenomenon differed from that of a *dedoublement de la personalité* in that it did not appear to be a case of 'subliminal consciousness' on the one hand or a supra-normal intellectual faculty on the other, but distinctly that of a purely *extraneous psycho-physical spontaneity or automatism*. It was *psychic*, for it presented conception; it was *physical*, for it presented sense intuitions; it was *spontaneous and automatic* for it acted independently of the usual trend of motor-phenomena on the one hand and of the wilful intelligence as used in ordinary experience on the other. This it automatically continued to do until later on in my experience, when I believed myself to be so completely en rapport with it that I considered the spontaneity practically identical with and in perfect accord with the actions of my own will. From this point on, there was a gradual diminution in the characters of the manifestations.

Le Baron also noted that 'complete self-surrender to the

psycho-automatism, as a deific telepathic ideal, resulted in the communication of a loftier flow of verbiage'.

Le Baron temporarily became a Spiritualist but abandoned his 'experiment' in April 1895, concluding that the glossolalia was less important than it pretended to be. He traced a high proportion of its words in a vocabulary of primitive Dravidian or British-Indian, non-Aryan, tribes, but recognized that the identification might be coincidental, as the phonetic elements in his glossolalia were English. In the specimens following it will be noted that a comparison of tongue with translation shows no correspondence in vocabulary such as would be expected where the same words appear several times.

Te rumete tau. Ilee lete leele luto scele. Impere scele lee luto. The old word! I love the old word of the heavens! The love of the heavens is emperor.

Onko keere scete tere lute. Ombo te scele te bere te kure. Sinte te lute. The love of the darkness is slavery! The heavens are wise, the heavens are true.

Sinte kuru. Orumo imbo impe rute scelete. Singe, Singe, Singe, Eru. The heavens are sure. The love of the earth is past! The king now rules in the heavens!

Ede pelute kondo nedode	I have been looking, looking for daylight.
Igla tepete kompto pele	Ages have flown and the years have grown dark;
Impe obode inguru lalele	Over the hilltops the sun is now shining,
Omdo resene okoro pododo	Far from the sky comes the song of the lark.
Igme odkondo nefulu kelala	Beauty is dawning, the darkness is passing,
Nene pokonto sefo lodelu	Far up the vales fly the songs of the light.
Impe telala feme olele	Into the cities the joy will be spreading,

Igde pekondo raog japate	Into the by-ways the light will be spread,
Rele pododo ogsene ly mano	Glory has come to the lost soul of man!

Le Baron suggested nine alternative theories to account for his tongues:

(a) Sentences are the work of a powerful unconscious imagination and do not possess the natural consonantal and vowel elements of a language at all.

(b) They are brand new ideas in old and foreign verbal husks, the forms of which were latent in man's subconsciousness at birth.

(c) The consonantal and vowel combinations are but the articulate shells of very ancient ideas latent in this man's subconsciousness at birth, but out of the shells of which the meanings have been eaten up or metamorphosed by some at present unknown law of mental evolution. They are not now to be considered as ideas at all.

(d) New and actual presentations of real and new ideas in a foreign tongue.

(e) A ludicrous and silly mistake of the man's imagination allied to some species of humorous hallucination, not to be considered seriously, a perjury, ghastly jest, very profound mental trick, loose jargon of a maniac.

(f) A species of scientific telepathy. The consonantal and vowel combinations come from some morally indifferent, sublimely good or awfully naughty source, and one which is subject to the will of man.

(g) Although he says he never knew nor heard these combinations before he uttered them, he may in some mysterious way be deceiving himself.

(h) It may not be beyond belief that he is unconsciously in possession of a similar principle or intuitive linguistic power said to be possessed at this day by the higher adepts of India, or the Grand Lama of Tibet, or the Rosicrucians, by the means of which an unknown language is spoken by purely intuitive processes unknown to the analysis of western mental philosophy.

(j) These consonantal and vowel combinations and their intuitive vocal adjustments may be startling scientific hints of mental forces latent in everybody, which, if studied, generalized, verified, systematized, and seriously investigated by philosophers might prove of incalculable benefit to the human race, but which could find no encouragement for expression in the nineteenth century because of the fierce and mocking intolerance of the conservative dogmas of the age.

These theories need no comment here.

Not the least puzzling feature of this case is Le Baron's apparent possession by the spirits of the medium's parents. A striking characteristic is the exultation which accompanied his glossolalia, seemingly identical with the joy which possesses the Christian speaker in tongues who has experienced Spirit-baptism. The same euphoria seems to arise from some non-Christian tongue as from Christian, indicating a similar psychological release in both cases. This fact could have significance for both psychologists and theologians.

8

The Twentieth Century: Christian Tongues

At about the time that Edward Irving was founding the Catholic Apostolic Church in London, James Latourette of New York gathered together a group of charismatic Methodists and others. They sought to reproduce the conditions of the early Church by indulging in 'Pentecostal exercises'. In 1845 the charismatic Oneida Perfectionists were founded in Vermont, and in 1851 the Irvingites leaped the Atlantic and established a church at Potsdam, New York. The New Apostolic Church, the result of an Irvingite schism, was founded in 1860. These and similar movements kept flickering the idea that the New Testament gifts of the Holy Spirit might still be the right of fully sanctified Christians.

Other possible factors in its survival were reactions against the sterile and over-intellectual Deism of the eighteenth century and, later, against Darwinism and the attack by science on religion. The renewal of interest in religious questions may have aroused in those temperamentally inclined to them the enthusiasm for spiritualism and psychical research and that zeal for the recovery of the charismatic aspects of religion which became world-wide in the twentieth century. When existence becomes complicated, materialistic, faithless and frightening, mystical and esoteric faiths, especially those which reward belief with demonstrable miracles, provide an escape from the terrifying complexities of life, together with conviction of a happier life beyond earthly existence.

Another factor was the improvement in communications. In the late nineteenth and twentieth centuries, newspapers broadcast the news of similar charismatic experiences which, a century earlier, would have caused a flutter only in the local community. Faster travel enabled evangelists to influence both sides of the Atlantic. Postal services, cheap printing, the spread of elementary education and literacy and, later, radio, television and the whole media apparatus of the modern world played their parts. News that glossolalia in Kansas had its counterparts in England, Scandinavia, Lithuania, India and Brazil made its practitioners think of it as a permanent world movement, God's message to and renewal of his entire Church in the twentieth century.

Doctrines not unlike those of Pentecostalism, even when there was no charismatic emphasis, became popular. The Moody and Sankey revivals, the Holiness movement, camp meetings in America, the Keswick and other conventions in England, the Salvation Army, Reader Harris's 'Pentecostal League' and other bodies and evangelists taught that the complete Christian needed a 'second blessing' of sanctification beyond 'mere' conversion, or that perfect holiness was possible. The Latter Rain Movement, a revival characterized by Holy Spirit baptism evidenced by glossolalia, was founded by the Spurlings, father and son, of whom the younger, expelled from the Baptist Church and ministry, formed a Holiness Church in 1892, regarded by some as the original Pentecostal Church.

The year before, Daniel Awry had spoken in tongues in Oklahoma, and for the last decade of the nineteenth century revival and charismatic ideas were rife among radical Protestants. In 1898 there was formed at Anderson, South Carolina, the Fire-Baptized Holiness Church which in 1911 allied with and took the name of the Pentecostalist Holiness Church, founded in 1899 in North Carolina.

But if a single beginning of modern Pentecostalism has to be named, Bethel Bible College, Topeka, Kansas, has as good a claim to be the source as any. Under their minister, the Reverend C. F. Parham, the forty students at the college, aware that there was something missing in their Christian experience and studying independently, concluded unanimously that one common and sure sign of baptism with the Holy Spirit was speaking in tongues. They prayed for the gift, which was conferred on Agnes N. Ozman after Parham had laid hands on her. On New Year's Eve 1900 there came from her lips a flow of syllables which neither of them could understand. The next day Miss Ozman spoke in tongues at a meeting in Topeka and was understood by a Bohemian who was present. Two days later Parham and twelve students spoke in tongues, and thirty eventually became glossolalic. The movement met with only local success, but in 1904 a mission led by Parham at Galena, Texas, took fire, resulting in hundreds of conversions and healings. Parham's followers received what they called 'the Pentecost' and claimed to speak in foreign tongues of which they were normally completely ignorant. A typical newspaper report ran,

> Last week a woman arose during the meeting and spoke for ten minutes, no one apparently in the audience knowing what she said. An Indian, who had come from the Pawnee Reservation in the territory that day to attend the services stated that she was speaking in the language of his tribe and that he could understand every word of the testimony.

The vagueness of the report, characteristic of a very high percentage of such stories, can be noted. 'A woman', 'an Indian' (no names given), 'stated' (to whom? when?). Parham opened another Bible school at Houston, Texas, one of the students of which, a black minister, the Reverend W. J. Seymour, later started the Azusa Street, Los Angeles, Mission, which was to have considerable importance for the Pentecostal movement.

In Britain the great Welsh revival of 1904 inspired phenomena akin to those of the Camisards. Young Welsh men and women, mostly in their later 'teens, although so brought up in English that they could not carry on a sustained conversation in Welsh, prayed publicly in the language with an idiomatic facility which would normally have indicated long and familiar usage. An interesting feature is that they spoke it with English accents, unlike the Camisards, who spoke their French correctly. The prayers, spoken mainly by comparatively illiterate youngsters, combined Bible and Prayer Book expressions and were uttered with coherence, beauty and piquancy of expression, richness of cadence and fervency which impressed observers. The speakers felt that their prayers 'came' to them at the time and that they could not help praying, which they did effortlessly and with pleasure. It was noted also that their appearance changed. They became pale and their eyes wore a far-away, listless look. One young man said that for some days after he had prayed at a service, people moved in the streets like ghosts in a thick mist. Coarse features sometimes became 'almost refined' and 'Madonna-like'.

It is perhaps worth mentioning here in passing that the ecstatic Welsh congregational cry known as *hwyl* has been related to plainsong which, in turn, is thought by some to be a conventionalized form of those 'singing tongues' possibly referred to in the New Testament phrase, 'spiritual songs'.

Following the Welsh revival came 'the Children of the Revival', when scenes of Pentecostal fervour, sometimes regrettably extravagant, broke out in a number of Welsh centres. The question, 'Why Wales? Why not the whole world?' inspired the Reverend A. A. Boddy, an Anglican vicar, to organize the Sunderland conventions, held annually from 1908 to 1914. These, though small, attracted religious leaders from Europe and America. Frequently, exquisite singing in the Spirit would sweep through the whole congregation, its members chanting in perfect harmony, some in their own, some in other tongues, yet all in one Spirit, spontaneous and free.

Further afield, Welsh missionaries led a revival in the Khassian Hills in India, and this in turn inspired a Christian widow, Pandiat Ramabai, leader of a mission at Mukti, Kadgarn, to prepare a team of thirty girls to preach the Gospel in the district. On 29 June 1905, they were praying for power when a tongue of fire seen on a senior girl caused another to run for a pail of water to put her out (is it flippant to see in this story a similarity to the incident of Sir Walter Raleigh's servant's throwing a bucket of water over his master when he first saw him smoking a pipe?). The 'baptism of fire' was followed by speaking in tongues when girls who knew no English prayed in it and in Greek, Hebrew, Sanskrit and unknown languages.

Recorded in a Church Missionary Society *Prayer Circular* of September 1906 is another incident where a sixteen-year-old Indian girl at a CMS school in Bombay prayed in a tongue. Canon Hayward, of Bombay Cathedral, found an interpreter who understood much of what she said. She was praying in Arabic for Libya, a country of which she had never heard.

Perhaps as a result of such incidents, perhaps independently, missionaries of different denominations and their followers began to speak in tongues, and the Pentecostalist movement broke out at Coonoor, Calcutta, Dhond, Allahabad, Gujarat, and other centres.

In 1906 Parham's pupil, the Reverend W. J. Seymour, was invited to Los Angeles. He aroused opposition, was locked out of his church and thereafter preached at No. 312, Azusa Street, where, on 9 April seven persons, including an eight-year-old boy, were baptized with the Spirit and spoke in tongues. The noise of the glossolalia drew curious crowds. By the next morning there was no getting near the house, those who approached it falling under the power, the sick being healed and sinners saved as they entered. The Holy Spirit fell upon the mission three evenings running 'so that the houses shook and the earth quaked'.[1] Although many of the press accounts were hostile, they publicized the mission, which lasted for three years. Many Pentecostalists regard that April day (whose phenomena so closely resembled those of the 'birthday of the Church') as the birthday of their own movement.

Pentecostalism spread in various parts of the world apparently spontaneously and independently of any system of doctrine or church organization, a fact which encouraged its adherents to see in it a work of the Spirit which 'bloweth where it listeth'.[2] The baptism, although an intensely individual experience, bound together its recipients in 'the unity of the Spirit'. In America a Norwegian, T. B. Barratt spoke in tongues as a result of reading of the Los Angeles revival. Barratt was Cornish by birth, his parents having emigrated when he was four, was fluent in English and Norwegian, and had founded the Oslo City Mission with its own journal designed for international preaching. His experience was probably the most important result of the Azusa Street mission, for Barratt became Pentecostalism's 'Apostle to the Europeans'. In October, 1906, back in Oslo, Barratt was confident that he had spoken in eight languages, including French and Italian. His experiences soon became front-page news, attracting reporters even from abroad.

Barratt in turn convinced Lewi Pethrus, a young Swede, whose longing for Holy Spirit baptism was fulfilled after a visit to Oslo in 1907. He spoke in tongues himself and later led a revival in Sweden which emphasized the baptism and the charismatic gifts which accompanied it. An evangelistic campaign by Pethrus in Copenhagen resulted in the conversion of a notable Danish actress who left the stage at the age of thirty-four and the height of her career. This caused a considerable stir in the Danish press and country and aroused opposition.

In the United States Pentecostalism moved generally from west to east, tongues appearing successively in California, Utah, Texas, Illinois, Indiana, Ohio, Pennsylvania and Maine. Stories of miraculous xenolalia stimulated an interest in foreign missions because it was believed by many that the heathen would be won for Christ by supernatural preaching to them in their own languages. Most are vague, such as that of 'an Indian from Mexico' hearing 'a woman' speaking German, a language he understood, and being converted. Some are more detailed but useless as evidence because of the lapse of time, such as a story recorded by Sherrill.[3] A Mr Harvey McAlister's brother, Robert, was 'in Los Angeles' (not necessarily an eye-witness) when the incident took place. A girl, Kathleen Scott, addressed a visitor in a language not her own. The man then announced to the meeting that he was a Jew, present under an assumed name, to take apart the sermons of Christian preachers and use them in lectures against Christianity. Kathleen had addressed him in Hebrew, revealing a knowledge of his name and other details and calling him to repentance. 'Then the man dropped to his knees and cried and prayed as though his heart would break.' Even though Harvey McAlister himself knew Kathleen Scott and had heard the incident also from her parents, the story is fourth-hand and 'hearsay evidence'.

The tale bears a 'folk' resemblance to that of Jacob Rabinowitz, a Jew prayed over at the First Assembly of God Church in Pasadena, Texas, by, among others, an Irishman named John Gruver who told him in Hebrew his father's name, although no one in Texas knew his family.[4] The conversion of a Jew is still a particular feather in the cap of the Christian agent responsible, and there are several stories of their conviction by bystanders who addressed them in Hebrew. Some of these appear to be doublets of each other.

Whether such stories were true or false, the movement spread. Azusa Street continued to exert its influence. Groups of Pentecostalists in Chicago, New York and Little Rock, derived from its mission, as did some in Winnipeg, London, Sunderland, Amsterdam, Oslo, Calcutta, Allahabad and Mukti. Missionaries at the Wuchow Schools, South China, read about it in a newspaper, and later one of them spoke in tongues at a prayer meeting. By September 1906 there were an estimated 13,000 Pentecostalists, a not inconsiderable total for a movement only a few years old. Spontaneous and unrelated outcroppings of tongues appeared in widely separated parts of the world which, through publicity and the ease of travel, pollinated each other. W. T. Ellis, travelling round the world in 1907 to investigate Christian missions, was convinced by the genuineness of tongues in India. Miss Minnie Adams, an Indian CMS worker, wrote a booklet about her charismatic experiences which resulted in the eventual foundation of the Methodist

Pentecostal Church in Chile. Archdeacon Phair came across tongues among baptized Red Indians in Winnipeg, and another minister, A. G. Ward, preaching to Indians with an interpreter, suddenly broke into speech to them in their own language.

The claim to have been the first Pentecostalist in England was made on behalf of Mrs Catharine Price, of Brixton, who early in 1907 worshipped in tongues in her room. She spoke in tongues again at a meeting the following evening, and in the summer opened her house for the first Pentecostalist prayer meetings in England. In the autumn Barratt visited Boddy's Sunderland Convention and tongues immediately followed. Mrs Boddy sang most beautifully in tongues, and two notable Pentecostal personalities received their baptism at Sunderland, Smith Wigglesworth, whose subsequent ministry took him to Scandinavia, Switzerland, Australia, New Zealand and America, and Stanley Frodsham who later in America edited the *Pentecostal Evangel*, organ of the Assemblies of God, and was an early historian of the Pentecostal movement.

Four inhabitants of Preston, Lancashire, convinced from study of the Scriptures that the gifts of the Holy Spirit had been lost through the Church's unbelief and not because God had withdrawn them, founded the Preston Pentecostalist Association, one result of which was the formation of the Congo Evangelistic Mission. At Halifax, Yorkshire, Southsea, near Portsmouth, and Ryde, Isle of Wight, there were other apparently spontaneous manifestations.

There were, however, opposition and disillusionments. The reasons for the former need not concern a survey of glossolalia, but the latter emphasized the fact that, whatever tongues were, they were not given, as many thought, for use in missionary work. As early as January 1908 the *Baptist Argus* of Louisville, Kentucky, published the result of an investigation into eighteen instances of Americans who thought this. A Mr McIntosh who had expected to preach at once in Chinese needed an interpreter for the simplest affairs of everyday life and admitted his failure. A dozen missionaries to Japan likewise admitted their inability to speak through tongues. Two of the dozen felt they had the gift of the Hong Kong dialect but failed there also, as did the Reverend A. G. Garr and his wife in India.

But the movement continued to spread and to affect more and more countries. In October 1907 Mrs Polman of Amsterdam, influenced by Scripture study inspired by news of God's doings in America, spoke in tongues, followed by her husband who received the gift at the 1908 Sunderland Convention. The leader of a small assembly in Amsterdam, he moved twice into larger halls because of growing congregations. In Germany the power fell on Pastor Jonathan Paul, a Lutheran minister, in September 1907. He spoke in tongues at Friedrichstadt with Paster Voget, minister of a church of three thousand members at Bunde. Singing in tongues was one of Paul's gifts. He claimed that a comparison of hymns in tongues with the German of the hymn sung to the given tune had enabled him to discover the meaning of some of the new words, and rejoiced that he had learned part of the language of heaven. The glossolalic version of a hymn rendered in English as 'Let Me Go' was as follows:

> *Schua ea, schua ea*
> *O tschi brio ti ra pea*
> *Akki lungo tari fungo*
> *U li bara ra tungo*
> *Letschi bungo ti tu ta.*

'Anyone can see,' commented Paul, 'how remarkably these words rhyme. And, what is more remarkable, there is more rhyme in this song in tongues than in the German words. When I made this discovery, I could not but praise God.'[5] Whether one sees in these comments that childlikeness which is the key to the Kingdom of Heaven or a pathetic naïvety, the movement spread in Germany as it had elsewhere. In 1908 the first German Pentecostalist Conference met at Mulheim and by 1912 the country was honeycombed with missions and assemblies.

Meanwhile Barratt, besides attracting the attention of the world press to the more sensational aspects of his Oslo mission, campaigned in Denmark, Finland and Switzerland, publishing his *Victory of the Cross* in Swedish, Finnish, Russian, German and Spanish. A notable convert was the Reverend H. J. Mygind, a former pastor of the Danish State Church, who maintained that the tongues were genuine xenolalia. In 1907 some Esthonian Christians were Spirit-baptized with tongues.

Back in the United States, A. J. Tomlinson, a glossolalic, in 1908 combined, under the name of The Church of God, Spurling's Holiness Church, Barham's Topeka communion and Seymour's Azusa Street Mission. Through schisms The Church of God spawned a number of other Pentecostal groups. The reasons for the factions make tedious reading and are irrelevant to this survey.

1908 saw the spread of tongues to Scotland, where about two hundred were Spirit-baptized by the end of February, and to Ulster, while in England that year's Sunderland Convention influenced Baroness von Brosch to carry back the message to the Baltic provinces of Russia. There were Pentecostalists in Australia and South Africa by the same year, as a remarkable instance of xenolalia was reported from Johannesburg. Maggie Truter spoke in a native tongue for a few minutes, then in High Dutch for about the same time, then in English. She gave an eloquent description of Jesus in Gethsemane in the English, rendering this perfectly in the other two languages, as Dutchmen and natives who were present confirmed. The speaker knew very little High Dutch and nothing of the native language. It would be convincing if such an event could be tape-recorded today. By 1910 an organized Pentecostalist group, The Apostolic Faith Mission, was operating in South Africa.

There was speaking in tongues also in 1908 in the Gemeinschaftsbewegung, a pietistic movement to awaken more fervour in the German State Church. Before the glossolalia started, its speakers gave 'a peculiar hissing or gnashing of teeth'.[6] Some of those who claimed to interpret the tongues 'saw' letters or writing which gave the meaning, others 'heard' it, others understood directly.

In the following year there began what hindsight shows to

have been possibly the most significant continental Pentecostalist movement, that in South America. In Chile a
missionary Methodist paster, W. C. Hoover, reacting against
the rationalizing liberalism of his Church leaders, led his
Valparaiso congregation towards Pentecostalism. Santiago
followed, and the Pentecostal Methodist Church was created.
The charismata in it were regulated, and today half the Chilean
pastors have not spoken in tongues. Pentecostalism suited South
America because its emotional element appealed to the natives
and the flexibility of its structures matched the social instability
of the continent. For these reasons, and through the missionary
zeal of entire congregations, it was to spread with astonishing
growth throughout almost every country south of Panama.

Also in 1909 the Pentecostalist Union was formed under the
presidency of Cecil Polhill, one of the Cambridge Seven of
China Inland Mission fame whose names are legends among
evangelical Christians. At first undenominational, although
requiring a belief in 'the Baptism of the Holy Ghost with the
Scriptural signs', it merged in 1925 with the Assemblies of God,
one of the principal Pentecostal communions. It sent six
missionaries to the East and Africa in two years, and the sense of
urgency brought about by a strong expectation of Christ's
immediate Second Coming led to tremendous emphasis among
Pentecostals on missionary work. Separate missionary training
colleges were begun for men and women.

In Britain the movement grew steadily, churches opening in
centre after centre of population. On Christmas Day, 1909,
there spoke in tongues J. Nelson Parr of Manchester, whose
importance was that he founded in 1924 the major Pentecostal
federation of the Fellowship of the Assemblies of God in Great
Britain and Ireland.

Barratt in Norway, recognizing that the policy of encouraging
Pentecostalists to work within their own denominations had
failed, prepared to establish a union of independent Pentecostal
assemblies and issued his 'General Principles'. These included
the statements that everybody could be filled with the Holy
Ghost as the disciples were at Pentecost, that tongues as well as

the other charismatic gifts were given to believers to a greater extent than ever since the days of the apostles and that when Spirit-baptism was accompanied by tongues, this was a special and precious token of the indwelling of the Holy Ghost.

Yet by 1920 Barratt, influenced by Pastor Paul, had learned to evaluate glossolalia more carefully. He no longer claimed that it was xenolalia. He recognized that other spirits could speak with tongues as, by the power of suggestion, could the unaided human mind. He admitted that tongues were not an essential accompaniment of the baptism and asserted the necessity of a moral investigation into the genuineness of the experience.

In 1910 there was a long Pentecostal revival campaign in Zürich. An International Pentecostalist Conference in Oslo in June 1911, attended by representatives from Denmark, England, Finland, Germany, Sweden and the United States, did much to strengthen the movement. In 1912 further emphasis was laid on the need for clear doctrinal statements – two more were given by Barratt in the following year – the use of missionaries and the protection of the original Pentecostal message.

Until the outbreak of the First World War, Pentecostalism grew in England, the United States, India, China and Egypt, and in 1914 America alone had thirty-five Pentecostalist missionaries in the field. In that year an important advance was made in the United States when what was to become the largest Pentecostal Church in the country, The Assemblies of God, was founded. The Central Bible Institute, the official Bible College of the American Fellowship, with 350 students, was also established.

In spite of the war, the Elim Foursquare Gospel Alliance, originally the Elim Evangelistic Band, came into being at Monaghan, Ireland. It was to become one of the most important Pentecostal communions in the British Isles. The following year a great impetus was given to the movement in Norway when Barratt's assembly at Oslo was officially established as an independent association. In the next sixteen years its membership grew from two to seventeen hundred while the total number of Norwegian Pentecostalists increased from 8,000 in 1930 to at least 35,000 in 300 congregations in 1960.

In the course of growth charismata largely disappeared. The majority of modern Norwegian Pentecostalists have never spoken in tongues, and the new Church has settled down very much as the early Church must have done. New and radical Pentecostal assemblies, emphasizing ecstasy and charismata, have come into being outside the recognized Pentecostal churches in Norway. So the pattern repeats itself and will do, one feels, until the end of time.

Meanwhile, in the Belgian Congo, the Pentecostalists faced a setback when their church at Mwanza was joined by a company of freed slaves with denominational prejudices who were returning to Lubaland from Angola. But 1920 saw a breakthrough when many magnified the Lord first in Luban, then in tongues, including 'beautiful English' and snatches of other European languages. A remarkable feature was that these languages had a clear 'r' sound which the Luban cannot normally pronounce. Another milestone in another country was the official registration of the Pentecostal Church in Batavia in 1924.

In England the period between the wars was a time of Pentecostalist expansion. The extravagances of the Apostolic Faith Church drove some of its members to start the Apostolic Church at Penygroes, which evangelized vigorously in Wales, the British Isles, Denmark, West Africa and Australia. The Elim Alliance entered England in 1921. The Assemblies of God in Great Britain and Ireland was born in 1924. Pentecostal leaders came to the fore and at public holiday seasons some forty or fifty simultaneous Pentecostal conventions were held. Of these the most noteworthy were the Easter conventions of the Elim Foursquare Gospel which filled the Albert Hall from 1926 to 1939 under Pastor George Jeffreys. Bible Colleges, Missionary Training Colleges and publishing houses associated with various Pentecostal denominations helped to spread the gospel of 'tongues'.

How great the impact of the doctrine was and is on the

religious life of Great Britain or, indeed, of any western nation, is difficult to say. When one is close to Pentecostalism one is aware of a fervour and ferment which seem to fill the horizon. But move away from its immediate environment and one finds that many people are unaware of its existence and that the fact of glossolalia is unknown to many churchgoers in the principal denominations. Yet Pentecostalism has been recognized by the World Council of Churches and, if statistics are to be believed, is numerically strong enough to have been called a third force in world Christianity after Catholicism and Protestantism. And neo-Pentecostalism seems increasingly to be creeping into the established Churches.

But this is to anticipate. Los Angeles was certainly made aware of Aimée Semple McPherson's The International Church of the Foursquare Gospel, founded in 1921. This had no official connection with the Elim Foursquare Gospel in England. Indeed, there was little similarity in spirit between the English variety of Pentecostalism which was bred out of puritanism by ecstasy and the Hollywood publicity methods used by Sister Aimée. Supported by a Bible School and its own radio station, the American Foursquare Gospel had grown by 1955 to a membership of nearly 63,000 in 604 churches.

American influence continued to be more than domestic. In Europe, as a result of efforts by the fully Pentecostal Russian and Eastern European Mission, with headquarters at Chicago, about 350 Assemblies of God with a membership of some 80,000 and a large annual conference at Odessa, existed until the leaders were arrested in 1930. In Poland there were 500 Assemblies of God in 1939. At Danzig a Pentecostalist Bible School existed until politics closed it in 1938. In the Baltic States there was an association of 900 members at Tallinn, Esthonia, and others in Latvia.

England was also inspired to missionary work as a practical result of a message in tongues given through Mr and Mrs Douglas Scott at a meeting at Sion College. The message and its interpretation resulted in assemblies and conventions of Pentecostalists being held in half a dozen French cities and the evangelistic effort's spilling over into Belgium and French-speaking Switzerland.

1939 saw an attempt at unity in England by a conference of Pentecostal Churches followed by another in 1940; and in 1939 a European conference was also held. These failed to agree on a common doctrine of tongues, there being four views:

(1) The converted believer should pray for and, when he is in a right spiritual condition, accept baptism with the Holy Spirit with signs following, *one* of which may be speaking in tongues.

(2) Glossolalia is essential – baptism with the Holy Spirit is proved by the baptizee's speaking with tongues then, even if he never does so again.

(3) The *sign* of tongues is different from the *gift* which enables the speaker to talk in tongues whenever the Spirit guides him to do so.

(4) Tongues are no proof of Spirit-baptism – individual Christians may produce glossolalia without it.

Pentecostalist leaders may be quoted against one another supporting all these views.

The Second World War handicapped but by no means checked Pentecostalist expansion. In 1939 there were some two dozen sects in America with an estimated 5,000 churches and 250,000 members, besides many small groups, many of them ethnic and representing almost every nationality in the United States. These grew by 1955 to thirty-five denominations with 18,834 churches and nearly 1,500,000 members (another twenty-three communions existed for which statistics are not available). Expatriates returning to Europe evangelized zealously so that, for example, Italy in 1955 boasted 399 Assemblies of God. The movement in America was helped by extra-ecclesiastical organizations such as the Full Gospel Business Men's Fellowship International, founded by Demos Shakarian, grandson of that Shakarian who had come from Armenia where a glossolalic movement had existed in the nineteenth century. The Fellowship's magazine, *Voice*, took the 'full Gospel' into circles which it would not normally have penetrated.

In addition a neo-Pentecostalist movement has spread in recent years in the orthodox denominations in both America and England. It is not easy to say how widespread this is, for non-Pentecostal glossolalics keep their practice private where it has been formally proscribed, as in Episcopalian Churches in California and Missouri, and, where it has not been condemned, in order to avoid ridicule, censure or divisiveness within their communities, Kelsey, historian of the Pentecostalist movement in the United States, estimates that during this century at least two to three million Americans have spoken in tongues and, guess though these numbers must be, they can scarcely be exaggerated. More important, quality has been added to quantity. Many modern glossolalics are not illiterate hill-billies intoxicated by camp-meeting revivalism, but intelligent and educated professional men including doctors, professors, lawyers, ordained ministers and priests of all the principal denominations (including a Jewish rabbi) and scientists of many different disciplines from biology to psychiatry. Official periodicals of many of the principal denominations give news of neo-Pentecostalism in their Churches with caution but not hostility.

Movements such as the Blessed Trinity Society, Holy Spirit Fellowships, Christian Advance and the Full Gospel Business Men's Fellowship, together with periodicals published by them, help to spread the gospel of glossolalia. Group experience in The Holy Spirit Fellowship is described in an article in *The Living Church*, organ of the national Episcopal Church of the United States.

> Without any emotional build-up or preliminary, and just as
> simply as he speaks in his own language to pray or praise
> God, a person will begin to speak in another language. . . .
> The interpretation . . . often will be in flowing and beautiful
> English, beyond the ability of the person speaking. So
> objective and real is this gift of interpretation that many

times, after the first interpreter has spoken, one or two others will say, 'I received essentially the same interpretation'. Occasionally, another person will continue further with the same interpretation, in the same style and vein. Listening to the whole process, one finds it difficult to deny that its source is God the Holy Spirit. [7]

One purpose of Christian Advance gatherings is to tell the story of the meaning which men and women have found in the experience of tongues.

In modern neo-Pentecostalism there is less emotionalism. The private use of tongues is more important than the public. Neo-Pentecostalism is more orientated towards clergy and professional men, is centred on the Bible rather than experience, is not divisive or separatist and is more disciplined, with strict observance of Pauline directives. Tongues are emphasized less and the other gifts of the Spirit are claimed.

In the rest of the world Pentecostalist expansion was rapid throughout the 1940s and 1950s and is continuing today, not only in countries like Sweden and Norway, where it might be expected, but in Portugal where, by 1957, more than a quarter of the entire Protestant communicant membership was Pentecostal. In the South American continent today over one-third of the Protestants are Pentecostal, Brazil alone claiming more than two million and boasting in São Paulo the largest Pentecostal church building in the world, designed to hold 25,000 worshippers. In 1962 the Assemblies of God, the largest of the Pentecostalist Churches, were represented in at least 76 countries – exactly half of the total of 152 mentioned in the *World Christian Handbook* of that year.

Ecclesiastical statistics are as suspect as most, but Pentecostalists throughout the world today number not fewer than six million and may be as many as nine million, perhaps about sixteen million, if children and non-communicant adherents are included. If it is assumed that all these believe in glossolalia and that most of them expect one day to speak in tongues, the phenomenon is seen to be not insignificant as a type of human behaviour. Perhaps one in every three hundred human beings in the modern world believes in Christian glossolalia, and if to these are added those whose faith it still is that the spirits can communicate in tongues through shamans, medicine men and mediums, their numbers are formidable. There cannot be many human beliefs so widely held and so extensively practised.

9

Tongues in Twentieth-century Spiritualism

The case of Mrs Laura Finch, who wrote Greek, a language of which she was entirely ignorant, was thoroughly investigated from November 1899 until 1904. It was first reported in the *Annales des sciences psychiques* by Professor Richet, a French psychic researcher of undoubted integrity and scholarship.[1] Mrs Finch wrote in a state of light trance with her eyes closed, sometimes with great effort, almost suffering, slowness and a convulsive trembling. She remembered nothing when she awoke.

A high proportion of her writing was traced to the *Dictionnaire grec–français et français–grec* by Ch.D. Byzantos, published by André Coromelas at Athens. Richet did not know of the book until sent a copy by Dr Vlavianos of Athens, whom he consulted about the case. He watched Mrs Finch writing many of the extracts which she did standing, seeming to copy characters seen before her in the air. In one passage of thirty-eight words there were two mistakes, both of a visual nature and such as no-one knowledgeable of Greek would have made, and in six further phrases 52 out of 56 accents were correctly given. The phrases were claimed to be relevant to the circumstances and to topics of conversation between Richet and Mrs Finch, and the professor commented that the writing demonstrated and almost proved the phenomenon of clair-voyant reading at a distance of a closed book.

Other explanations Richet suggested were (a) conscious fraud; (b) unconscious memory of things seen and forgotten; (c) the intelligence of a spirit interpenetrating Mrs Finch's intelligence (there was some material which could have indicated activity from Antoine-Augustin Renouard, Richet's great-grandfather). The arguments against fraud were Richet's certainty of Mrs Finch's integrity; the fact that she knew no Greek (though the professor acknowledged the impossibility of proving a negative); her Greek was modern where two primers she possessed (but had never studied); were ancient; the *Dictionnaire* was almost unknown in France; the mistakes were those of a copyist ignorant of the script; a total of 1,535 signs, including letters and accents, was written in scarcely an hour, containing 42 mistakes of a visual kind, and this feat, Richet maintained, was beyond human memory. A passage from Cicero, difficult to understand without special knowledge and study, was quoted in the *Dictionnaire* and translated into Greek but not into French. Mrs Finch used this in a way relevant to a conversation with Richet, thus intelligently using a Latin phrase she did not understand translated into modern Greek of which she was ignorant. All the quotations came from the Greek–French section of the dictionary which only someone knowing Greek would use. If fraud were the explanation, Mrs Finch would also have had to use Plato and the New Testament (sources of other 'copied' texts) with relevance to topics of conversation. She stopped in mid-career, there being a hiatus of four years. She was not a Spiritualist, for she did not believe in the survival of the soul in her conscious state (though she did in trance). She gained no material reward. She was not an exhibitionist for at the beginning she insisted on anonymity.

Against (b) was the use of the Ciceronian phrase, as much a difficulty for the subconscious as for the conscious mind, and the prodigious extent of the memory needed. Had Mrs Finch at some time glanced through the dictionary without remember-ing she had done so, she would have had to choose phrases from at least a dozen pages relevant to topics of conversation, to have chosen to use Greek instead of French, and to have remembered some of this with all its accents for five years.

Richet concluded against (c) that there was no real evidence of communication from his great-grandfather and still less from anyone else. There could possibly have been thought-transference from someone. He pointed out, however, that Mrs Finch had quoted from four different works and used always an apt and relevant phrase. He found the facts impossible to explain, but maintained that facts established beyond doubt must not be ignored and that unexplained did not mean inexplicable.

After Mrs Finch had seen Richet's article she wrote further Greek extracts and one Hebrew. She wrote of herself,

I present, however, at extremely rare intervals, a faculty of writing in languages unknown to me, a faculty which is scarcely clairvoyance, and is certainly not of a physical nature. Messages in foreign or unknown languages have also been received through me by means of *raps* without contact, at equally rare intervals. An interval of two years marked one of these periods of inaction in xenoglossy. On another occasion, the interval lasted for seven months and this was followed by two efforts, separated from each other by a few days, when, I believe, something like one thousand Greek characters were written – a language I am totally unacquainted with. Each productive period has been accompanied by a sensation of heat and strain in my head, and was preceded by days when I experienced a kind of persistent but very feeble clairaudience and clairvoyance, when I seemed consistently to hear rapid whisperings in languages unknown to me and see visions of characters and hieroglyphics, which passed all too quickly for me to be able to write them down. Then this all seemed to crystallize and, except on two or three occasions, when the writing was done in a state of trance, or the message was given by means of 'raps', the phenomenon of vision, after these preliminary fugitive stages, assumed a steadiness which enabled me to copy down the characters held up, as it were, before my eyes.

Whilst, on the other hand, the faculty of clairvoyance seems to be at my command, and can be exercised in a comparatively normal manner, which permits of self-observation and study of the faculty, on the other hand, the production of Xenoglossy and of 'raps' appears to be entirely out of my conscious control; at least, up to the present, and I am incapable of producing either the one or the other entirely at will. I am obliged to wait some tidal wave, as it were.

Three hypotheses were put forward by other authorities. Sir Oliver Lodge[2] suggested that an intelligent control, wishing to give as a test phenomenon something remarkable, might constrain a medium to copy texts from a hardly accessible book, their source not being revealed for some time. But if an intelligence could so well overcome the difficulties of communication from the other side as to achieve so much, why could he not have identified himself more definitely? All such communications frustrate by stopping at a point where evidence acceptable to an open-minded student seems capable of being given. It is as if the spirits delight to tantalize.

Mrs Verrall,[3] a noted automatic writer of Greek and Latin, agreeing that the visual mistakes proved Mrs Finch's ignorance of Greek, postulated two controls, X1 possessing the knowledge to read Greek capitals, and X2, a mere copyist. She quoted evidence which powerfully argued the simultaneous possession of knowledge and non-knowledge. X2 could have been Mrs Finch herself, for such knowledge and non-knowledge can be demonstrated by hypnosis. A somnambulistic subject, told to walk across a room which he has been told is empty, will circumnavigate a chair in his way which he does not see with one stratum of his mind but must see with another in order to avoid it. If questioned, he will reply that he walked without deviation across the room and that there was nothing in the way.

The Hon. Everard Feilding and Miss Alice Johnson argued for

fraud.[4] They denied that the quotations were relevant to the topics of conversation between Richet and Mrs Finch, reducing the difficulty of the case to one of learning so much Greek by heart. But, *cui bono*? Why should an anonymous non-Spiritualist lady of apparent integrity trouble to learn screeds of an unknown tongue for no stated purpose?

The explanations that best fit the facts are supernormal though not supernatural. Clairvoyant reading of distant books may in fact be a rare human faculty. Or living minds may be able to communicate unconsciously and irrelevantly, having been put into touch with each other by shifting psychic conditions which may in the mental world be parallel with or analogous to the physical conditions which produce mirages in the desert. In such a way Mrs Finch could have received impressions from a reader of the dictionary who could communicate to her both the visual appearance of the Greek words and enough understanding of them in French (for presumably *he* would have some acquaintance with both languages) as to enable her to use quotations relevantly.

Even more remarkable than Mrs Finch's clairvoyant Greek was the clairaudient Sanskrit of Mr William Dudley Pelley, author of *Seven Minutes in Eternity*. Hearing a voice speaking an unknown tongue, he dictated twelve pages of the sounds at longhand speed to a stenographer who marked the vowels so that they could be read phonetically. Some weeks later, 'an erudite philologist' found over a thousand words of 'pure Sanskrit' in the script, 'composing a sensible message that had to do with present-day happenings in the world's affairs'. Grateful as readers should be to the obliging intelligence who communicated his message at dictation speed, to enable Mr Pelley to refute 'superficial scholars', it would have made a stronger case if the philologist, or even the stenographer, had been named, and the message reproduced in original and translation.[5]

A striking case is recorded in the *Proceedings of the Society for Psychical Research* of sittings of Dr F. van Eeden, a Dutchman, with the medium, Mrs Thompson.[6] Van Eeden asked his questions in Dutch without translating them and got immediate replies in broken English but not Dutch. This is, therefore, a case not of xenolalia but of understanding a language which the medium did not know.

Mrs Thompson's usual control was an entity called 'Nelly', but on 7 June 1900 a young friend of van Eeden who had committed suicide after a preliminary attempt in which he had tried to cut his throat, partially took over. Van Eeden felt that the evidence became striking.

> During a few minutes – though a few minutes only – I felt absolutely as if I were speaking to my friend himself. I spoke Dutch and got immediate and correct answers. The expression of satisfaction and gratification in face and gesture, when we seemed to understand each other, was too true and vivid to be acted. Quite unexpected Dutch words were pronounced; details were given which were far from my mind, some of which, as that about my friend's uncle in a former sitting I had never known, and found to be true only on enquiry afterwards.

The extract that follows, one of several recorded, is an example of the kind of communication which comes through a *good* medium and shows how what is evidential to one person can appear to another as mere extra-sensory brain-picking by a gifted sensitive.

After a long silence, Mrs Thompson seemed very restless, feeling her throat with her hands. Her control, Nelly, spoke.
Nelly: 'He wants you to speak Hollands. Hollands.'
Van Eeden spoke a few words in Dutch, asking if his dead friend heard and understood. A very expressive pantomime followed in which Mrs Thompson took van Eeden's hands firmly as if to thank him very heartily, making different gestures.
Nelly: 'He understood . . . (speaking hoarsely, like the dead friend). . . . What's "vrouw poss . . . poss?"'
van Eeden: 'Vrouw post – ik versta je.' (This was the exact

114

pronounciation – the final 't' being but slightly sounded in
Dutch – of a name very familiar to van Eeden. 'Mrs Post' was
a poor workwoman who used to come to his house every day.
When the sitter had spoken these words, Mrs Thompson
laughed very excitedly and made emphatic gestures of
pleasure and satisfaction, patting his head and shoulders, just
as his friend would have done.)

Nelly: 'He is so glad you recognized him. He is not so
emotional, usually. What is "wuitebergen . . .
criuswergen"?' (This is very nearly the right pronunciation of
the word 'cruysbergen', the old name of van Eeden's place,
Walden. He commented, 'It is remarkable that it was not at
all like the pronunciation of the word as if *read* by an English
person, but as if heard. This name is still in use among us,
and my dead friend used it always. The new name, Walden,
which was often in my mind, and which I even pronounced
before Mrs Thompson, never came in her trance.')

van Eeden: 'Ih weet wat je zeggen wil, zat het nog eens.' ('I
know what you mean, say it again.')

Nelly (tries again and says): 'Hans.' (Nelly then 'went away'.
Mrs Thompson awoke and could taste 'some anaesthetic
stuff', probably idoform, used in healing the friend's
throat-wound. Her trance state suddenly returned.)

Nelly: 'That gentleman *was* pleased and delighted.'

van Eeden: 'Why does he not give his name?'

Nelly: 'It is like sum, thum or like Sjam. Not quite this.
Please, do you pronounce it properly.'

van Eeden: 'Yes, indeed, it is Sam.'

Remarkable claims were made by Mr H. J. Browne, a
Melbourne banker, in his two books, *The Holy Truth* and *The
Great Reality*. Early life in Africa enabled him to speak the
Kaffir language. When a Kaffir guest visited his home, his
eleven-year-old daughter, an automatic writer, though ignorant
of Kaffir herself, wrote several Kaffir names which astonished
the visitor, followed by a message in the language, several words
of which Mr Browne did not understand. He read them to his

visitor who understood all but one which Mr Browne could not pronounce correctly until his daughter wrote, 'Click with the mouth'. This reminded him of a trick of Kaffir pronounciation which enabled him to say the word properly. The entity who had influenced his daughter's hand to write proved on enquiry to be an old friend of Browne's, 'H.S.', who when alive could talk Kaffir and had written the message at the request of the visitor's spirit friends.[7]

One of Mr Browne's sons wrote what purported to be sheets of Ancient Persian as fast as a shorthand writer but as 'regular as copperplate'. An Oriental scholar, Dr Figg, denied that the writing was Persian, whereupon Mr Browne gave a friend some of the sheets to submit to the 'gentleman in charge of ancient MSS at the British Museum'. The latter announced that they had similar characters written on stone about 7,000 years old, that the language was 'Tartar-Persian' and that he could translate it. The extract proved to be an elaborated account of what had already been told through the mediumship of the daughter, that the inspirer of the writing had been a Persian prince when on earth. He had been made to study military tactics by his father and he gave 'an interesting account of ancient civilization and of his life and doings'.[8]

This account is sixth-hand, reported by Bozzano, quoting *Light*, quoting Mr Charles Bright, a reporter of the Australian Spiritualist review, *The Harbinger of Light*, quoting Mr Browne, quoting 'a friend', quoting 'the gentleman in charge of the ancient MSS' (no name given, nothing to corroborate the alleged findings). One feels that such an epoch-making document, throwing light upon an ancient civilization, from such an alleged source, would have caused some stronger reaction than the comment that it was 'an interesting document', and that the 'gentleman in charge' would at least have kept a copy for the Museum archives. Perhaps he did – but there is no record here of his having done so.

An example of xenolalia in trance induced by hypnosis is given by Henri Sausse in his '*Des Preuves? En Voila!*'[9] An entity manifested himself through an eighteen-year-old girl and claimed to have been an ecclesiastic in life. He wished to be called 'The Grand Vicar', saying that he could not reveal his name for family reasons. He spoke through the medium with great fluency and eloquence, interlarding his discourses with Latin phrases of which he furnished the translation, since none of those who heard him nor the medium understood the language. He recommended them to pray with fervour and conviction before opening the sittings and often added a Latin Oremus to the given prayer. On 14 December 1911, the Grand Vicar, at the request of the sitters, caused the medium to write down the Latin of a message and Oremus and their translations. These were shown to Professor Rossigneux, a teacher of Latin, whose opinion it was that they were monastic Latin, probably written by a priest. The words were ill-arranged, and the translation, though good, smacked of the seminary.

Sausse found Rossigneux's comments conclusive. Yet in a Roman Catholic country it would be surprising if any girl reached the age of eighteen without having heard a good deal of ecclesiastical Latin and some of it probably translated. This case, although interesting in its personification of 'The Grand Vicar', would seem to be another case of abnormal memory.

Bozzano, quoting *Light*, recounts the experiences of Count Chedo Mijatovitch, Serbian Plenipotentiary in London in 1912.[10] Some Hungarian Spiritualists having asked him to consult some good medium through whom he might seek guidance from an ancient Serbian sovereign, he visited incognito a Mr Vango whom he had never before met. Vango told him that the spirit of a young man was present, talking a language of which he did not understand a word. This sounded unlike the middle-aged king who had died in 1350 who was in the minister's thoughts, and he asked the medium to reproduce at least a single word spoken by the spirit. To Mijatovitch's astonishment, Vango uttered the Serbian words, *'Molim vas pishite morgoy materi Nataliya da ye molim da mi oprosti'* ('I request you write to my mother, Natalia, that I beg her to forgive me'). The count recognized that the spirit of the murdered King Alexander was communicating, a fact confirmed by further reference to confidential advice which he had given him two years before his assassination.

Vango reproduced the words in a peculiar manner, syllable by syllable backwards, thus: '*Lim, molim; te, shite, pishite*', and so on. In experiments with psychography, cases of 'inverted writing' are often found in which the medium writes the words backwards from right to left, obliging the experimenter to read the message reflected in a mirror. Something of the same kind can happen in hypnosis when a somnambulistic subject can feel in his left ear, say, a pinch which the hypnotist inflicts on his own right ear.

On 16 May 1912, Count Chedo and a Dr Hinkovich sat with Mrs Wriedt, an American direct-voice medium, who knew only her own language and yet is credited with having spoken at least thirteen foreign tongues. A dead doctor friend of Hinkovitch conversed with him for some time in Croatian, Chedo understanding every word. On 24 May the Count, accompanied by Professor Margaretta Selinka, 'the most scientific woman of Germany', was addressed by his mother in Serbian. Madame Selinka talked with her late husband and her own dead mother.[11]

The captain of the *Makara* showed a London *Times* reporter a letter describing a strange script written by a Mrs B. This was later shown to a Professor G., 'one of the great archaeologists of the world'. He identified it as hieratics, the popular form of hieroglyphics used by priests in Asia Minor up to about 5000 BC. Only a handful of people now alive could have written the document in the twenty minutes taken by Mrs B. The message thanked the lady for having communicated and described how differently people travelled now from then, quaintly contrasting the motions of camel and ship and concluding with an accurate description of the cabin and the state of the sky and sea.[12]

This account is a bald summary of an incident repeated by Bozzano, quoting *Light*, quoting *The Times*, quoting a letter sent apparently by one ship's captain to another. One would like to get closer to the anonymous Mrs B. and Professor G. and, still more, to see the script and translation.

Mrs Piper, a very celebrated medium, had as her guide a French doctor of Metz called Phinuit. He could not talk French – xenolalia in reverse, as it were – and his name was not found in the Metz archives. When asked why he did not speak French, he replied that he had so many English patients that he had forgotten his maternal tongue!

On 5 February 1883, Pearl Leonore Pollard was born, in due course married John H. Curran, of St Louis, and died on 4 December 1937. Thorough investigation of her background showed her to have been of very moderate education, very ordinary, honest and with nothing in her career to provide the material communicated through her by an entity calling herself 'Patience Worth'.

Patience first announced herself on 8 June 1913, via an ouija board, subsequently adding that she had been born in England, possibly at Dorchester in 1649 or 1694, lived there till she was 21, and then went to America, where she had been killed by Indians. Her inclusion in a book on glossolalia is justified by the fact that her English was so archaic that it was as foreign to Mrs Curran as Spanish or German would have been.

The spelling out of words letter by letter on the ouija board developed during the next five years to direct mental communication of tremendous speed – 3,000 words in one and a half hours and 5,000 words in a single session. 1,600,000 words, 'all literature', were written in five years. Different kinds of literature were communicated, and during an evening Patience would run from one composition to another and back without a break, with infallible memory resuming exactly where she had left off.

Much of the writing was published. It included *Telka*, a blank verse poem of 70,000 words communicated in 35 hours; *The Sorry Tale*, a novel dealing with the time of Christ; some short stories; a very large number of poems; and a considerable collection of aphorisms. Twenty-two poems were written in one evening, of which five were included in an *Anthology of Best Poems for 1917*. Sometimes twenty-five to thirty short poems would be introduced in an evening spontaneously on subjects suggested by those present. One example of such an instant production, given on the subject, 'A Field of Daffodils', was:

> . . . The great God, in a sudden mercy,
> bent and kissed the field;
> And lo! the soil was pregnant,
> and gave forth a golden smile.

The language is curious. It is a composite of dialects with a very high proportion of words drawn from Anglo-Saxon, and impossible to identify with the dialect used at any time in any part of England. The words are used always in their original sense, with no modernisms, and could not be used thus with the speed with which they were communicated even by a scholar who had made a special study of English etymology and dialects. Mrs Curran had never given an hour to such study. And, curious as the language may be, the opinions of many eminent critics recognized in the material literature of a very high quality.

A possible clue to Patience's surname is the fact that Mrs Curran's family moved to Fort *Worth* when she was eight months old. Records show, however, that there was a family called Worth living in Dorsetshire in the seventeenth century, although no Patience is to be found in printed genealogies.

Asked why she had chosen Mrs Curran as an amanuensis, Patience replied, ' I have said it to be a trick o' throbbin'. The wench be attuned unto the throb o' me'. Yet Patience emerged as a distinct personality quite different, apparently, from Mrs Curran, with a deep devoutness, profound thoughts couched in language often lovely and considerable acid humour that did not suffer fools gladly. Mrs Curran's relationship with her was like one with another human being.

The medium's conscious mind and sometimes her health and emotions could interfere with communications. On the other hand she could smoke, interrupt herself by breaking off to take part in the general conversation or answer a telephone, and Patience's 'dictation' would then be resumed at the exact point of interruption. This was also the case from one sitting to another, even if months intervened. Once, when the chapters of a far advanced novel were mislaid, Patience dictated them a second time. The lost document was found and the second dictation seen to be an exact replica of the first.

Hypotheses attempting to account for Patience Worth appear in a later chapter, but here it may be said that she was outstanding, even unique, in four ways. First, she is a rounded, highly individual and remarkably complete personality in her own right, unlike and independent of Mrs Curran. If she is only a dissociated personality, she is probably the most highly developed one ever to have emerged, and her incubator was a woman who, unlike most of those producing such personalities, seems to have been psychologically completely undisturbed. Second, Patience's personality impresses the reader with its integrity. She is a Puritan, devout and conscious of God, yet saved from bigotry by her awareness of the beauty of God's creation and unafraid of being moved by it. Her acid common sense and her contempt for folly make her an uncomfortable companion at times, but they are balanced by her poetic insight and her appreciation of goodness. She impresses as a woman, rather than as a 'spirit', whom the reader can respect and whose views he can appreciate even if he disagrees with them. Third, the quality of her communications is as far beyond the fragmentation and triviality of the average mediumistic revelation as the sun is brighter than a candle. And, finally, any explanation of her other than as some kind of discarnate personality, seems inadequate. Patience Worth does not prove the survival of men after death, but she is a powerful argument for it.

Perhaps the last word may be left to her. Among subjects fired at her in a single evening which elicited thirty-two short poems and seven aphorisms was her own name. She wrote:

> A phantom? Weel enough,
> Prove thee thyself to me!
> I say, behold, here I be,
> Buskins, kirtle, cap and pettyskirts,

And much tongue!
Weel, what has thou to prove thee?[13]

Contemporary with Mrs Curran were the activities of Margery Crandon who was prominent in American psychic circles in the 1920s. She communicated in Chinese and other languages, but modern investigation seems to confirm the opinion that she was a most ingenious and persistent fraud unparalleled in the history of psychical research. So strong is the evidence for deception in so much of her activity that all of it must be suspect, and further investigation of her alleged xenolalia may be omitted here.

An incident reminiscent of the communication in Morse already noted (page 78) concerns a sensitive, Mrs Conant, who prepared to write automatically for a stranger. Her hand rose and fell in an irregular manner, the pencil making a 'ticking' sound upon the paper. She thought the sitting a complete failure until her visitor revealed himself to be a telegraph operator who wanted confidential information from a friend, also a telegraphist, who had just died. He had received what he wanted by means of telegraphic ticks used in the transmission of mundane messages.[14]

A cloud hangs over another medium of the 1920s, George Valiantine, a comparatively uneducated American sensitive, because he was associated for a time with the suspect Margery Crandon and because he was, later in his career, allegedly caught out in trickery to do with physical phenomena. He does seem, however, to have been genuinely gifted as a direct-voice medium, and many remarkable incidents concerning his mediumship are recorded. In one, a Welshman, Caradoc Evans, carried on a question and answer conversation in Welsh with his dead father.[15] This could not have been prepared in advance, unless Evans were a conspirator. In another, Countess Tyong Deitiongham talked also to her dead father, in two Chinese dialects spoken by them when he was alive mingled in a way which no European would use.[16] A Japanese conversed with his elder dead brother in Japanese[17] and a Spanish cook with the spirit of her dead husband in a mixture of Basque and corrupt Spanish.[18] The records are detailed and, on the surface, well-attested, and the variety and obscurity of the languages allegedly spoken by Valiantine are inexplicable in our present state of knowledge unless the spiritist explanation is accepted.

Probably the most remarkable incident of Valiantine's mediumship is recorded in Professor Whymant's *Psychic Adventures in New York*.[19] The account well illustrates the difficulties faced by the psychical researcher. At first reading it is a convincing story of spirit communication but one which, on critical examination, raises doubts and queries. Whymant, knowledgeable in Chinese and some thirty other languages, an authority on the Orient and unpredisposed at the time to Spiritualism, attended a series of séances with Valiantine at the home of a New York lawyer, Mr William Cannon. After communications made in various languages, Kung-fu-tzu, the name by which Confucius was canonized, was repeated, followed by Chinese which Whymant could not follow at first but came to realize was in the style of the Chinese classics edited by Confucius 2,500 years ago. Scholars of archaic Chinese used approximately the same accent and style when they intoned passages from the ancient books.

Whymant tested the communicating entity with personal questions about Confucius and posers of the type with which all students of Chinese have wrestled in their studies of the Confucian canon. The questions were answered without pause or fumbling almost as soon as put. The supreme test was met when Whymant asked the voice to throw light on a poem from the Shih King anthology, its text so obscure and corrupt that no scholar could understand it. The whole poem was immediately repeated in such a way that its meaning became plain. Whymant took down the revised version and checked it next day in the New York Public Library. He found one error in the voice's version which was corrected by 'Confucius' at the next sitting before he even had time to refer to it.

Whymant was sceptical of many communications made at the dozen séances he attended because of their banality. But he records hearing fourteen languages spoken, including Chinese, Hindi, Persian, Labourdine Basque, Sanskrit, Arabic, Portuguese, Italian, Yiddish, German and modern Greek. The voices came sometimes two or three at a time, when Valiantine himself was talking with his neighbours.

The account may be challenged on the following grounds. Since Chinese script is not phonetic, no modern Chinese scholar can have any idea of how Confucius's Chinese sounded. It might be recognized by its style, but the translations given in an appendix to Whymant's book are said to be utterly unlike the style of the Chinese classics, while the flowing language of the transcript is described as bogus and certainly not Confucius's. The name Kung-fu-tzu was not invented until centuries after the sage's death (not a telling argument). The quality of Whymant's Chinese has been questioned, although he taught at two universities. He took down the Shih King poem in total darkness. His motives (consciously or subconsciously wanting to score over other Chinese experts), his scholarship and his integrity have all been questioned. There are no known grounds for the alleged motivation. Although Whymant's account is the only first-hand one published of these sittings, there is no reason to suspect its truth or his integrity. His scholarship may be doubted if Whymant mistook the style of Confucius as badly as other Chinese scholars allege. In the absence of recordings his word has to be taken for the truth of what happened, and the arguments by scholars against the authenticity of the alleged Confucian Chinese are not to be dismissed lightly. On the other hand, experts in ancient languages disagree surprisingly, and the emended translation of the Shih King poem reads convincingly to a reader ignorant of Chinese.

On Good Friday 1926 a twenty-eight-year-old Bavarian girl, Teresa Neumann, cheerful and ardently religious, who had been intensely ill from 1918 to 1920, produced stigmata.[20] She lived through the passion of Christ, pronouncing words and phrases of Aramaic, including some spoken by Jesus on the cross. Among these were the words for: crucified; Jews; hail, master; unrecorded words spoken by the disciples when Jesus was betrayed; Father forgive them; verily I say unto thee, today thou shalt be with me in Paradise. Eminent Orientalists attested that Teresa was without doubt speaking Aramaic, although it is a language so completely extinct that it is said to be almost impossible to reconstruct it accurately. For 'I thirst' she correctly used '*As-che*' where the experts would have used '*Sachera*', and Bozzano, reporting the case, asked whence Teresa produced this and other accurate though unexpected expressions. That she had the faculty of reading closed books at a distance seems denied by the correctness of her pronunciation. She apparently heard the words by clairaudience, and many who observed her were convinced that she was in communication with some contemporary of Jesus who had witnessed his passion.

Fairfield records that Teresa spoke other languages.[21] In 'the State of Exalted Repose', one of three well-defined forms of ecstasy into which she passed, she talked good High German with a majestic voice, quite unlike her usual broad Bavarian. She was credited with understanding unknown tongues, but there appears to be no documented or even corroborated account of this ability.

Florizel de (or von) Reuter, born 1893 in the United States, came to Europe with his mother when he was seven and lived there thereafter, becoming a world-famous violinist. He wrote three books, *Psychic Experiences of a Musician*, *The Consoling Angel* and *A Musician Talks with Unseen Friends*.

Florizel's mother was the medium through whom his early experiments were conducted. Before these took place, he attended his first séance at Los Angeles in June 1925 when he conversed through the medium Mrs Stella White with Paganini in Italian. At a second sitting he addressed the alleged spirit of a violinist, Pablo de Sarate, in Spanish and was answered intelligently by the medium in English. These experiences prompted him in 1926 to buy an Additor-Hesperus, an apparatus consisting of a board of polished wood along one side of which the alphabet and numbers one to ten were printed and a round box with a protruding pointer which moved automatically and indicated letters when a finger or fingers were lightly laid upon it.

For many days mother and son experimented unsuccessfully and were on the point of giving up when an apparently nonsensical passage was given. This was found, however, to be German written backwards, the last word being H C I (*'Ich'*), and the message reading 'I guard, I protect, I observe, I warn, I watch. Seven duties have I'. Later messages in the same inverted style referred to matters which Florizel knew but of which his mother, the writer, was ignorant; and although she spoke German fluently, the extreme rapidity of the inverted script made complicity on her part impossible.

The de Reuters were no means linguists, the mother knowing English, German, French, Spanish, Italian, Swedish and Latin. Communications were received in all these languages from February, 1926, through to May, and, in addition, Russian and Hungarian, which neither mother nor son knew, were written phonetically. In the languages known to them words were frequently used outside their vocabulary. Florizel partly summed up the first phase of his experiments thus:

(1) Writing with the apparatus took place under conditions which effectively prevented the writer from consciously directing it. His mother was often blindfolded and the letters on the board too close together for the distance between them to be calculated.

(2) About twenty different Intelligences communicated, of whom three had been friends in life, a number were acquaintances and four became intimate spirit-friends.

(3) Nine languages were used, of which two were completely unknown.

(4) Inverted writing was used in German, English, Italian and Swedish, spontaneous questions being correctly and lucidly answered in it without an instant's pause for reflection.

Even more remarkable communications were to come. Paganini reappeared several times, defending himself against the charge of dissoluteness and using a number of words unknown to the de Reuters. Emile Zola (or at least an intelligence separate from that of the automatist) wrote French far beyond the ability of the de Reuters. Traits characteristic of other communicators in their earthly lives appeared, and sometimes essays were written on theological and other problems either unconsidered by de Reuter or on which he held opinions directly contrary to those expressed.

Florizel developed automatic writing in Italian, French and German which was partly clairaudient, partly telepathic. Sometimes he heard or seemed to hear the word spoken the instant the pencil began to write it; sometimes the word about to be written would suddenly flash into his brain. In the following two years further communications were made in other languages unknown to the de Reuters (although, as a violinist travelling all over Europe, Florizel had superficial contact with many of them). In addition to those already mentioned Norwegian (spoken by Grieg whom de Reuter had met when he was alive), Polish, Dutch, Turkish, Persian (but a variety of it spoken only in India), Arabic and Lithuanian were written.

It is not possible in so brief a survey to give an adequate summary of the experiences narrated and of the details given which, on the surface, make an almost unanswerable case for the spiritist hypothesis. If all the information given in de Reuter's three books are the literal truth it is difficult to see what explanation there can be of them other than that the communicators were either the spirits of dead people or entities masquerading as them. Subconscious memory does not explain the logic of the answers given in unknown tongues to the comments and questions of the sitters, and if cryptesthesia (that is, the faculty of acquiring subconsciously facts unknown to our outer consciousness) be the explanation, it is cryptesthesia of a quality unknown elsewhere in the annals of psychical research.

A conspiracy on the part of the de Reuters is possible. It could have been that for some reason they decided to fabricate evidence. Perhaps, like the manufacturers of the Piltdown skull, who, one theory is, wanted to demonstrate the fallibility of a theory of evolution and were killed in the First World War before they could expose their fraud, they wished to prove the gullibility of some believers. Perhaps they wanted to bolster belief in Spiritualism, as some Christian priests have used false miracles at the tombs of saints to confirm the faith of the ignorant, the end justifying the means. There is no evidence at all that they had either of these objects and no person's integrity should be attacked without evidence. But if such were their objects, who better able to achieve them than a constantly travelling violinist accompanied by his mother and jealously guarding one or two evenings here and there to be private with their friends? Acquaintances in London would not have known what Florizel and his mother did or whom they saw when they were in Rome, nor their acquaintances in Vienna how they spent their time in their hotel suite in Paris. It would have been easy to write accouunts of séances which took place in the presence of Baron von Nutzing and Madame Natalia Blandenski (names invented) in which visiting spirits spoke German or Russian. Turkish or Urdu could also come through, not be recognized and be submitted to and translated later by an interpreters' bureau or an embassy. A careful selection of dates when the de Reuters were quietly at home and no check could be made on what they were doing, a catalogue of people present at the séances who could not be traced, a little elementary research into uncommon languages, a certain amount of simple stage-management – all these are possible. Given two years to make preparations and arrange his life for the purpose, a professional writer could produce a book or books as circumstantial and convincing as de Reuter's. The fewer people in a conspiracy, the better; and what more efficient conspirators could there be than an only son and his mother, close to one another and constantly in each other's company and confidence?

Against such a thesis, there are many incidents in the books which were verifiable at the time they were written. De Reuter needed neither money nor fame from the books, for one or two concerts would have given him as much as they earned altogether and his international reputation as 'Paganini Redivivus' provided enough of glory. Artistes of his eminence live in the glare of publicity and can scarcely risk losing their reputations for the sake of a silly game. Yet the books trouble because the communications seem too good to be true. The best messages sent through the best mediums of highest integrity are at their best rarely as good as the de Reuters' average. It may seem carping for a psychical researcher to look for convincing material all his life and suspect it when apparently found. A man sensitive enough to be a genius of a violinist and in tune beyond the normal with a mediumistic mother could form with her a psychic battery of sensitivity of outstanding power, and the books do not belittle the mistakes that were made as well as record the successes. Yet they seem to have made little impact in psychic circles when published, being met, seemingly, with the kind of response that serious parapsychologists today make to popular occultism.

In the 1930s appeared the phenomena of the 'Rosemary' communications. Amenhotep III, c.1406–1370 BC, an Egyptian Pharaoh, married a Babylonian princess whose existence is known to scholars but not her name. In 1931 this princess, giving the names Telika Venturi and Nona for short, allegedly communicated through 'Rosemary' (a pseudonym), described as a cultured English girl. It was claimed that 'Rosemary' though she had never seen an Egyptian dictionary or grammar, speaking in partial trance, recovered the pronunciation, known to no living scholar, of the Egyptian spoken during the XVIIIth Dynasty some fourteen hundred years BC.

Rosemary's mediumship was recorded by Dr Frederic H. Wood, a musician, and Mr Howard Hulme, a holder of the Oxford University honours Certificate in Egyptology. The latter, who lived two hundred miles away from the others, played his part mostly by letter but held a number of sittings with them.

The communications were at first in English. They awakened in Rosemary not only memories of a former incarnation in Egypt when, as a temple-dancer named Vola she had known Nona, but at least three other lives which she had lived on earth since that time. Later, Rosemary developed clairaudience of Egyptian words as she was passing from semi-trance to her normal state. Nona would sometimes precede, sometimes close a sitting with a group of from six to sixteen word phrases, each from one to seven syllables in length. Rosemary hearing them clairaudiently dictated them to Wood who took them down as best as the foreign accent allowed him to do in English vowels and consonants. The phrases were then sent to Hulme who returned them transcribed into orthodox Egyptian phraseology, supplemented by hieroglyphic symbols and translated into English both literally and approximately.

Wood acknowledged four possible sources of error. Rosemary might neither have heard nor repeated correctly fragmentary syllables retained from a torrent of rapid speech. Egyptian, guttural and nasal, needs an 'alien' throat and Rosemary's was adapted to English. He himself might have recorded inaccurately. Hulme might have analysed the phrases inaccurately. He might have translated them wrongly.

Nona wrote through Rosemary's hand of the difficulties of communication. She sometimes said more than her medium heard, and Rosemary sometimes retained only part of a sentence. Yet as many as sixty-six Egyptian phrases were recorded at one session. In 1934, in one of his rare sittings with Rosemary, Hulme had prepared a long list of questions which the medium refused to see before the session. Nona answered these without hesitation, using speech, writing and gesture for nearly two hours to throw light upon the strange guttural aspirates, peculiar consonants and construction of the language, dead for three thousand years. Never before, it is claimed, has so ancient a tongue been communicated through a medium by a spirit.

The claim presents difficulties to both believer and sceptic. Since no living scholar knows how the ancient language was pronounced, there can be no standard with which to compare any allegedly correct pronunciation. Ancient Egyptian, like some other languages, was written only in consonants. If, therefore, one takes a simple word represented by ST and the symbol V to stand for any vowel; the following permutations may arise: VST, SVT, STV, VSVT, VSTV, SVTV, VSVTV. With differing vowel sounds, some of them possibly double vowels, these represent combinations running into three figures.

The arguments in favour of the genuineness of the language and its pronunciation are as follows:

(1) Over 900 phrases of ancient Egyptian were communicated in something over five years, enough for a dictionary sufficiently complete for average purposes. Over 2,000 words, phrases, short sentences and whole paragraphs had been recorded, numbered, dated, edited and, for the most part translated, by March 1940.

(2) Since the consonants, it is claimed, were correct, it can be presumed that the vowels, used fluently and consistently, were equally correct.

(3) The vowels were used and pronounced consistently in words and phrases used years apart and in different contexts (not a convincing argument in the light of Hélène Smith's consistent 'Martian').

(4) Period characteristics, survival of archaisms, grammatical accuracy, the use of exceptions to grammatical rules habitually used by the ancient Egyptians, peculiar popular terms, ordinary elisions, figures of speech, the rapidity of speech with the slurrings and fusion of words common to all vernaculars, the complete lack of consciousness of any difficulty in using idioms and phraseology which English Egyptologists find difficult, all indicate a communicating intelligence colloquially familiar with the speech idioms used in Egypt during the XVIIIth Dynasty.

(5) The language was recorded on gramophone records at the International Institute of Psychical Research, under test conditions, on 4 May 1936. This fact shows that Rosemary, Wood and Hulme were not afraid of any outside investigation of the phenomena.

Nona communicated through Rosemary sometimes in

English, sometimes in Egyptian. She claimed to be an advanced spirit who had returned to a lower plane to act as teacher and had, presumably, to revive her memories of ancient Egypt and its language. Dr Wood found the separate personality of Nona, expressed through her spontaneity and independence of thought, very impressive. Rosemary's Egyptian may have come back to her with the memory of her former incarnation as Vola. The Egyptian and English were on different 'wave-lengths' so that adjustment from one to the other took a little time.

Rosemary's own account of the process of communication was that she 'felt' the language-phrases as inaudible speech, impressed on an abnormal brain which seemed to exist between the normal brain and the skull, filling her whole head and making it feel tight and ache. The words came without prior thought and were not retained at all. Dr Wood categorized Nona's communications as relative xenoglossy, responsive xenoglossy, and bilingual xenoglossy. The first was Egyptian for which no translation was offered at the time but shown in subsequent translation to be relevant to matters discussed with Nona or to contain new information that she wished to impart. The second consisted of Nona's answers to questions put to her. These were sometimes in Egyptian; sometimes in English or by a translation of Egyptian phrases in reply to a question put in English; sometimes in Egyptian to a question asked in Egyptian; sometimes in a bilingual form, English and Egyptian used in either order. Experiments were made in which Hulme gave Wood questions in Egyptian to put to Nona which the doctor memorized as sounds only. Neither he nor Rosemary knew the substance of the question, yet every time the answer was given by Nona promptly and informatively. Some of the reported questions and answers appear extremely evidential – but depend for their accuracy largely on Hulme's unsupported word (although Wood himself learned ancient Egyptian later). The third occurred when Nona gave both the Egyptian phrase and its English translation, always in idiomatic English probably derived from some subconscious part of Rosemary herself.

One small but telling incident may be noted among many.

Once Rosemary, on a visit to Brighton, left her handkerchief on the sea-wall. An hour later she heard many times a clairaudient phrase, *shenóo sherant*, and remembered her missing handkerchief, which was recovered for her by Mr Hulme. He analysed the phrase a few days later to find that it meant 'wrapper of the nose'.

Dr Wood believed the Rosemary case to be unique in that 'it has provided the best evidence hitherto obtained to show that individuality, identity and memory not only survive the death of the physical body but persist for thousands of years in our sub-conscious selves'[22] and that Nona might never have established the connection, 'had she not been able to find a medium in whose subconscious mind lay a clear memory of the language once spoken by them both'.[23]

Since no living person knows what the vowels of Ancient Egyptian were, even experts in Egyptology could not be expected to give a satisfactory and unanimous verdict on Rosemary's language. An Oxford don, versed in Egyptian, suggested that Rosemary 'picked up' the words from Hulme's attempts to converse with her. Professor Lexa, of Prague, on the other hand, allowed that 'the medium certainly uses phrases which are Egyptian'.[24] Dr Wood quoted other 'confused opinions' to 'show how little scholars know about Egyptian speech'.[25]

One of the most prominent direct-voice mediums of recent years is Mr Leslie Flint, one of whose tape-recordings includes a conversation in unidentified 'ancient tongues' between a man and a woman. Mr Flint does not exhibit much xenolalia, though the accents in which his voices speak English are many, varying from Scottish, Welsh and Cockney to the refined accents of Ellen Terry. His published life story shows that he received only a board-school education, so that the production of these voices with their variety of accents, vocabulary and timbre are almost as much a 'speaking in tongues' as was Mrs Curran's Patience Worth dialect. The autobiography is an answer also to the canard that Mr Flint learned his voices as a performer on the music-halls in his youth. There is no truth in this allegation.

Mr Flint has submitted himself to rigorous testing, including being seated in a soundproof cabinet designed by electrical experts, without any inhibition of his voices sounding from the air outside and around the apparatus. As usual, the believers accept the validity of the tests and the sceptics reject it. A Society for Psychical Research study in April 1940 found the balance of evidence for the existence of a particular foreign entity unconvincing. 'The sitting terminated abruptly when "Sister Maria" [who was uncertain whether she was Italian or Spanish] was asked *Parlate Italiano*, when she explained in voluable broken English that this tongue was much better for the communication' (report of investigator B). Investigator C, on the other hand, reported that Maria, on being asked by sitter D in Italian whether she spoke that language, replied in English that she wished to practise the language and appeared at least to understand her native tongue. D reported, 'Maria was unable to reply to me in Italian . . . I have heard of one case with this medium when Italian was spoken fluently.' In his fuller report D wrote, 'She said, however, that she was then working on an English vibration but she volunteered on a future occasion to speak either French or Italian. It would be interesting to see if she can do so.' The impression left by the file of reports is very mixed. But Mr Flint's tape-recordings are impressive for their length, contents, sustained quality of speech in various accents and different natures of the alleged personalities communicating. If they are the products of trickery – and no evidence has been produced to show that they are – he is either a superb actor or has his voices supplied by fellow-conspirators, of whose existence there is again no evidence.

In the last decade there has appeared a new phenomenon which, it is claimed, represents a breakthrough in psychical research. *Breakthrough* is, in fact, the title of the English translation and enlargement of the late Dr Konstantin Raudive's book describing his investigation into what are sometimes called inaccurately 'Raudive voices' and are better named 'electronic voice phenomena'. The book was originally written in German in 1968 under the title of *Unhoerbares wird Hoerbar* ('The inaudible becomes audible')

The story begins with the recording on tape by Friedrich Jürgenson, a Swede, of bird-song. He noticed on his tapes, in addition to the notes of birds, very faint voices about which he wrote two books, whose titles may be translated 'Voices from space' (1964) and 'Radio links with the dead' (1967). Dr Raudive, born in Latvia and a naturalized Swedish citizen, heard some of Jürgenson's tapes in 1965, was convinced of the genuineness of the voices and devoted the rest of his life to their recording and study.

Breakthrough names five methods of recording that have been used, describing the technical details and precautions that need to be taken. They are microphone recording, radio recording, radio–microphone recording (which enables the voices to enter into discussion and answer questions), frequency-transmitter recording, and diode recording.

The human ear does not at once pick up the voices (which are of varying quality, differ in pitch and rhythm from, and are twice the speed of ordinary speech) and has to be attuned to them for periods of up to three months before it can begin to hear the phonemes. But it is claimed that they can be heard by anyone with a fair sense of hearing, regardless of his views or prejudices. The voices use words from as many as six different languages in a single sentence and communicate like telegrams, their messages cut to the minimum and sometimes symbolic rather than literal. Their variety is considerable, including communications from Dr Raudive's deceased mother, aunt, cousin and many friends and Tolstoy, Dostoevski, Gorki, Nietzsche, Jung, Sir Oliver Lodge, John F. Kennedy, Churchill, Lenin, Stalin, Trotsky, Hitler and Mussolini. It is claimed that the voices can hold meaningful conversation with the living and that they are indeed communications from the dead. Opponents deny that two-way communication has occurred and that distinct personalities are manifested in the voices.

The phenomena have been argued at length in articles and correspondence in the Society for Psychical Research *Journal,*

Light and *The Psychical Researcher*, among others, and D. J. Ellis, Perrott–Warwick Student in Psychical Research, 1970–2, made them the object of his study. Jürgenson, interviewed in *The Psychical Researcher* by Peter Bander, stated that he accepted only voices that were beyond doubt and from which all listeners heard the same from the beginning. Prophetic messages convinced Jürgenson's colleagues, and electronic experts discerned a similarity in voice-prints between recordings of the same speakers alive and dead. The voices appeared so real to Bander and the conversations so relevant that their very quality inspired unease in him – they seemed too good to be true.

Yet debate continues to be fierce and experts flatly disagree. Some deny the objectivity of the voices, attributing them to sounds interpreted falsely by the human ear (psychiatrists argue that a single taped word played on a repeating loop can inspire listeners to hear up to forty other words). Even if the words are objective, subjective hearing of them may thus deceive.

Other explanations offered are that they are the psychokinetic projection of Dr Raudive's mind or of the minds of the participants, the evidence for this being that the polyglot languages were those he knew himself and that idiosyncrasies he used himself in speaking German were repeated by the voices. It is suggested that Raudive was a medium. Against this, Colin Smythe, publisher of *Breakthrough*, received German, which he does not know, and tapes containing 'at least' eight languages were received by Raymond Cass who speaks only English and German. Spacemen and elementals are also suggested as possible sources of the somwhat poor communications.

Each electronic expert quoted on one side can be matched by an equally distinguished specialist on the other. Natural causes, indistinct fragments of radio transmissions, mechanical noises and unnoticed remarks, interpreted by imaginative guesswork, wishful thinking and tricks of human mishearing are enough, the opponents say, to explain the voice phenomena. Perhaps the most realistic comment that can be echoed is the conclusion of D. J. Ellis who, after his two-year study, said that it is 'premature to claim any of the radio voices as paranormal'. But the interview with Jürgenson claiming voices of far better quality obtained since Raudive's death came two years after Ellis's investigations, and he and his allies would doubtless disagree with the scholar's findings. Jürgenson's material includes an uninterrupted twenty-four-minute conversation.

Claims are made from time to time that subjects regressed into allegedly previous lives by hypnotists have spoken the languages which they talked then and of which they are wholly ignorant in their present incarnations. Some of these do not stand up to examination and others are exaggerated. Dr Ian Stevenson, however, who is well-known for his scholarly investigations into and writings on reincarnation cases, has published a detailed review and report of a case of apparently genuine responsive xenolalia, that is, of a language in which the subject carried on lengthy intelligent conversations without ever having been in contact with it or known it in her present life.[26]

The subject was 'T.E.', a thirty-seven-year-old housewife of Jewish parentage who was born and grew up in Pennsylvania. Regressed by her husband, a physician, under hypnosis in 1955–6, she became a man, Jensen Jacoby, speaking in a deep male voice in either broken English or Swedish – in three lengthy sessions she spoke almost entirely in Swedish. Although his locality and time could not be identified with any certainty, Jensen appeared to have been a Swedish peasant who had lived some centuries earlier either in Sweden or New Sweden in America and had met a violent death. Stevenson and seven other scholars, including three Swedish-speaking persons, three, also Swedish-speaking, who studied the tapes, and an American who understood Scandinavian languages, agreed that this was a genuine case of responsive xenoglossy. There seems to have been no opportunity during her life for 'T.E.' ever to have learned Swedish or to have had contact with Swedish-speaking people. Stevenson's forty-three page report of his seven-year investigation of the case, its discussion in twenty-five pages, in which he considers fraud, cryptomnesia, extra-sensory perception, reincarnation and possession, and a 165-page transcript of the tapes, give the reader all the data from which to form his own judgment. Stevenson favours either reincarnation or possession as a possible explanantion, with an inclination towards the latter; and his opinion is the more acceptable in view of the scholarly restraint of this as of all his writings.

Every now and again an individual appears psychically gifted far beyond the average. Such, if all that is written of him is true, is Matthew Manning whose book, *The Link*[27] includes a wide spectrum of psychical experiences, including automatic writing in Arabic script in different handwritings. These were translated by Professor Suheil Bushrui of the American University of Beirut who judged that they could not have been reproduced from memory. One was translated, 'Life consists of many forces that live within us to the end of time . . . of the body does not frighten us because we shall all come together in the end. And death shall destroy all differences.' A second was too fragmentary to make immediate sense though it contained a number of Arabic words but became clear when it was explained in an English script received later that a certain George Laing, mentioned twice in the Arabic script, had been murdered in Saudi Arabia. Unfortunately, 'little else was discovered about George Laing' except the name of the alleged murderer, the place of the murder (Sakaka) and the fact that Laing had joined the community in Saudi Arabia in 1943. The account would have been strengthened if these facts could have been verified, and there is no suggestion that any attempt was made to do this.

The faculty of talking in tongues often accompanies automatic writing and other psychic gifts, and appears to be more widespread than is usually recognized. Cases come to my notice three or four times a year, and I possess a number of tapes of such glossolalia which their speakers are convinced are genuine languages and contain messages of importance for the world. Such tongues, unfortunately, are nearly always claimed to be ancient languages such as Aztec or Egyptian, which have the handicap that, since they were not phonetically written, no one can certainly know how they were pronounced. So far, none of these tongues has been identified nor its message deciphered.

Some reported incidents, of the type appearing from time to time in newspapers and magazines which give more or less sensational accounts of the spread in witchcraft and black magic and warnings against dabbling in such, support the doctrine that demons speak in tongues. A named Baptist minister, for example, claims to have talked in Greek and Aramaic with a girl, also named, who was possessed by some forty devils, and that they replied to him in the same languages. It is a regrettable fact that reports and articles are seldom completely accurate and need to be investigated at first-hand if they are to be used as evidence.

One example may be quoted. An article entitled 'The Eternal Question' in the *Daily Telegraph* colour supplement of 27 September 1964, stated that the medium, Mrs Twigg, had interviewed Mrs Randall, a Dutchwoman married to an Englishman and in appearance and accent entirely English. 'Mrs Twigg,' said the article, 'immediately started talking to Mrs Randall in Dutch, calling her by a nickname only her father, who had been Dutch, ever used.' Mrs Twigg, whose integrity is undoubted, made no such claims herself, and the Randalls, with whom she put me in touch, reported that Mrs Twigg had ended a series of messages in English purporting to come from Mrs Randall's deceased father, with the words, 'I don't know what he says. . . It sounds like "Tot ziens, Bollie".' *'To ziens'* means *'Au revoir'* and *'Bollie'* means 'Little Head', Mrs Randall's father's name for her when she was a little girl.

There is a difference between 'immediately began speaking Dutch' and the facts (remarkable enough), and many stories of xenolalia will be found to suffer from similar exaggeration.

Mrs Twigg hears her communications clairaudiently and repeats what she hears. She has spoken in Hungarian to an apparently English sitter who was Hungarian; quoted Swahili from a phrase-book used by a dead husband communicating with his wife; and used some disjointed words in Czech. Foreign languages come 'in a string of phonetics' and she repeats these without knowing their meaning.

The questions arise that if the entities communicating through mediums are indeed spirits, how do they communicate with each other in their non-physical world and how is it that they are confined to the languages they used on earth when they communicate with us? One alleged communicator asserted that spirits do speak to each other as it would be disagreeable to live in a world without sounds, and claimed that they could acquire a knowledge of languages unknown by them on earth 'by impression'. Others deny the need of languages, asserting that those having a right to share their thoughts 'vibrate in harmony' with them. It was only when they entered the 'earth-vibration' that they were compelled to try to express themselves in the language that was formerly their only means of mental and spiritual intercourse.

Judge Edmonds held the opinion that spirits communicating with humans used the different languages of the various countries to which they might be attracted and might be understood by those whom they addressed. A Danish 'spirit', asked how she spoke English so well, said that her thoughts were somehow transformed into English, as in Denmark they became Danish. She heard the human replies as 'thought-forms'. Bozzano affirmed that communicators use their native tongues with the same personal idiosyncrasies they used in life, though a 'foreign' spirit would have a hard time speaking through a medium who knew only English – the communicating spirit is affected by the medium as clear water flowing through a rusty pipe emerges stained. Spirit-helpers, familiar on earth with other languages, help, and communicating spirits, if themselves sufficiently psychically developed, can dispense with this help after a few trials and speak in a language 'all Greek' to the medium. Spirits seldom use language among themselves but think in unison.

Two types of mediumship can perhaps be distinguished, that in which entities speak or write *through* the medium, and that in which the medium acts as a focal point for entities to manifest themselves independently while using his psychic 'current' as the source of their power. Communications coming *through* the medium will be affected by the medium's mind and personality, as described above. But where the medium acts as a focal point, a source of psychic energy whereby entities can speak with direct voice or materialize, the recorded stories seem to indicate that they are at least partly, perhaps wholly, independent of him. A theory of direct-voice speaking, for example, is that spirits draw ectoplasm from the medium from which they form an invisible larynx through which they can speak. All that is required of the medium here is the personal quality, whatever that may be, to provide the apparatus to enable the spirit to communicate. Likewise, languages heard clairaudiently could come from the spirits themselves. All that the medium has is the ability to hear communications unheard by normal ears and made independently of him, and repeat what he hears. He may or may not be able to get his tongue round some of the sounds, but they are independent of his mind. Materialized spirits are reported as usually speaking in their own language, 'a fact which suggests their psychic independence.'

All this is based on the assumption that spirits exist at all and that they can communicate with the human world. Whether these assumptions are true or not must later be discussed.

10

The Charismatic Movement

Throughout the history of religions there have been two conflicting yet complementary impulses. Both are essential to the development of a faith and yet their existence side by side imposes tensions that are sometimes unbearable.

The first impulse may be called the prophetic. A religion, normally inspired by a charismatic leader, begins usually within the context of another, as Christianity, inspired by Jesus, began within Judaism. The adherents of the mother faith, settled in their beliefs evolved over centuries and expressed in well-tried patterns of ritual, resent the challenge to their authority and habits of thought which comes from the new movement. Contempt, opposition, persecution, follow quickly upon each other. Many 'prophetic' movements peter out under the attacks of authority. If they survive, they do so by the conviction, heroism and enthusiasm or fanaticism of their followers. Sometimes they become one more element in the general corpus of belief, sometimes they take over the mother faith completely, sometimes they break or are broken away and become a new faith in their own right.

If they survive, whatever form their survival takes, they develop after two or three generations into the second pattern, the 'priestly'. They become respectable. Worship comes to be conducted decently and in good order under the supervision of a venerated sacerdotal caste arranged in a settled hierarchy. This regards ethics as more important than enthusiasm and correct doctrine than charisma. Routine brings about dullness and, in time, dissatisfaction. A few enthusiasts, again usually inspired by a charismatic leader thrown up at a psychological moment, try to recapture the original inspiration (hence, in Christianity, the repeated efforts to 'get back to the Primitive Church' regarded, in spite of considerable evidence to the contrary, as a golden age of concord and amity in the unity of the Spirit). If the new enthusiasts escape or survive charges of heresy and schism, they normally start reforming movements within their religion which, because of the quality, commitment and self-sacrifice of their lives, attract other earnest and devout believers. The reform grows in reputation, flourishes, attracts adherents of lesser quality, those who, in T. S. Eliot's words, commit 'the greatest treason' of doing 'the right thing for the wrong reason', becomes powerful and wealthy and decays into respectability, even corruption. The charismatics of later generations are forced to start other movements to slake their spiritual thirst, and the pattern is repeated.

Christian church history has many examples of this process. Montanism, the first recorded glossolalic movement after New Testament times, seems to have been a reaction against the increasing respectability of the Church and an attempt to recapture the first enthusiasm. From the days of Christ until the Reformation, whenever the Church entered a period of stagnation, a new movement or a reform of an old one, revived it. Augustinians, Benedictines, Cluniacs, Dominicans, succeeded one another. The Reformation happened largely because, within the Catholic Church, the monastic impulse, which supplied the vehicles for 'prophetic' reform, perished in a changing world. Some other way of recapturing the first rapture had to be found. So the Jesuits and the Catholic Reformation continued the process within the Roman Church and various forms of Puritanism within the Protestant. Once the Church had divided, the way was open to further divisions, and 'prophetic' movements usually became schismatic sects –

Methodism, for example, separating from Anglicanism and itself dividing into a number of conflicting Churches. On a smaller scale, prophetic and priestly movements continued within the independent Churches. Thus, the Anglican had its evangelical revival in the early nineteenth century and its Tractarian Movement (at once a priestly and prophetic one) in the late.

Many of the early 'prophetic' movements can be seen clearly, perhaps with the hindsight of history, Benedict, Dominic, Luther, Calvin, Loyola, Wesley, stamping their personalities on the movements they inspired. The charismatic movement of the twentieth century may be unique in that, although there are personalities who have made their names in it, none of them can be regarded as its founder nor even *primus inter pares*. It began spontaneously, like the wind which 'bloweth where it listeth' as independent ripples within established denominations. It was a forerunner of the ecumenical movement which has been the main feature of the Christian Church during the present century; it was in a very real sense an ecumenical movement in itself. For, whatever their other differences may have been, charismatics who had shared the experience of one or other of the gifts of the Spirit, tongues, healing, interpretation of tongues, felt that they also shared a unity of the Spirit which swallowed up denominational differences.

The reasons for the movement have already been mentioned. There was first dissatisfaction with the smugness of Victorian Churchianity and its class-consciousness. The Established Church was upper- and middle-class, its pew-rent payers separating themselves from *hoi polloi* by the power of their purses; and the Free Churches catered for the lower classes who, by attendance at them, turned themselves into the deserving poor (though, possibly, not as deserving as those who squeezed into the back and side pews of Church of England churches). Second, the shock to faith of the science-will-explain-everything outlook that began with Darwin drove many by reaction into a search for mysticism and demonstrable miracles. For Christians this meant an emphasis on the work of the Holy Spirit, for others a search for communications from the spirits. Finally, the materialism which contrasted with the religiosity of the nineteenth century and has been developing in the twentieth into a belief that man shall not live by bread alone but by motor-cars, coloured television, time-and-a-half on Saturdays and double time on Sundays, has disillusioned many. The world is demonstrably not happier for a higher standard of living – perhaps it does need a vision without which the people perish.

So Pentecostalism began in the early 1900s, both in America and England, as movements usually independent of each other within established Churches. Yet, although it proved ecumenical in uniting believers across the denominations, it proved divisive within them. The arrogance and extravagance of glossolalics, acknowledged by their own historians, and the intolerance of their opponents drove out the Pentecostalists to form new denominations which, in turn, often subdivided through schisms. What should have been an expression of the unity of the Spirit, charismatics and others recognizing and fulfilling their different functions in partnership in the Body of Christ, as Paul pictured the Christian community, became in America literally dozens of additional denominations, and in England several.

So, during the first half of the twentieth century the Pentecostalist Churches developed along their own paths, regarded by the older denominations with that suspicion that the orthodox (the 'priestly') have always felt for the enthusiasts (the 'prophetic'). Of recent years, however, changes on both sides have resulted in a movement towards each other. Whereas in the beginning every member of a Pentecostal Church would have been expected first to be converted; next, perhaps via sanctification, perhaps not, to experience baptism with the Holy Spirit; and to prove that this had happened to him by signs following, always of tongues, according to some Pentecostal denominations, or sometimes with manifestations of other gifts, according to others; now there are large communities most of whose members and many of whose pastors have never spoken in tongues, and probably never will. Yet they believe in the charismata and would be indignant if it were suggested that they were not part of the charismatic movement.

The movement back to recognition has also been helped by the fact that, apart from their doctrine of Holy Spirit baptism, most Pentecostal Churches have orthodox theologies. English Pentecostals, for example, are mostly covered by the evangelical blanket and share their theology with one or other of the Free Churches or the Low Church variety of Anglicanism. Many German charismatics are Lutheran, and some share with French Pentecostals an adherence to Reformed (Calvinist) doctrine. Some Pentecostals, especially in North America, are Quaker in their theology, while the South American movement, originating in Methodism, has in large measure remained Methodist. Many indigenous Churches, especially in Africa, owe their origin to European missionaries who were Methodists or Baptists or Salvation Army before they were Pentecostalists, and caught from their founders fragments of their earlier theologies which have made it easier for them to come to terms with other Churches. Even those that are so nationalist, independent in thought and sometimes syncretistic that they can scarcely be classified as Christian at all, maintain a bridge with the charismatic movement by exhibiting all the gifts of tongues and healing that are to be found in orthodox Pentecostalism; and across this bridge they can pass in a future when nationalism has lost its first fervour into the international community of the world Church. Interestingly, there has been a strengthening of Pentecostalism in at least one mother country by the entry of former colonials – the West Indians have brought into England their own brand of enthusiasm in much the same way as the negroes of North America have developed theirs in the United States.

Numerical strength has a part to play, for, however much the respectable godly in the fashionable West End church may turn up their noses at the noisy rabble in the tin tabernacle in the slums, world Christianity cannot ignore a movement which has millions of adherents throughout the world and is in many parts

1 Giotto's 'Pentecost'

2   The Oracle at Delphi, from Christian, *Histoire de la Magie*

3   The town and isthmus of Corinth from the Acropolis

4 The French Camisard leader
Jean Cavalier (1680-1740)

5 The Reverend Edward Irving, MA

6   A meeting of the Shakers

7   The Mormon Tabernacle, Salt Lake City

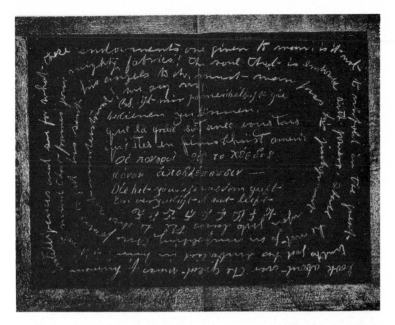

8 Slate writing in five different languages produced by Slade in Berlin, 1878

9 Hélène Smith's 'Martian' Script, 1898

10 Amy McPherson

of it numerically stronger than any other Church except the Roman Catholic.

For the picture presented by Pentecostalists in England and America at the beginning of the century and even now was not and is not a world view. In Anglo-Saxon and European civilization, Pentecostalists came principally from the depressed classes and the ignorant. Although these welcomed the occasional middle-class convert, they distrusted his education and, if he proved apostate, regarded that as the cause. The formation of their own Churches in England also imposed a painful conflict of loyalties upon many believers. Some inevitably remained in their former denominations. The range of the Anglican Church, with its right wing almost as Catholic in doctrine and ritual as any Roman and its evangelical tradition capable of as great starkness as the most unpretentious Free Church chapel, was able to accommodate neo-Pentecostals, provided that they kept quiet, talked in tongues only in private and did not disturb the peace of the bishops or the congregations. The same restraint was required of neo-Pentecostals in the French, German and Swiss Reformed Churches and the German Lutheran. In the United States, with its looser ecclesiastical organization and structure, its lack of a state Church and its insistence upon freedom of worship, it was easier for worshippers to enter the newly-formed Pentecostal communions. It would be impossible to prove the point, but it may be surmised that in England many Pentecostalists remained in their own Churches reserving their tongue-speaking for their private devotions without letting anyone know of their practice, and that they were to be the seed of the neo-Pentecostalism that is now bearing fruit. In America the majority made a clean break with their former denominations and began anew.

The picture was very different, however, in other parts of the world. To some extent in Africa but very powerfully in South America, Pentecostalism became ecumenical in a wider than theological sense. Where Indians of many different origins, negroes, descendants of Spanish settlers and other white men exist in every variety of colour and class, Pentecostalism has gathered within its embrace men of every type and from the whole range of society and education. The charismatic movement in South America has been democracy in action. Church services in which the congregation plays the major part contrast strikingly with a culture which in the past tried to impose itself from above and outside upon the oral native tradition of many of the inhabitants. The requirement that every Church member shall be an active evangelist not only swells the movement numerically to a dramatic degree but gives him self-respect and dignity, and renders the whole Church independent of foreign missions. What is more, such worshippers have little time to be over-nice in details of theology. They agree upon the main structure of their belief, which is enough for them, and are too busy doing to be overmuch concerned with theology.

The strength of the 'third wave' was such that in 1961, at the New Delhi meeting of the World Council of Churches, two Pentecostal communions were admitted to membership. In 1968, Christian Kurt, leader of the Mulheim Association of Christian Fellowship in Germany, which includes communities within the established Churches of Germany and the Pentecostal Free Churches, was the first Pentecostal to address a Faith Assembly of the World Council of Churches.

The movement of the Pentecostalist Churches towards the world community of Christians found a corresponding move in the established Churches. In the 1950s there was a charismatic revival in the 'main-line' denominations of the United States. It began, unexpectedly, in the Episcopalian Church, where it aroused considerable opposition from some of the bishops and proved to be regrettably divisive in some congregations. But it rapidly spread to other denominations, and its adherents, while remaining true to their own Churches, could join in fellowship with each other in organizations which transcended denominational differences. Such a one is the Full Gospel Business Men's Fellowship International which reaches circles that no preacher could normally touch. The Oral Roberts University, Tulsa, Oklahoma, founded by the son of a Full Gospel preacher, who had been cured of a speech impediment by a Pentecostal healer and had earned a reputation as a religious broadcaster, also spread the neo-Pentecostal gospel. The journalistic talents of John L. Sherrill on the popular level and the more scholarly history of the movement by the Reverend Morton T. Kelsey, an Episcopalian priest, have brought the news of recent happenings to a wider public both in the United States and England. It is not easy to say how great the movement is nor how widespread its influence may be on the Christian Church as a whole and on the wider society beyond. But one gathers that the signs indicate that neo-Pentecostalism is on the march.

In England today small groups of tongue-speakers using their gift in private prayer circles or in their individual devotions, though often with the knowledge and approval of their priests and ministers, are more widespread than is commonly recognized. For, contrary to usual opinion, it is not difficult to speak in tongues, once the possibility of doing it is known. (The practice is none the less valuable for that to those who are temperamentally suited to use it properly.) The Fountain Trust, founded in 1964 to serve the renewal of the Church in Britain and beyond 'sees the world-wide charismatic movement as one of God's ways of renewal for the whole Church. It regards the recovery of the power and gifts of the Spirit as an essential part of this renewal' and 'sees renewal chiefly in corporate rather than merely personal terms'.[1] Loyalty to their own Churches is, in fact, a characteristic of neo-Pentecostalists, most of whom are aware of and try to avoid the dangers of divisiveness.

This does not mean that they do not differ from each other in theology. Charismatics in the Free Church tradition may believe in the two or three stages in the development of the believer – conversion, then (perhaps) sanctification, then baptism with the Spirit with signs following. This is not far from the 'Second Blessing' and 'Holiness' ideas held by many Protestants. They are also likely to be Puritan in their eschewing of tobacco, alcohol and worldly pleasures. Anglican neo-Pentecostals, especially the trained theologians among them, reject Spirit-baptism as a process differing from water-baptism, both being for them two stages of one operation. By this operation the candidate receives the gift of the Holy Spirit which the bishop at confirmation prays may increase in him more and more until he comes unto God's everlasting kingdom. The whole tenor of the words of the baptism and confirmation services equates water-baptism as the outward and visible sign of the inward and spiritual grace of Spirit-baptism. If the confirmand becomes a charismatic, his charisma is a gift neither greater nor less than the unspectacular 'ordinary' gifts granted to other men, and it should be, for him, part of everyday Christian development. Neo-Pentecostalists may also be very far from belonging to the under-privileged types from whom the early charismatics came. They may be intellectual and 'worldly', smokers and drinkers and theatre-goers and fond of the good life in every sense of the expression.

It is therefore not strictly true to say, as has been said, that neo-Pentecostalism is no more than a repetition of classical Pentecostalism on a higher social level. There are differences in theological outlook and interpretation and fundamental dissimilarities in attitude. Pentecostalists, especially in the 'third world', practise the priesthood of all believers in that every member of a congregation plays an active part in worship and evangelism. The older established Churches still tend to be flocks who leave the main business of the Church to their pastors because 'that's what they're paid for', and the difference between a Pentecostalist preacher and an Anglican is that between an orchestra conductor and a soloist. Yet, for all the disparities in outlook and behaviour, there is in the charismatic movement a truly ecumenical unity of the Spirit which could change the face of Christianity.

Remarkable is the existence of a neo-Pentecostalist movement in the Roman Catholic Church. Romans recognize that Pentecostalism came from sources outside the Catholic Church and is an example of God's action transcending that of the Church. This itself is a remarkable admission which would have been unthinkable twenty years ago. The Roman Catholic bishops accept the charismata as having a Biblical basis, but naturally wholeheartedly reject the Pentecostalist theology of tongues. Simon Tugwell, a Catholic neo-Pentecostalist, who presented a piece of extempore, though prayerfully prepared, singing in tongues of three Catholic sisters in a BBC broadcast, defends the use of glossolalia by stating that an essential part of Christian praying is prayer that we cannot ourselves fully understand and that tongues 'is a particularly straightforward embodiment of this principle'.[2] They can be used to help the speaker grow into a fuller and richer experience of the Christian life as a whole.

Part of the purpose of this book has been to present a survey of many types of tongue-speaking in different cultures with the object of seeing if they have anything in common. Tugwell makes the point that there is no phenomenological difference between Christian and occult glossolalia and healing. From the outside and psychologically they look alike. They become Christian by fulfilling their function which is to be 'for the common good, for some reasonable purpose in the community'.[3] The emphasis on community is a golden thread running through the whole of the modern charismatic movement. Its possible importance for the ecumenical movement as a whole cannot be over-emphasized.

The charismatic movement could be like other 'prophetic' movements, lose its fervour, become respectable and have to be replaced by another wave. There are, however, world factors which could avert the process or at least change the pattern. The shrinking of the world through broadcast and televised news and ever faster travel, the growing interdependence of the nations, the greater respect of cultures for each other so that Christians can learn from Buddhists and Europe from Asia and Africa and vice versa, some of the more positive values of sundry counter-cultures, the realization of man's responsibility to nature as a part of creation rather than its lord and master and the global nature of ecological problems, even the knowledge that for the first time in history the human race can destroy itself, all these factors may pollinate movements of thought and spirit and bring them to unexpected types of fruition. It may be

151

that in the distant future, though one appreciably nearer than would have been dreamed possible two generations ago, the Christian Church may be reunified. The ecumenical spirit of the charismatic movement may play a large part in achieving this. But part of the movement is that it has touched individuals of other faiths. Jewish rabbis have spoken in tongues. Spiritualists, many of whom are as highly idealistic and of as religious a cast of mind as any adherents of other faiths, can claim that their speaking in tongues and healing are often manifested for the good of the community and thus meet Tugwell's criterion. Perhaps the charismatic movement can aim at a still greater unity and the fulfilment of the old vision that one day 'the earth shall be full of the knowledge of the Lord as the waters cover the sea'.[4]

11
Psychological and Medical Glossolalia

Speaking in tongues caused by moments of crisis, physical injury or mental disturbance and illness is widely reported in medical literature. If it is accepted that the memory retains everything that has been poured into it throughout life, although at levels too deep for much of it to be normally available, most of the reports are unremarkable. A few are extraordinary and, if they had taken place in séances, would understandably have been taken for spirit communications. Following is a selection of such cases, which could be multiplied many times over, beginning with simple ones and progressing to more complicated.

My late wife, born in Assam and bilingual in English and Bengali until she returned to England at the age of seven, forgot the eastern language entirely except for a snatch of lullaby and a few odd words. Working as a British Council guide when she was in her forties, she was showing two Eastern Pakistanis (as they were then called) the sights of London when they all but stepped in front of a bus. She shouted in Bengali, 'Look out!', a phrase she did not even know she had ever used, to the amazement and amusement of her guests. Furthermore, until they told her, she thought she had shouted the warning in English.

An English officer under hypnosis spoke Welsh (a language

strange to his listeners) which he had spoken as a child but had forgotten,[1] an experience shared by a hospital patient who spoke Welsh after a thirty-year absence from Wales. A physical injury to the head caused this, recovery from which caused him to forget his Welsh again.[2] A blow to the head caused another patient to lose his knowledge of Greek and apparently nothing else.[3] A German woman, married to an Englishman and accustomed to talk English, in illness lost her English completely and could talk to her attendants only through her husband acting as interpreter,[4] while another lady in delirium talked Breton, having had a nurse from Brittany when she was a child.[5] A very large number of similar cases could be quoted in which bilingual patients lost one language (sometimes their native tongues) and could converse only in the other. Sometimes they spoke only the first language they knew, sometimes the last, as in the instance of a clergyman who, with a disease of the brain, could speak only Hebrew, the last language he had learned;[6] while an Italian who died of yellow fever in New York at the beginning of his illness spoke only English, in the middle of it French and, on the day on which he died, Italian.[7] The approach of death seems abnormally to bring back

The approach of death seems abnormally to bring back childhood languages. A Lutheran clergyman of Philadelphia stated that the many Germans and Swedes in his congregation, when near death, always prayed in their native tongues, sometimes unspoken by them for fifty or sixty years.[8]

A more complicated case of recovery of past languages is that of a woman in delirium from 13 to 16 March 1902. On the thirteenth and fourteenth she talked Hindustani, which she had not spoken for sixty-six years, on the fourteenth Hindustani mixed with English, and on the fifteenth English, French and German. Her history was that she had been born in India where she had been cared for by Indian servants until she was three and had spoken only Hindustani; that she had then been sent to England before she was four and had learned English; and that she later learned French and German as fluent as her English. Her doctor observed that her case was a dramatic instance of a not uncommon phenomenon but remarkable for its perfection, completeness and good authentication.

He commented,

> It seems as if structural memories were laid down in the nervous system in strata, the memory of each successive experience overlying the memories of previous experiences; and as if, in senile loss of memory, the removal of the upper layers allowed of an over-activity of those that remain.[9]

The enhanced ability in music and fluency of language that have already been noticed in some religious glossolalics are also to be found in patients and sometimes among the insane. A man suffering from slight delirium connected with erysipelas of the head sang 'with great precision' some Gaelic songs, though he had not spoken the language since his youth and had no gift for music.[10] A girl of sixteen whose illness caused her continually to fall asleep sang a hymn in her sleep incomparably better than she could when awake.[11] Jung described a girl who 'used only literary German which, in marked contrast to her uncertain and confused bearing in the waking state, she spoke with the utmost confidence and mastery'.[12]

A family, often hearing music at night, traced the sound to a maidservant who, when awake, was dull, awkward, slow and without any talent for music. When she was seven the girl had slept in an apartment next to one occupied by a violinist of considerable skill, had become ill and had been cared for by the family whose servant she became. In her sleep she warbled exactly like 'the sweetest tones of a small violin'. She began by muttering, making noises like the tuning of the violin and then, after some prelude, imitated elaborate pieces of music clearly and accurately. Later she imitated an old piano in the house and the singing of the family, discussed a variety of subjects with justice and truth, conjugated Latin verbs correctly and spoke several French sentences accurately which she had heard from a Frenchman whom she had met in a shop. It was almost impossible to wake her from the sleep in which she performed these feats, but when sixteen she began to observe those in the

155

room and answer questions with astonishing acuteness. At twenty-one she 'became immoral' and it was believed that later she became insane.[13]

Coleridge's tale in *Biographia Literaria*[14] of the young woman who was the subject of Göttingen gossip during his stay there is well known. In fever she talked Latin, Greek and Hebrew, their source being traced to an old Protestant pastor who had taken her in and whose custom it was to read aloud from his favourite books in those languages. Coleridge's acceptance of the story was uncritical but the tale can be easily paralleled by other similar and better documented, such as that of an old unlettered Scottish woman who declared to her pastor that she had a message from the Lord. She then delivered in English, a tongue not normally used by her, a truly eloquent passage about Dissenters. It transpired that as a young woman she had been housemaid to an eloquent English minister whose views on Dissenters she supposed she was delivering from God himself.[15]

Sufficient enquiry nearly always traces the sources of real languages and destroys the claims that outlandish ones have been spoken. An outbreak of hysteria at Morzine, a French village on the Swiss border, resulted in those afflicted speaking in German, Latin and 'Arabic'. A medical doctor from Dijon traced the German to neighbouring Swiss cantons and Germany itself, and the Latin to church services where the inhabitants had heard it from childhood. All the alleged examples of Arabic were reduced to one, and no one in the village or locality had ever known or spoken the language or was qualified to recognize it.[16]

Some cases of mental illness produce glossolalic phenomena of a quality equal to that of religious ecstasy or trance-mediums. A girl, cataleptic once a week and epileptic two or three times in the interval, had spent six months in France five years previously. She had learned only a very little of the language. Yet, before her cataleptic seizures, she went into a state of ecstasy, recited poetry in French and delivered harangues about virtue and godliness in the same language, speaking correctly and fluently. Her doctor, calling her an excellent example of a

trance-medium, cynically commented, 'The materialistic influence of bromide of potassium, however, cured her catalepsy
and epilepsy, destroyed her knowledge of the French tongue
and made her corporeal structure so gross that the spirits refused
to make further use of it for their manifestation.'[17]

Mental illness is the cause of some xenolalia which the
speakers themselves and other believers ascribe to reincarnation.
A girl experienced, for example, alternating dual personalities
of which A was the primary, B the secondary.[18] B thought
herself the reincarnation of a Spanish woman. At times she
spoke automatically in a tongue which consisted of fragments of
Spanish with possible traces of Italian. This proved untrans-
latable into English. It was learned later that at her convent
school the girl would have heard three Mexican girls talking
Spanish to each other, and could have unconsciously assimilated
their speech. Shortly after her father's death, the shock of which
precipitated her condition, she became strongly attracted to a
man of half-Spanish blood and Spanish appearance. This event
furnished the emotional appeal which precipitated B. She may
have learned some words from him, but a sample of her Spanish
contained historical references which suggested that she had
overheard the three Mexicans orally repeating lessons in Spanish
history, and there were traces also of expressions of piety. In
addition to common small Spanish words and proper names
there were words which sounded Spanish but were not.
Probably the derivation of many of these could have been traced
by investigation.

Quoted by F. W. H. Myers[19] is the case of Fraulein Anna O.,
aged twenty-one, an accomplished linguist, who, distressed
beyond the normal by the death of her father, became ill in
1880. She suffered from hysterical aphasia (incapacity of
coherent utterance caused by lesion of the cerebral centres for
speech) and paraphasia (erroneous and involuntary use of one
word for another, as of one syllable for another). Sometimes she
was altogether speechless. Sometimes she talked German in an
ungrammatical, negro-like fashion which often accompanies
trance or secondary states. Sometimes she spoke English,

apparently believing it to be German, but understood German. Sometimes she spoke English, her phrases neat and well chosen, and could not understand German. In her most lucid hours she spoke French and Italian and had no memory of her English states, and vice versa. She read only French and Italian and, if she read aloud, translated very fluently by sight into excellent English, apparently unaware that the books were not in that language.

Hypnosis later revealed that each specific hysterical symptom arose from some incident which had happened in the anguished hours by her father's bedside. Once, bewildered and exhausted, an attempt at prayer found outlet only in a remembered line from an English children's hymn. This seems to have given her the persistent suggestion of English, as the last phrase uttered before aphasia sets in often persists for the aphasic as his single utterance.

A. Maeder made a detailed analysis of F.R., whose mother-tongue was German, when the patient was 41.[20] Suffering from dementia praecox and paranoia, he was isolated at the age of sixteen with some thirty other patients. He spoke to no-one but carried on long monologues with imaginary friends and enemies and filled exercise books with language which nobody understood any more than they understood his spoken words. Sometimes a French or German word appeared. Maeder studied F.R. by free association and by the description he gave of objects and pictures. Hidden sense was discovered behind his gibberish. Much time and patience disclosed a rich vocabulary and revealed its meaning. His language unfolded a myth in which F.R. was a great man, strong, powerful and generous, engaged in an epic struggle against his enemies who were led by Satan himself. He called his language *'Die excellenzsprache'* or *'La Salisjeur'* or *'Salisschur'*. *'Avoir Salis'* meant 'to have relations with high society', Les Salis being one of the oldest aristocratic Swiss families. F.R.'s language contained unique terms belonging to the delirious ideas of the patient, its etymology being more varied than would be expected. It was very rich in words relating to the human body, which he looked upon as a *'grossière mécanique . . . avec robinets, récipients, chaudières, régulateurs, distillateurs, distributeurs*, etc.' Maeder gives examples of the vocabulary and analyses many of the terms used.

For F.R., language lost its shades of meaning but was like a mosaic. The syntax was merely infantile. The reason for his development of his own language was that he lived in a personal fantasy world which needed such an aristocratic or individual tongue. German was only a dialect, the language of common men. As professionals had technical terms and peoples of the world spoke foreign languages, so he must have his own *'langue des Excellences'*. It was for his personal use, and he made no effort either to communicate or be understood. 'We end,' wrote Maeder, 'by recalling the two principal points in the study of the glossolalia: the importance of the emotional use of words (l'effectivité) and of its infantile nature.'

There can be few cases more remarkable or complicated than that of Ninfa Filiberto, a girl of sixteen, of Palermo, under the care of Dr Nicolo Cervello who, in 1853, published a pamphlet on the case entitled 'The Story of a Case of Hysteria with Spontaneous Somnambulism'. This was translated in the *Journal of the Society for Psychical Research*, December, 1900,[21] and also into French.[22]

Ninfa, very nervous and sensitive from youth, though healthy, was seized with convulsions on 26 December 1849. On 22 May 1850 a second attack of convulsions was followed by loss of consciousness, and a worse attack occurred on 27 June. After still more convulsions in spite of medical treatment, she regained her happy disposition and seemed cured by 9 August.

On the tenth there was pain and paralysis of the left arm, followed by further pains and delirium on the thirteenth, when she did not recognize her parents. She wished to write on the twentieth but no one at first understood her script; then it was realized that she was writing in reverse, with an astonishing speed. She was given twenty-eight sweets which she counted in reverse, beginning at once with 28. She saw everything upside-down. There were many attacks of unconsciousness, and on 26 August she lost the use of her right arm. She smelled and saw through her elbow. Her sufferings continued until 10 September, although the convulsions eased. On that date she began to write again, but used numbers instead of letters, which she wrote with tremendous rapidity. On the twelfth began a new kind of writing, not numbers but letters of a completely unknown alphabet. Its connection with the normal alphabet was eventually established and her writing could then be understood. On the thirteenth she adopted another alphabet impossible to decode. She wrote in vertical lines. She did not understand the doctor's language and spoke herself in a new one. During her frequent trances she spoke French and Italian. Later on the same day she was given a Greek grammar. It pleased her and soon she used it for the rest of the day writing Italian words in Greek characters and, for the first time since 20 August, without writing backwards. But she did not speak or understand Italian at this time. The only way to make her understand phrases was to call out the Greek names of letters one by one. For her part, she spoke a completely unknown language with such fluency that it seemed her own. It was supposed to be modern Greek for she said in another somnambulistic phase, 'I have been in Athens. I have seen that dear city, where the people speak as I do.' She said in trance that she could have spoken every kind of language – on that same day she would understand and speak Greek, the next day French, the next English. On the fourteenth she did not understand Greek or Italian but only French, a language she knew in an elementary fashion. She was given an Italian–French dictionary, whereupon she read the French phrases but could not read the Italian. When told she had spoken Greek the day before, she laughed and said that she had never understood Greek or any language but her own – she was a Parisienne living at Palermo. She laughed at her interviewers' French accents and pronunciation.

When she woke the next day she knew a little French but no English, and her father introduced her to two English-speaking friends in the presence of eight people in all who understood the language. Then she spoke excellent English, wondering why her tea had not been brought (it should be noted that tea is never drunk in Sicily in the morning). She conversed easily and at length with the Englishmen, but refused to write the language until strongly urged, when she wrote the date with the mistake 'Fifteen September'. Later that day her voice became very faint and sometimes she became completely speechless. She asked for an English book and pointed at different words which formed sentences she wished to say. When the Englishmen talked together she seemed to understand them, and remarked how fortunate it was to meet two compatriots abroad. She commented on the bad accents of Sicilians speaking English. In the evening she said that she would speak Italian the next day.

> On the 16th she announced that she was born in Siena, and described minutely the works of art existing in that city. I do not know whether others will agree with me, but I declare that to hear her speak the purest Tuscan appeared to me still more marvellous than her speaking English. It is impossible for one not born in Tuscany to express himself with the delicate modulations of that harmonious tongue.

Ninfa Filiberto continued in this state until the eighteenth. She had predicted that her paralysis would entirely disappear on that day, a prediction which came to pass, but the curious point is that at the moment the paralysis disappeared, the invalid, who had been speaking the purest Tuscan, passed brusquely, in the middle of a sentence, into her Sicilian dialect. From that moment she remembered nothing of the language she had spoken. During her illness, the girl's confessor, convinced that she was devil-possessed, tried to exorcise her, but to no avail.

Dr Hahn, commenting on the case in *Annales des sciences psychiques*, says that a neurologist, arguing from the multiplicity of convulsive attacks, motor and sensory alternations, will see in them an abnormal, aberrant form of hysteria, while admitting the great difficulty of including this case in the standard category of the illness. The occultist will explain it by the influence of spirits manifesting through the somnambulistic subject. Parapsychology can see in it evidence for travelling clairvoyance and clairaudience.

On the face of it, this remarkable case makes almost all other instances of glossolalia appear trivial. As Dr Hahn comments,

> Neither psychological automatism, nor subliminal consciousness, nor the externalization of sensitivity or of a double, is sufficient to explain this remarkable aptitude which the subject had of speaking a language which she had never learned nor heard spoken. He would be led rightly or wrongly to invoke the influence of spirits incarnate in the subject. All question of fraud being put aside, there remains 'this extraordinary fact, marvellous, of the substitution of a foreign language scarcely or never heard by her, and which she spoke fluently, with ease, and with an almost complete correctness, with no mistake against the genius of this language which she seems to have managed without a foreign accent, and with every nuance of intonation that could be desired'.

Unfortunately, much that it is necessary to know if the case is to be judged accurately can never be known. It is not certain that Ninfa spoke Greek, and, if she did, it was after seeing the Greek grammar, when the speed of composition, which seems to have been a feature and symptom of her mental illness, could have enabled her to speak with the fluency she showed (since no one understood her, the language could have been Graecized gibberish). Her French and English appear to have been fluent, but it is not known what opportunities she had had of hearing them spoken, nor the content of her conversation – was it small-talk trivia, or was her knowledge of subject and vocabulary tested by probing questions? The capacity for remembering and the powers of reproduction and imitation of material subconsciously absorbed can be demonstrated to a remarkable extent by subjects under hypnosis, and Ninfa was a girl whose condition could have made her hypersensitive in these respects. Unless her knowledge of languages was tested beyond what she might have heard – and there is no evidence of this – her speech, though paranormal, cannot be shown to have been due to supernatural influences. As for the speaking in Tuscan, this, too, could have been imitation – it cannot be shown that she had never heard Tuscan spoken – and her knowledge of Sienese art could have come from her studies. It is not known how much detailed knowledge she showed, and it is not uncommon for sixteen-year-old girls to be interested in and superficially knowledgeable about schools of art that take their fancy. The case is a remarkable one, but not beyond the degree of strangeness in many met with in abnormal psychology. And there is always the underlying query, the gap between what really did happen and the report of it.

The above cases seem to show that language known or even subconsciously heard, once absorbed into the brain in any way, becomes part of its permanent furniture. Under conditions of sufficient impetus, such as danger, breakdown of control and inhibitions, or the temporary deterioration of the more recent 'layers' of the personality, due to physical or mental illness, these languages can burst out in surprising fluency. When they are allied with the abnormal powers of imitation, reproduction and memory which many human beings can be shown to possess under hypnosis and other trance conditions, and which perhaps exist in everybody to a greater extent than is commonly realized, there is explanation sufficient to account for a high proportion of apparently supernatural glossolalia. Before he begins to consider a supernatural explanation, the investigator must at the very least make certain, first, that the speaker in tongues could never, at any time in his life, have heard the language he is talking – an almost impossible task in the majority of instances. Secondly, the intelligence allegedly speaking the language through the glossolalic must be tested thoroughly by question and answer about subjects so esoteric and varied that any chance of their having been overheard is out of the question. Only if these conditions are met should the possibility of some entity's communicating through the human organism be entertained. Even this is only a beginning – for who or what are the entities that communicate?

12

Debate and Discussion: Christian Tongues I

The survey of tongues which occupies the first part of this book answers a number of questions but leaves some problems unsolved. As with all psychic and spiritual subjects, attempts to find a solution to them will differ according to the prejudices of those who propose them, whose attitudes may be divided roughly into three types.

There are first the materialists who deny the existence of the spiritual. While admitting that the laws of nature are not as rigid as thought by the scientists of fifty years ago and that there are in them paradoxes inexplicable to man in his present state of knowledge, they believe that further discovery will in time throw light upon these dark problems. If they consider psychical research a legitimate field of study at all, they may concede the existence of extra-sensory perception with the proviso that again further research will explain its phenomena and that these will be found to be physical powers of that most complicated of all computers, the human mind. They can point with some justification of their viewpoint to the mass of psychic material which amazed our grandfathers. This, in the shape of dissociated personalities and other abnormal psychological conditions once thought to indicate spirit possession or the communicating dead, together with the physical phenomena of the séance room and the spontaneous activities of the poltergeist, all have their 'explanations' which they find sufficient. Nothing exists in their view that undermines their materialistic faith, for the inexplicable will one day become explicable and – though they would be unlikely to use a biblical quotation to support them – there is nothing 'hid that shall not [eventually] be known'.

Opposed to them are those who believe that matter is the illusion, spirit and/or mind the reality. They can point to the findings of modern physics that the ultimate 'bricks' of matter are particles of electricity which are apparently without weight, dimensions or substance. Existence is for such believers a dream from which humans will awake after death to a life whose impact will compare with their present experience as their most ecstatic earthly moments of conscious living compare with their soonest-forgotten and flimsiest wisps of dreams. Psychic experiences and mystical revelations are glimpses of reality seen and heard as if flashed from 'beyond the misted curtains, screening this world from that . . . faint and . . . lit with flame from far'.[1] For them there will always be phenomena which will never be explained until death becomes the gateway to the spiritual dimension their hearts know exists and to knowledge unobtainable in the present life.

Between these may be found a third group who, in Eddington's words, consider the universe more like a great thought than a great machine. It is the material world that is 'shot through with the glory of God' and, if they look for salvation at all, they see it in the promise of 'a new heaven and a new earth'. They reject the dichotomy of matter and spirit and, if they believe in life after death, see it as an expansion of present understanding and experience rather than an 'other' form of existence. In considering speaking in tongues they may gravitate either to the first or second group, according to their philosophical or religious emphasis.

For the materialists no glossolalia or xenolalia can be anything but natural phenomena. Even if some instances are not entirely explicable now, there is sufficient reason, from the many natural explanations that do exist, for a belief that all such phenomena will one day be perfectly understood. The second group, while admitting that great areas of tongue-speaking can be naturally explained, contend that there are cases which can only be given a supernatural interpretation. In drawing the threads together, therefore, it must be asked if such cases do, in fact, exist; and, if they do, examine all the possible theories that have been put forward to explain them.

There are clearly not enough data to argue any case from classical and Old Testament times. The phenomena in Acts, chapter 2, were due probably to cryptomnesia, which may equally be the explanation of the other instances of certain tongue-speaking in Luke's book, and also of some of the glossolalia of the Corinthian church. It can be deduced that at Corinth there also appeared, as a recognized and regular part of worship, other forms of glossolalia (tongues of angels?) which, because they were neither understood nor recognized, needed interpretation. These may have been very like modern Pentecostal tongues and therefore open to the same explanations, or quite different – there is no way of knowing, although, if they were different, it is difficult to imagine in what way. Believers in Pentecostalism would maintain that they were similar in that all Christian tongues were and are inspired by the Holy Spirit and that the Scriptural record of the Corinthian practice is the warrant for the modern exercise of the gift. If the similarity is accepted, then the conclusions of linguistics and psychology which can be drawn from present-day tongues can be applied to those of Corinth.

Anthropologists usually cast their nets wider than to study in detail the narrow business of the tongues to be found in their various cultures. The glossolalia they have found seems, however, to fall into clearly-defined classes. Medicine men and women and shamans may use the language of another tribe, unknown to the members of their own community and therefore wonderful. Or they may use archaic forms of their own tribal language, handed down probably for many generations from medicine man to medicine man. Similarly descended may be a special 'medicine man' language which may be attributed by the speaker to ancestors, ghosts or spirits, or totem animals, and be no more than esoteric gobbledygook. Finally, a language may be used imitating those with which the speakers have hearing acquaintance, such as white men's tongues, and there are also examples of languages spoken through cryptomnesia. There appears to be no evidence of genuine, responsive xenolalia (that is, intelligent conversation carried on in a recognized language completely unknown to the speaker) in any native culture studied by anthropologists.

The records of Christian glossolalia up to the Reformation are so meagre and savour so much of other saintly wonder stories that a critic can be forgiven for doubting all of them. The usual explanations of cryptomnesia and inspired nonsense can be given to many. Where any written record exists, as in the instance of Abbess Hildegard, analysis shows the tongue to have been a derived language, seemingly incubated in the sub-conscious mind and brought to the surface by a mystical experience. Pachomius and Hildegard both invented alphabets for their languages, as did Hélène Smith hundreds of years later. Even where evidence of xenolalia is produced, as in the process of canonization of St Francis Xavier (sufficient, apparently, to silence the *Promotor Fidei* or Devil's Advocate), the counter-evidence of Xavier's own accounts of his linguistic difficulties and the growing exaggeration of the claims of his supporters as the centuries pass are enough to enable hostile critics to dismiss the claims as legend.

The accounts of non-Catholic tongues – Shaker, Mormon, Irvingite – contain not a shred of real evidence of xenolalia. Camisard tongues were remarkable for the purity of their French and the youth of their speakers, but are all explicable in terms of abnormal psychology. Stories of Christian tongues in the nineteenth and early twentieth centuries would be wonderful if they were true; but they contain so much vagueness, show so many signs of myth-formation (a study of them by an expert form-critic would be interesting) and, when investigated, have so little evidence to support them that again hostile critics can be forgiven for dismissing the whole collection.

A typical example of a doublet formation is to be found in two stories, both recorded by J. J. M. McCrossan, B.A., B.D., formerly a teacher of Greek in Manitoba University.

One night, after a great evangelistic meeting where scores had been saved, we saw the evangelist overcome by the power of God while in prayer, and we heard him speak Chinese. We recognized the language because we had so often heard it spoken; but God, in His goodness, had a Christian Alliance missionary standing by our side, a man we knew, trusted and loved. He had been a Chinese missionary for over eighteen years. He whispered to us, 'He is praising God in the very Chinese dialect I preach in; he is speaking it perfectly, and, oh, how he is praising the Lord Jesus.' He then interpreted sentence after sentence to us. It was indeed wonderful, as we both knew that the evangelist was absolutely ignorant of the Chinese language.

On another occasion we heard an American woman, when filled with the Holy Ghost, praise God in Norwegian. We knew it was either Norwegian or Swedish, for we had heard these languages so frequently in Minneapolis. However, our gracious Lord had a Norwegian gentleman standing by our side, who said, 'Brother McCrossan, I know this woman. She is an American and utterly ignorant of my language (Norwegian) and yet she is speaking it perfectly, and, oh, sir, I have never heard anyone praise the Lord Jesus as she is doing.'

The remarkable parallelism of the two accounts and the anonymity of all the protagonists indicate a possible confusion of memory and at least a set pattern of thought in their narrator. If the accounts are accurate reports of two separate occasions, just as McCrossan had sufficient acquaintance with Chinese and Norwegian to recognize them, so might the evangelist and American woman have had enough respectively to praise God in them cryptomnesiacally.[2]

And the apologists for xenolalia often make a poor showing. Thus Archibald M'Kerrell,[3] basing his case on an incorrect

exegesis of Isaiah 28:11, quotes samples of language he had
heard spoken by four men and eleven women as follows:

Hippo-gerosto-hippo-senoote – *'Foorime oorin hoopo tanto
noostin.'* – *Noorastin-niparos-hipanos-bantos-boorin.* – *'O
pinitos'* – *elelastino-halimungitos-dentitu.* – *Hampootini-
farimi-aristos-ekrampos.* – *'Epoogos vangami.'* – *Beressino-
tereston sastinootino-alinoosis* – *'O fastos sungor, O fastos
sungor, O fastos sungor'* – *depipangito-boorinos-hypen
eletanteti-eretini-menati.*

These, he argues are obviously languages for eight reasons:

(1) In each of them can be heard monosyllables, disyllables
    and polysyllables (but this is also true of nonsense
    language).
(2) The modes of inflexion and terminations resemble those
    in other known languages, for example Latin and Greek.
    (Greek and Latin were widely known in the early
    nineteenth century among educated people and the
    latter was still used professionally. Both could easily have
    been overheard and a bastard form of them reproduced
    from the subconscious by people in a state of ecstasy.)
(3) Radical parts of words and entire words themselves were
    common to other known languages, for example, Greek
    and Latin. (M'Kerrell's knowledge of other languages
    does not seem to go beyond Greek and Latin, and he
    might have found it difficult to substantiate his claim of
    'other languages'. And in any nonsense language there
    can be found words which can be traced to some language
    in the world.)
(4) In the specimens, 'g' before 'i' is hard, not the modern
    pronunciation of the Roman 'g' but the Greek gamma.
    'This of itself is a most invincible proof that this tongue
    is a language.' (But one would expect Britons to use a
    hard 'g', as in gibbon, giddy, gift, gig, gild, girl.)
(5) *Hoopo* 'seems to declare the ancient Greek "ore
    rotundo"'. (Even if this contention can be taken

seriously, isolated words do not give sufficient strength to an argument for language.)

(6) The elegant reduplication of the same syllables as in *elelastino* are so like language and so unlike chance sounds. (On the contrary, repetition of syllables is a feature of nonsense tongues.)

(7) The same adjustment of words which is common to language appears, 'words of smaller and greater length, arranged at such distance as to give sufficient variety to the aspect of the language'. (Quite apart from the difficulty of being certain of word-divisions in ecstatic speech written down either in shorthand or from memory, developed glossolalia shows many of the characteristics of the speaker's mother-tongue, and this variety of length of words would echo that in his native language.)

(8) The characters of the tongues differed – some were stately and sonorous, some sweet but emphatically energetic, some coarse, hard and guttural. (One would expect different individuals to produce different tongues, but M'Kerrell's specimens show little variety and linguistic analysis would almost certainly show that differences were in the manner of delivery rather than in the nature of the speech.)

The Christian characters of the speakers were, M'Kerrell claims, additional proof. These may be accepted as proof of their honesty and sincerity in their *belief* that they were speaking in tongues, but honest sincere believers have been mistaken before now.

In M'Kerrell's experience, interpretation was given either word by word, or as a whole following the interpretation of the tongue. He noted the clairvoyance of some interpreters. 'Sometimes, to the deep amazement of auditors, their most powerful thoughts are produced before them by the speaker, and rebuked.'[4] Let us hope that none of them shared the experience of the sitter at a spiritualist séance who had a pornographic book in his pocket and was addressed in Latin with, 'There are nasty-minded people here – away with such!'

The witness of linguistic scholars is unanimously against the claims that genuine languages are spoken. With reference to Spiritualist xenolalia, Flammarion, the noted French psychical researcher, comments drily, 'I have not been asked to verify them and I am not asked to say here anything but what I am absolutely sure of.'[5] Henke records that in hearing a hundred or more people speaking in tongues at Chicago revival meetings, he heard no one speak in any of the six languages he knew.[6] In its simplest form the glossolalia was 'a mere babbling or screaming; and where it was more developed, there has been a constant tendency towards a repetition of certain syllables'. Mosiman traced many supposed examples of real speech in foreign languages but failed to discover an authentic case. He never heard a German word in assemblies where it was asserted that they spoke German, and he gives details of half a dozen cases which, when investigated thoroughly, produced nothing.[7] Nils Block-Hoell, while admitting the possibility of a genuine miracle, confesses that he has not 'succeeded in presenting a convincing example of xenolalia of which a satisfactory rational explanation cannot be given'.[8]

It is argued, notably by Sherrill, an apologist for tongues, that the odds against an expert recognizing any terrestrial language are enormous, to say nothing of 'tongues of angels'. There are, he claims, nearly 2,800 languages and dialects spoken in the world today plus all the languages spoken in the past.[9] But the Reverend William E. Welmers, a Presbyterian minister and expert linguist, disagrees. Linguists, he claims, know something about representative languages of every known language family in the world. If any of the thousand languages of Africa were spoken, there was about a ninety per cent chance that he himself would know it in a minute. Not only was one sample of tongues of which he had made a 'sympathetic study' unlike a genuine language but was followed by an utterly disproportionate interpretation. He concludes, 'Our evidence is still admittedly limited, but from the viewpoint of a Christian linguist the modern phenomenon of glossolalia would appear to be a linguistic fraud and monstrosity, given even the most generous interpretation of First Corinthians, 12–14.'[10]

Welmers may have been unfortunate in his one sample, for Bloch-Hoell says, 'At more than 50 Pentecostalist meetings I have attended I have never heard inarticulate glossolalia, only the language-like or word-like form.'[11] He mentions the interesting fact that a grammar of glossolalia has even been published,[12] though one would imagine that such a grammar would differ from country to country. And even where a very limited language appears, it may have significance. Pfister made a study of a man of twenty-four who, when seventeen, had made utterances which no one could understand. Pfister took down a large part of his limited vocabulary and explained each word in it, showing its source and meaning.

> His exhortations expressed his own desires to study and get religious clearness, and how he ardently wished to be a preacher and to marry a certain girl. It was a distortion of language made in order to disguise the utterances of the most secret things of his soul that nobody could understand, and yet he could vent all that was in him. His glossolalia proved infectious and he later developed a cryptographic unknown language, and finally there came to be some liturgical stereotypy.

There was a family glossolalic tendency for 'His sister's unknown tongue played a good deal upon English and his mother's upon Italian, but both were very infantile.'[13]

Sherrill, recognizing that all the case-histories he quotes came from involved and possibly prejudiced people, played tapes for the better part of an hour to six linguists, two specialists in modern languages, three in ancient, and one an expert in the study of language structure. No language was identified by any of them. But one said that one tape had been structured like modern poetry which depends upon sound as much as upon verbal meaning. 'I felt that although I didn't understand the literal sense of her words, I did catch the emotional content of

what she was saying. . . . It was a hymn of love. Beautiful.'
They frequently identified language patterns on the tapes and
distinguished made-up gibberish instantly.[14] The expert who
claimed that he could catch the sense of what was said can be
believed, for Pentecostalist tongues are often manifestly praise,
adoration and sometimes grief and yearning. The words may be
a non-language and demonstrable as such when studied, but
they express emotions obviously deeply felt by the speaker.

Glossolalics who have had some contact with foreign words
may incorporate some of them into their tongues. If these words
have been picked up at a religious service, as would be likely
among Pentecostalists visiting or being visited by fellow-
worshippers, they will be religious and, in many instances,
recognizably so. Fellow-believers, convinced that the collection
of sounds has a literal meaning and recognizing a word here and
there, may be prepared to swear their Bible-oath in all honesty
that the whole passage was spoken in the language suggested by
the words they understood, and interpret its meaning
accordingly. The interpretation will be helped as much by the
intonation, gestures, general expression of emotion and
conventional ideas of the believers as by the words.

The advent of the tape-recorder has not produced the definite
evidence for or against Christian xenolalia that disinterested
seekers after truth would like. It is easy enough to record
run-of-the-mill glossolalia in Pentecostalist meetings where it
regularly takes place. It is another matter to record a miracle – to
happen to have by one a tape-recorder when a Jew is being
converted because several of those round him are spontaneously
telling him the secrets of his life in Hebrew. Yet it is only that
kind of recording which can produce the quality of evidence
needful to satisfy an unprejudiced enquirer.

Tape-recorders have been used to collect Pentecostalist
glossolalia for detailed analysis, notably by Dr W. J. Samarin,
Professor of Linguistics at the University of Toronto, who has
published a number of scholarly articles and monographs on the
phenomenon.[15] Referring to the often-alleged recognition of
foreign languages, he says,

A person hearing or thinking he heard Swahili words would tend to "hear" a lot more in Swahili. This is clearly the case with Sango, a *lingua franca* of the Central African Republic. Europeans, particularly Frenchmen, think that the incidence of French words is so high in this language that it is really a kind of bastardized French. Statistical studies have revealed how wrong they are.[16]

The claim of two Englishmen to speak Temne, a Sierra Leone language, was rejected categorically by a native speaker of Temne, and a 'lengthy recording demonstrated, to my satisfaction, that the discourse was glossolalic'.[17] More interesting still as throwing light on xenolalia is the fact that

> Several people have told me when they were abroad, their children – out of desperation we would say – created their own pseudowords in talking French or Japanese, for example. In the latter case, what was remarkable was that almost all adults, even the Japanese, thought that the child was really talking Japanese.[18]

Samarin is not unsympathetic to Pentecostalists who, he thinks, have had a bad press. 'We are not justified in saying that people who experience glossolalia are fundamentally or temporarily in an abnormal psychological condition. . . . Moreover, there is evidence to indicate that for many people glossolalia is a cathartic experience.'[19] And again,

> The common attitude towards glossolalia is far from being scientific in the proper sense of the term, and is based partly on prejudice, partly on ignorance, and partly on laziness. Prejudice has led to a judgemental attitude towards Christian groups (like the Pentecostal ones) that practised glossolalia; and ignorance results from inadequate exposure to the great variety of experiences that glossolalia is associated with.[20]

But he is convinced that what might be called 'supernatural' xenolalia does not exist.

It should be noted that an interesting feature of these reports is that they are often set in a certain frame. It consists of the following elements; on a certain occasion person A utters a glossic discourse which is identified by person B as being his own language, whereupon some witness to the event (including either A or B) takes it as a God-given sign for some kind of decision. This stereotype kind of oral transmission of purported history requires its being considered a kind of folklorist genre.[21]

Samarin estimates that there are 4,000 to 7,000 languages on earth not yet studied, but he asserts that though new languages are constantly being discovered, 'We know enough now . . . [to] assert that the glossas are not normal human languages even though they may reveal some of their characteristics.'[22] His verdict is that Christian charismatics would be unable to provide a case of xenolalia that would stand up to scientific investigation, and, if it did, it would probably prove to be cryptomnesic.[23]

Samarin also notes the striking difference in interpretations given of glossolalia and alleged xenolalia.

When somebody identifies an utterance as being a known language, like German or Chinese, he refers only indirectly to its content; there is as far as I know, no translation, as one would expect if the second person really knew the language. It is only with glossolalia that there is an 'interpretation'.[24]

This is not a translation word by word or phrase by phrase (*pace* M'Kerrell) but as a 'unitary semantic block, almost always as a very generalized praise of God',[25] and the information is not conveyed linguistically but transmitted via codes and channels other than those which constitute a natural language. 'The empirical measure of this is that the audience knows considerably more after a performance than it did before'[26] – though it must be admitted that the knowledge is seldom if ever original and could equally be expressed in the vernacular. On the other hand, a number of individuals, sensible, normal and

of good education, and belonging to main-stream denominations, such as the Anglican and Baptist, allege that they have
heard tongues followed by interpretations which had something
to say personally and directly to them.

An interesting feature of the habitual glossolalist is that in
time recurring segments of his tongue can come to develop
meanings. Pastor Paul, quoted by Lombard, claimed that '*ea*'
meant 'Jesus'. He then tried to say 'dear Jesus' and 'my Jesus' in
tongues and observed that in each case a different glossic word
preceded '*ea*'. Lombard points out the naïvety of the
assumption that another language will be like one's own – in
German, the pastor's native tongue, a noun is preceded by its
attributes.[27]

To return to Samarin, his findings can be summarized under
three further headings, (a) the relationship between Christian
and non-Christian glossolalia; (b) the psychological/physio-
logical conditions for the production of tongue-speaking; (c) the
nature of glossolalia as a linguistic phenomenon. He notes that
Le Baron's glossolalia and modern American tongues are so
much alike that they must be accepted as manifestations of the
same linguistic phenomenon. Tape-recordings of two schizophrenic patients were also similar to glossolalia. He quotes the
account of a man who, when he was sixteen, burst out in a fit of
anger at an older brother who had habitually taunted him and
remembered that, while speaking, he had had no idea that he
was not talking a language known to him. Only after he had
stopped did he realize that he did not know what he had said.
'The experience was so bizarre that he wondered at the time if
he had spoken the language of a preincarnation.'[28] Another
man, now in his sixties, commonly uses glossolalia in a jocular
way when, he says, he cannot express himself as he would like.
The two examples he gave, both remarkably like other samples
of glossolalia, illustrated an apology and a burst of anger; 'the
two utterances, given less than a minute apart, were
phonologically different, as far as I could tell without having a
tape-recording of them. In other words, they were like two
different glossas',[29] similar, perhaps, to the different glossas

experienced by those Christians who have been conscious of speaking consecutively in a number of tongues on the same occasion. Some non-religious languages, whether of children in play or adults in spiritism, are indistinguishable from religious ones in their segmental shape 'but the more complex ones are far more complex than any religious ones I have examined or heard'.[30]

Opinions differ about the cause of glossolalia, most explanations being physiological or psychological. But as tongues occur when people are *not* emotionally worked up, overt emotionalism is now played down. 'Much more investigation needs to be done on the correlation of psychological factors – for example, intelligence and personality types – to glossolalia. I doubt that any significant correlations will be found unless very specific kinds of behavior are the foci of study.'[31] There are social factors in the production of all anomalous or marginal speech. When man departs from normal language he follows certain paths, but it is not clear what triggers the departure in every instance. The physiological state is not the sole causation of the glossolalic process. Samarin rejects trance as the causation of glossolalia. Characteristics which are said to prove trance are found elsewhere without dissociation, and are absent in other instances where glossolalia is accompanied by trance.[32]

As far as Christian tongues are concerned,

> the only necessary, and perhaps efficient, requirement of
> becoming a glossolalist seems to be a profound desire on the
> part of an individual for a new or better religious experience
> . . . all glossolalists are unwittingly in collusion to
> perpetuate a myth: that there is something strange and
> miraculous about tongues. If it were known how easy it was to
> talk in tongues, there would be few, if any, glossolalists.[33]

Yet first experiences are not always easy, however fluent the glossolalist may become later, and there have been examples of believers, like Irving, who would have regarded tongues as their supreme spiritual achievement yet could not attain them.

Experiences differ from great freedom and pleasure to agonizingly difficult.

If a study of personality types of tongue-speakers could be made, 'Hopefully such a typology will be scientifically more useful than some traditional ones in that it will be based on the structural facts of behaviour and will not depend on non-verifiable notions like unusual psychological states or God.'[34]

Samarin's study of glossolalia as a linguistic phenomenon shows that it is not gibberish. It has a patterning of sound generally typical of real languages, the principal linguistic feature being the remarkable number of phonological units at the various levels of macrosegments (sentences), microsegments (words) and phonemes (syllables and sound units), which can be studied and analysed.[35] This does not agree with Welmers's view (note 10, p. 264) that glossolalia is extremely limited, but he was evaluating one sample only. Certain linguistic features of glossas prove their difference, however, from normal languages. They are more repetitious in both macrosegments and microsegments, and have a reduced inventory of sounds (one specimen uses only seven consonants and three vowels), though some genuine languages also have a small number. The speaker normally reproduces the features of his mother-tongue, maximizing what is common in it and diminishing what is uncommon. Thus, if an 'ee' sound is very commonly used in the mother-tongue and an 'eo' very rarely used, 'ee' will appear even more commonly in the glossa and 'eo' even more rarely. Echoism (onomatopoeia) is used; in my own experience of hearing tongues, the onomatopoeia is not so much in the use of words which sound like the thing they represent as in the exaltation of feeling in expressing praise, love, judgment or warning. There is a tendency towards regularity of cadence – this is, perhaps, due partly to the quality of the tongue as a public monologue, in the same way that a preacher's delivery is different from his conversational speech-rhythm. There is preference for open syllables, those ending with a vowel or vowel-sound (eeny, meeny, miny, mo) though it must be noted that both open syllables and the use of restricted sounds are characteristic of some natural languages.

Samarin does not believe that religious glossolalia is normally pathological or dissociative, or different in essence from non-religious tongues: any attempted explanation of their causes and methods must take into account other spontaneous, ephemeral or 'meaningless' utterances in non-religious contexts. He asserts that 'many people have reported being awakened at night by finding themselves talking in tongues' and quotes three cases of people whose acquisition of 'religious' tongues was spontaneous and unmotivated.[36]

> the first is that of a sixty-eight-year-old woman who reports that when she was thirty-seven and already the mother of eight children, her husband took two of her sons and deserted her. When this happened, she began to pray; soon she was praying in tongues. At this time in her life she had had no contact with glossolalists and knew nothing about tongues (except, I suppose, what she had learned from reading the New Testament). The second case is that of, a Dutchwoman who, as a member of the Dutch Reformed Church, had had no exposure to glossolalia. However, following a serious illness, she began to have dreams and visions and to experience 'the presence of Jesus'. It was at this time that she began to utter 'new words', whose phonetic shape was very different from that of Dutch. Only many years later did she come in contact with other charismatics. The third case is likewise that of a woman with no previous contact whatsoever with glossolalia. She reports that at a small group prayer meeting she unexpectedly began to speak in tongues on thanking God for a miraculous healing.[37]

Since I began my research into tongues, three or four cases a year have come to me from amateur sensitives, most of them thinking themselves unique in possessing the gift and certain that they have been given a message from divine or spiritual resources for the world.

So there is glossolalia as behaviour learned from the

communion of which one is a member, the Pentecostalist working for, and expecting sooner or later to attain, the baptism with the Spirit with the sign or gift following of tongues. And there is spontaneous glossolalia. But in both cases – and in non-religious glossolalia – Samarin contends that the tongues are repressive speech and that they are 'only the product of a set of processes that "works on" linguistic information acquired by the speaker'. 'There is a "glossolalic process" that results in linguistic forms of various lengths, a pseudo-language but also found here and there in ordinary language.'[38] I believe – though this is not Samarin's view – that family codes and vocabulary are minor examples of this process, and slips of the tongue may give rise to a whole mythology; as, in my own family, all breakfast cereals are 'crackly' (to the discomfiture of sundry au-pair girls who have tried to buy 'crackly' in the local shop); my first wife once said to me, '*Lookity lookity walwah*', when she meant, 'Look at the clock and tell me what time it is' (I 'interpreted' her fragment of 'tongue' and obeyed it instantly); and my eldest daughter, an actress, once expressed a desire to emulate Dame Aggy Peshcroft, who became for a time a notable family character and gave rise to a whole language of Spoonerisms of which the eminent divine would have been proud. All glossolalia, Samarin suggests, 'is a single pheno-menon of linguistic "regression" whose basic component is a stream of speech produced unconsciously with early-acquired rules of phonotion but more or less consciously modified according to socially meaningful values and attitudes.'[39] The speaker 'returns to processes that characterized his language learning in early childhood, at a time when he was first learning the part of language most obvious for a child – its phonetic representation'.[40]

It must be admitted that just as unprejudiced and scholarly psychic investigation in pre-tape-recording days rarely, if ever, came across cases of xenolalia in Christian, Spiritualist or other circles which stood up to thorough critical examination, so there is little tape-recording of either glossolalia or xenolalia which can be classed as supernormal in origin. There is some –

Stevenson's Jensen Jacoby (page 137) is an instance. There is, however, no record that can be played back known to me of Christian xenolalia resulting in conversion such as the stories that are to be found in Pentecostalist literature. The difficulty of having apparatus ready to record what must be spontaneous and unexpected has already been mentioned. There is the further difficulty inherent in all psychical research that the very frame of mind which wants to capture and study such evidence may inhibit the phenomena and upset the delicate conditions in which they occur. These are real difficulties – it might be equally hard to prove the existence of lightning to those who demanded for its proof photographs taken of it only on film that would be ruined by its flash. And it is difficult to believe that so great a quantity of alleged experience is founded on nothing but misreporting, exaggeration and deception. By the very nature of their respective idealisms, there must be some men and women of integrity beyond the average among the Christians and Spiritualists who claim to have had wonderful experiences of xenolalic communion in the Holy Spirit or with the spirits of their departed friends; and though integrity is no guarantee of a scholarly and critical approach, there must be statistically among the tens of thousands of adherents of Pentecostalism and Spiritualism a few individuals who are both accurate in their observations and honest in their reporting. Yet the burden of proof lies with them, for it is they who have asserted that these things are true. As a man is presumed innocent until he is proved guilty beyond all reasonable doubt, so an alleged event must be assumed natural and capable of normal explanation until proved otherwise beyond all reasonable doubt to open-minded and disinterested people who have really studied the evidence.

Some Christians with first-hand experience of speaking in tongues would clearly not accept Samarin's findings as being applicable to themselves, and they must not be dismissed without a hearing. Pastor Barratt wrote,

I was filled with light and such a power that I began to shout as loud as I could in a foreign language. I must have spoken seven or eight languages, to judge from the various sounds and forms of speech used . . . I know from the strength of my voice that ten thousand might easily have heard all I said. The most wonderful moment was when I burst into a beautiful baritone solo, using one of the most pure and delightful languages I have ever heard.[41]

Elsewhere he writes,

How could I know that they were [eight] different languages? I felt that the position of the mouth was different. The power took my lower jaw and my tongue and forced the languages out clear and distinct while nothing kept the power back in me. Once my windpipe hurt me. I think at that time it was Gaelic. I know that language.[42]

The sense of speaking a number of different languages, common to many speakers of tongues (and, indeed, I have tapes of different 'languages' spoken by the same speaker which, to my inexpert ear, sound different), would seem to contradict the assertion that phonetic elements are in the pattern of the speaker's mother-tongue. Yet the phonetic elements in my tapes may be disguised and the conviction of speakers may be subjective. When Barratt wrote of his 'Gaelic', 'I know that language', did he mean that he spoke it, had heard it, or could recognize it?

The German, Pastor Paul, could not pray in his native tongue when the glossolalic urge seized him,

for none of my German words fitted into the position of my mouth. . . . But now something wonderful happened. It seemed as if a new organ was forming in my lungs which brought about sounds which would fit into the position of my mouth.[43]

He, too, was conscious of then talking in a second, quite different, language.

Experts disagree on the ability of any human being to speak any language. Some maintain that many languages cannot be spoken fluently by foreigners because of the utterly different mouth formations required. But Tyler, an exponent of the opposite view, talks of 'the close uniformity of man's organs of speech all over the world, the general similarity which prevails in the phonetic systems of the most general languages.'[44] If he is right, the genuineness of xenolalia is not to be denied *a priori* on the grounds that an individual human mouth and larynx cannot adapt themselves to an unaccustomed language. The perfect pronunciation of xenolalia inspired by cryptomnesia, observed several times from the Day of Pentecost to modern times, seems to support Tyler's view, and the extraordinary powers of imitation of handwriting and speech in automatic handwriting and mediumistic communication (if not the work of discarnate spirits) are other evidence.

There is a further possibility to be considered as an explanation of the stories of Christian xenolalia which result in the conversion of unbelievers. It has been suggested that there have sometimes occurred 'miracles of hearing' in which the same words have been 'heard' or at least understood by several bystanders in their own different languages. This type of intuitive understanding is not impossible. When my late wife said, '*Lookity lookity walwah*' I heard the actual syllables she used but understood immediately what she meant and carried out her wish without hesitation or question. The Japanese adults mentioned by Samarin who thought that foreign children were speaking genuine Japanese might well have attributed meaning to the words provided by their own cast of thought. The militant atheist or fanatical believer may easily belong to the not uncommon psychological type whose missionary zeal or energy of persecution is an expression of repressed uncertainty deep in the subconscious mind. Such a man, exposed to normal glossolalia, could hear in it his own doubts and sense of guilt expressed in his own language. If such an explanation seems far-fetched, the doubter has only to read standard works on abnormal psychology to come across many instances of even stranger phenomena known to medical science.

To sum up, no instance of genuine inexplicable xenolalia resulting in conversion is known to have been recorded on tape. This is not to say that no case has ever occurred nor that one never will be recorded. Nor does it mean that tongues have no other use than to bring about miraculous conversions and that the lack of satisfactory evidence for these implies that they are completely false or useless. Their significance in Christian worship today has yet to be examined. But, like Flammarion, the honest researcher, whatever his personal beliefs, must say, 'I am not to say here anything but what I am absolutely sure of.'

13

Debate and Discussion: Christian Tongues II

Since all unrecorded Christian tongues are a matter of history and cannot be recaptured, and since no man exists who has examined every claim to conversion through xenolalia and found it false, the determined believer can reject the findings of linguistic scholars if he wishes. He can maintain that nothing is impossible with God, that no man, however scholarly, can set limits to the work of the Holy Spirit, and that there have been genuine cases of xenolalia and conversions through it, unknown to and unexamined by the sceptics.

To the Christian who accepts the verdict of scholars, there are, however, other defences which may be made of tongues. Charismatic groups with their expectations of an outpouring of the Spirit in the last days which, they say, are now upon us, could maintain that the growing practice of glossolalia is a sign of the times. Some individuals postulate an ecstatic 'language of Divinity', with no counterpart among human tongues, in which the humblest saint can enjoy supernatural converse with God. It is irrelevant that this can be proved to be no true human language and shown to consist of elements from the worshipper's mother-tongue, for its purpose is to establish a direct contact between God and the individual. That there is real contact is proved by the holy joy that the worshipper experiences and the sanctified life that he leads as a result.

185

Even if there were no such results, the practice of glossolalia, Pentecostalists would say, is Biblical, and Christians must faithfully follow the instructions of Scripture, whatever sceptical experts appear to prove. Pentecostalist theology holds that a believer is first converted and should then be water-baptized by total immersion ('sprinkling' does not count). He should then prepare himself by prayer, waiting expectantly upon God, and by sanctified living for the baptism with the Holy Spirit with signs following. Spirit-baptism is often administered by the laying-on of the hands of an already Spirit-filled pastor or other believer. There may be additional requirements in details of belief and behaviour in different Pentecostalist sects and variations in the belief concerning tongues (see page 105). Some physical sign is almost always required, and this is often provided by motor-automata – physical shaking, heat flush, twisting of the body as if by an electric current, or the lying prostrate and twitching of the body as in an epileptic fit. 'It seemed to me as though an awful electric storm had broken loose and I was hit by all God's lightning' is one subject's description.[1] Visual phenomena are sometimes seen by onlookers and auditory sometimes heard – auras round the speakers, tongues of fire upon their heads, visions of angels ('seen even by sinners', as one superior saint puts it), the noise of rushing winds – though such sights and sounds may very well be subjective hallucinations due to expectations inspired by Scripture references.

A book tedious to all but theologians interested in the minutiae of Biblical exegesis could be written on the Scriptural passages actually and allegedly concerning speaking with tongues. A summary of the arguments inspired by key passages for and against the Pentecostalist position can be given briefly as follows.

Charismatics claim two Old Testament passages as prophecies of 'tongues', Isaiah 28:11, 12, and Joel 2:23. The former is given increased authority by being quoted by Paul in his Corinthian dissertation on tongues, 'For with stammering lips and another tongue will he speak to this people.' In the context the passage tells of an invasion of Israel by the Assyrians – if his people will not learn obediance to Jehovah, they will be taught a harsher lesson by invaders talking a foreign language. There seems no justification for an allegorical interpretation, and Christians who do not accept the verbal inspiration of the Bible may even dare to say that Paul misused the quotation in the first place.

Joel mentions the literal facts of the Palestinian climate, 'the former rain and the latter rain'. Because James 5:7, 8, links the patience of the farmer waiting for the rains with that of the believer awaiting the Second Coming of Christ, Pentecostalists claim that the 'early rain' was the coming of the Spirit at Pentecost and the 'latter rain' the outpouring of the Spirit in the period (which is the present age) immediately preceding Christ's return. Opponents of their position accept the passages at their face value and find it strange that fundamentalists, who set such store by the literal truth of the Bible, should be so ready to seize on allegorical meanings when it suits them.

John the Baptist said, 'I indeed baptize you with water but one mightier than I cometh . . . [who] shall baptize you with the Holy Ghost and with fire.'[2] Pentecostalists claim that this and similar passages teach that every believer has to experience two baptisms, one with water and one with the Holy Spirit. The orthodox reply is twofold: first, that these passages are forecasts of Pentecost, 'the birthday of the Church'. The Holy Spirit came to God's people in power and has been with them ever since, and his coming in that fashion is no more to be repeated than a physical birth can be. The second answer is that John's baptism was not Christian baptism. The latter is with water *and* the Holy Spirit together, ratified and completed by confirm-ation or some equivalent of it which is the sacramental equivalent of Pentecost for the average believer.

Mark 16:17, 18, runs, 'And these signs shall follow them that believe . . . they shall speak with new tongues.' It is generally accepted by New Testament scholars today that the verses following Mark 16:8, are a later substitution for the torn-off end of the original parchment. Hoekema states that the external evidence of the Uncials is against the passage being genuine.[3] Brumbach asserts that the evidence of the Uncial and Cursive MSS is for rather than against and that 'on the whole, the evidence as to the genuineness and authenticity of this passage seems irresistible'.[4] When flatly contradictory interpretations are given of the same evidence, the ordinary reader may be forgiven for feeling bewildered. It can be safely said, however, that, in our present state of knowledge, most New Testament scholars would agree with Hoekema against Brumbach. And Mark provides a further difficulty for Pentecostalists in using the same tense for 'they shall take up serpents' as 'they shall speak with tongues'. The handling of serpents has exactly the same Biblical authority as the speaking with tongues. Snake-handling cults do exist, but the practice is not found in Pentecostalist Churches. Furthermore, scholars are not agreed as to whether Mark's 'new tongues' means glossolalia or something quite different.

One would expect the Acts of the Apostles which, it has been suggested, should more accurately be called the Acts of the Holy Spirit, to provide ammunition for the Pentecostalists' 'Fire'-power. Acts 1:5, 'For John truly baptized with water; but ye shall be baptized with the Holy Ghost not many days hence' is a reference to Pentecost upon which no theological theory can be based. A key passage is obviously the account of Pentecost itself in Acts 2. Here the debate is as to whether the account refers to an experience that each individual believer *must* undergo some time after his regeneration or only to an historical event that took place on the day of Pentecost. Critics ask why, of the three signs given (wind, fire and tongues), do Pentecostalists pick on tongues, especially when the prophecy was that believers should be baptized with the Holy Ghost and *with fire*. Should not an appearance of fire always accompany Spirit baptism, and, if not, why not? (A once-and-for-all reason for tongues can be given – they were a sign that the Holy Spirit would enable the apostles to communicate the truths of the Gospel to all the world.) After the apostles' experience at Pentecost, Peter immediately won three thousand converts by urging them to repent and be baptized for the forgiveness of sins, and they would receive the gift of the Spirit. There is no mention of tongues in their case (though literary and historical critics state rightly that an 'argument from silence' must never be stressed too much), and the plain meaning of the passage seems to be that the repentance which brings the remission of sins is also sufficient for Spirit-baptism, and that these are not two separated experiences but one. At the least, they can be one.

The preaching of the Gospel to the Samaritans in Acts 8, and their reception of the Holy Spirit had results which Simon the Magus 'saw' and which caused him to try to buy the power of bestowing the Spirit from Peter and John. Pentecostalists sometimes claim that what Simon saw was tongues, but no mention is made of them. Would he not have been described as hearing rather than seeing them? But this passage does support two experiences, for the Samaritans believed and were baptized and after an interval received the Spirit.

The story of Cornelius (Acts 10 and 11) asserts that 'Peter was still speaking when the Holy Spirit came upon all who were listening to the message' and the Jewish believers who had accompanied Peter 'were astonished that the gift of the Holy Spirit should have been poured out even on Gentiles. For they could hear them speaking in tongues of ecstasy and acclaiming the greatness of God.'[5] It could be argued that since the Jewish observers could understand that Cornelius and his friends were acclaiming God, the tongues were not glossolalia at all but simply joyful shouting of psalms, canticles and praises which these God-fearers might have learned from their attendance at synagogue worship. Again, conversion and Spirit-baptism happened simultaneously without any interval. It has been suggested that the coming of the Spirit first to the apostles (who were orthodox Jews), second to the Samaritans (who worshipped the God of Israel but impurely), third to Gentile God-fearers (who were attracted but not fully committed to him) and fourth to out-and-out Gentiles who had received only John's baptism, was a step-by-step extension of Pentecost in ever-widening circles to include the whole world, and that this was the reason for the speaking of tongues on two and possibly all these occasions. For at Ephesus, too, 'when Paul had laid his hands on' Ephesians who up till then had not even heard that there was a Holy Spirit, he came upon them and 'they spoke in tongues of ecstasy and prophesied'.[6] Paul's question to the Ephesians, 'Did you receive the Holy Spirit when you became believers?'[7] again suggests that conversion and receiving the Spirit were normally parts of the same experience and blessing.

It is interesting to note that in all these cases tongues were bestowed upon whole groups, not individuals here and there; that in Samaria, Caesarea and Ephesus they were bestowed on people who did not ask for them; and that, although the disciples tarried at Jerusalem for a promise, the nature of the fulfilment of which they had no idea, none of the other three groups was in this position. There is no other mention of glossolalia in Acts. The only clear instances after Pentecost of baptism with the Spirit are Cornelius and the Ephesians – it could be argued that the very special cases of the first admission of God-fearers and then Gentiles to the Church was the reason for this – and on these two instances, together with Acts 2, the Pentecostalist case of tongues accompanying Spirit-baptism rests; for even Brumbach admits that 'in I Corinthians, Chapters 12–14, there is not the slightest hint that the gift of tongues is associated, in any direct sense, with the filling of the Holy Spirit'.[8]

Pentecostalists assert that the phrase 'filled with the Spirit', which appears *passim* in the New Testament, designates a post-conversion Spirit-baptism, attested by glossolalia. Against their view it can be argued that the filling is sometimes repeated. The disciples are described as being 'filled' on two separate occasions; on eight occasions the expression is used with no mention of tongues against one only when glossolalia accompanies the filling, and on some of these the use of tongues would have been highly inappropriate (as in Peter's appearance before the Sanhedrin, Acts 4:8). 'Sealed with the Spirit' is another phrase said to mean Spirit-baptism, but to the disinterested reader every passage containing this phrase seems obviously addressed to all Christians concerning blessings shared by them all.

Non-Pentecostalists argue that, since there are some twenty instances of mass and individual conversions recorded in Acts in which people were brought to salvation without mention of tongues, Spirit-baptism with glossolalia was not the normal New Testament pattern. Against their contention is the Pentecostalist assertion that conversion is normally only the first step.· Tongues could have occurred without their being mentioned, especially if they were so normal that mention of them would have been superfluous. In any case, Spirit-baptism with tongues would have followed in due course as converts progressed in the Christian life.

In short, the few historical accounts of tongues in Acts and the nearly complete silence of the other New Testament books – the key passage, I Corinthians 12–14, being a reply to an almost chance question from the Corinthians – provide a flimsy foundation on which to erect so important a doctrine of the Christian life. No directive for Christian living is contained in these passages; at best there is only an example which some may choose to follow, others not.

The Corinthian experience shows marked differences from that of Acts. The Corinthian tongues were accompanied ˙by interpretation, those of Acts were not. The purpose of the Corinthian tongues was edification (building up the faith) of the individual Christian speaker or of the church, that of the Acts xenolalia was an expression and confirmation of the outpouring of the Spirit which gave an opportunity of evangelizing non-Christians. Corinthian tongues were part of normal worship; Pentecost was a unique occasion. The former were a continuing gift under the speakers' control, the latter a temporary and probably irresistible initial experience. Baptism of the Holy Spirit resulting in tongues is not mentioned in the one reference to baptism in the Corinthian passage, chapter 12, verse 13, where, in the context, one would expect to find it. Rather the contrary; for the verse runs (my italics), 'For indeed we were *all* brought into one baptism, in the one Spirit,

191

whether we are Jews or Greek, whether slaves or free men, and that Holy Spirit was poured out for *all of us* to drink'. A disinterested reading of the verse clearly indicates one experience shared by all believers, not a distinct Spirit-baptism.

Pentecostalists argue that chapter 12, verse 28, clearly establishes tongues in the Church as a permanent gift. 'Within one community God has appointed . . . apostles . . . prophets . . . teachers . . . miracle-workers, then those that have gifts of healing, an ability to help others or power to guide them, or the gift of ecstatic utterance of various kinds.' Their opponents contend that Paul was describing the Church as it was in his day, not as it should necessarily remain for all time. 'Apostles', for example, died with the Twelve and with Paul himself, unless 'apostle' is given a more general meaning.

Paul also had the outlook of a Christian of his day. He seems confidently to have expected the Second Coming of Christ at any moment, and his thoughts on almost every subject were coloured by this (how differently, surely, he would have written on Christian marriage had he foreseen a Church that was to last for two thousand years). In describing the Christian community of his day, he was not establishing a rigid pattern to be followed all down the ages.

Pentecostalists say that Ephesians 5:18, commands believers to seek Spirit-baptism ('And be not drunk with wine but be filled with the Spirit'). But both imperatives are present and continuous in sense – 'Keep on refraining from drunkenness and keep on being filled with the Spirit'. There seems no justification here or anywhere else in the New Testament for the theory of the 'second blessing'. Conversion is a single experience with a past, present and future; a Christian can say, 'I have been converted' and even name a date and hour when he passed from darkness to light, though he may equally be unable to, if he has grown into the faith since babyhood. He is 'being converted' as he continues living in the faith, and this may be either a steady unconscious growth or a series of leaps, if he is at all a mystic, from spiritual *crise* to *crise* – a whole series of 'second blessings' yet none of them a Second Blessing with capital letters. He can look forward to 'being converted' in the sense of being fulfilled in conversion, though this perfection will not happen until he is the other side of the grave. On balance, it must be admitted that the Pentecostalist doctrine of the second blessing of baptism with the Holy Spirit has no basis in Scripture which would be accepted by all Christians as having that meaning.

If the Corinthian letter gives authority for tongue-speaking among Christians, it gives equal authority for interpretation of tongues, and this is the justification for the practice among those Christians for whom the Bible is a verbally inspired authority. In the early days of Pentecostalism such interpretation was not common because it was believed that all or most glossolalia was xenolalia. When it was realized that much was not, both public criticism and Pentecostal biblicism created a demand for interpretation of public speaking in tongues. The result is that most Pentecostalists today obey St Paul's injunctions that there must be an interpretation to follow the tongue and that if no recognized interpreter is present, then the glossolalic must restrain himself and use his tongue *sotto voce* for his own devotion.

In the past, in some congregations, interpretation was the prerogative of the pastor, but this is not usual today. Interpreters are usually different from glossolalics, but sometimes the same individual who has received the gift of tongues may also interpret his own glossolalia and that of others.

It is stressed by nearly all those who have written on the gifts that interpretation is not translation and that a paraphrase of the spiritual content of the glossolalic message is given. The interpreter normally follows impressions in the region of ideas, and his experience has been judged parallel to that of the 'inspirational speakers' who appear at Spiritualist meetings. This is the reason that a tongue lasting one minute may be interpreted by a vernacular rendering lasting five.

Opponents of charismata, besides telling the kind of story of false interpretation quoted elsewhere in this book, deny that any true rendering of what may be in the mind of the glossolalic is ever given. At best, they say, the translation or paraphrase is a false one, though usually given in all sincerity by someone who has suggested himself into thinking that he has the gift of interpretation. At worst it can be a merciless attack on individuals and groups by opponents who interpret tongues as divine support for their own grudges and factiousness. I have myself heard what was obviously a torrent of praise given an interpretation of such internecine bile as I found shocking almost beyond endurance in such a context and, in truth, blasphemous.

Yet some interpreters do claim the ability to translate exactly. A Reverend Mr Sheat asserted that after prayer and waiting for about an hour, he apprehended how one succeeded in interpreting. A word was given him in a 'foreign' tongue and its translation in English followed immediately. Then the two were repeated, which clearly indicated that they signified the same thing. 'Since then, when someone speaks in tongues, the interpretation comes to me as soon as I seek it.'[9] This is not unbelievable, for Hélène Smith translated her 'Martian' in the same way, her vocabulary remaining consistent over a number of years.

Early on, Barratt enumerated four methods of interpretation:

(1) After a person has finished his tongue, the meaning of the spoken words is comprehensively interpreted, but is not translated word by word.
(2) The interpretation may be a simple outline of the glossolalic message.
(3) It may be given little by little and sentence by sentence.
(4) It may be given word by word.

He says that the first two forms are the commonest. The interpreter 'will be in the Spirit at the time when the utterance in other tongues is given, so that the words will be registered on his spirit and he will feel the urge to speak what God gives him'.[10]

The giving of a true interpretation is not to be dismissed as impossible. There are instances where human beings are, at least temporarily, so in tune with each other that they seem to think the same thoughts, and where they begin the same sentence at the same moment, or one begins a sentence which the other completes in the identical words that were in the mind of the first. There seems to be no *prima facie* reason why a genuine sympathy between two believers in the same Holy Spirit should not, in the heightened sensibility which their worship may inspire, produce a genuine interpretation, more or less exact, of a tongue.

There need not even be a community of background, thought or religion. William J. Macmillan quotes an experience which illustrates the possibility of paranormal understanding between men of entirely different cultures. A Harley Street psychologist used to send him 'any curious personality with whom he came into contact', and one day sent him

> a Tibetan monk complete with yellow robes and an
> interpreter. For the first few minutes we spoke through the
> interpreter. Then to my utter astonishment I discovered that I
> could understand him more easily if no attempt was made at
> translation. The interpreter was banished from the room.
> Each of us, speaking in his own tongue, had not the slightest
> difficulty in following the other's thoughts.[11]

The author of this story was a healer and a sensitive, and it is not unlikely that among the Pentecostal worshippers are some sensitives whose apprehension follows a pattern similar to his.

A more puzzling aspect to the non-Pentecostalist Christian is the banality and, on the surface, the downright lies of many interpretations. Already quoted as untrue is the interpretation, 'Jesus is coming soon', given since Pentecostalism began, if 'soon' has to be explained by such devices as a thousand years being but one day in God's sight. And it may be asked, what is the point of tongues at all if God's message has to be translated. Why not the message direct without the tongue?

There is a twofold answer to this. First, tongues frequently reinforce messages given in the vernacular. Secondly, they do provide, with interpretation, a way for God to communicate directly with a group of Christians assembled in worship. Sherrill, an apologist for tongues, acknowledges that many interpretations are suspect because of their theatrical nature, lack of correlation between the length of the tongue and its interpretation, and the stereotyped nature of the message, expressed often in King James's English. He quotes a personal experience, however, in reply to these criticisms.[12] He had helped a delinquent, who continued to go wrong, and had decided that trying to stand between him and the consequences of his misdeeds had never been in the boy's real interests. At a tongues meeting a woman gave a glossolalic message, immediately interpreted by a man, 'Do not worry. I am pleased with the stand you have taken. This is difficult, but will bring much blessing to another.' Sherrill, who had been accused of being a fair-weather friend, felt that these words were meant specifically for him. They

> hit me with a power that is indescribable. . . . Indeed, they
> gave me the courage to stand by my decision in the weeks that
> followed even in the face of a great deal of pressure. Events
> have since proved that this was indeed the right task . . .
> emotion of absolute certainty that was my interior reaction to
> that message and its interpretation. I [did not] question, at
> the time, that these were God's words to me. . . . Later, of
> course, I toyed with all kinds of other meanings the words
> could have had. But I couldn't argue away the fact of my
> feelings at the time. Here was something I had not read in
> Paul's letters and could not have guessed, that God might
> accompany the messages with a corroborating conviction in
> the hearer.

Such an experience could be discounted because of its subjective nature – what is strongly felt may, nevertheless, not be true. On the other hand, a subjective experience cannot be disproved except by events, and in this instance the events supported the experience. Even so, there is nothing beyond the belief of the participant to confirm that the message came from God. Parallels could, no doubt, be quoted from Spiritualist circles where help had been given by beneficient spirits who had 'passed on' or even from pagan circles where a god had given an equally convincing experience to a worshipper.

Barratt observed that in public meetings the contents of interpreted glossolalia were often determined by what had been previously in the mind of the inspired speaker or had been temporarily hidden in his subconsciousness. 'With regard to the many cases of glossolalia which I personally have heard, the interpreted messages were always related to what had been previously spoken about at the meeting.'[13] Gee supports this view: 'We have noticed that usually, if interpretation is given, it is only something which the preacher would have almost certainly said in the ordinary course of his sermon.'[14] This would seem to be an argument against the necessity or usefulness of tongues, although employed as one in favour of them. One would expect a message from the Holy Spirit to be something more than a reinforcement of the thought of a sermon – especially when many sermons are somewhat trite and cliché-ridden.

In summary, the arguments against tongues are that all recorded glossolalia and, by reasonable inference, all un-recorded, are pseudo-languages; that Biblical authority for the practice is at best extremely doubtful and open to other explanations by Christians every whit as devout and sincere as Pentecostalists; that interpretations are usually trite and, where seemingly valid and useful, subjective and closed to objective judgment. Miracle stories of conversion through xenolalia, even if any exist that can be shown to be true, are open to the moral objections that may be made to all miracles; first, that in compelling men to believe by an intellectual *force majeure*, God robs them of their free will; secondly, that the use of a miracle to convert a particular individual and the neglect of the same means to convert a myriad other lost souls show a favouritism quite unworthy of the Source of all morality.

The replies are that the inference that all unrecorded glossolalia are pseudo-languages is unjustified in that only a tiny proportion of tongues has been recorded; that tongues were obviously a normal part of the worship of at least one New Testament church and that Scriptural authority for the doctrine and practice of glossolalia *is* sufficient; that subjective experiences are borne out by subsequent events; and that, whatever the moral objections to miracles, the Bible is full of instances where individuals were healed or their souls saved by them.

There is a further defence which can be made by Pentecostalists who accept the evidence that all glossolalia is pseudo-language. If the theory already mentioned (page 58) that plainsong is a conventionalized form of singing in tongues (and not the invention of the 'Reverend Gregorian Chant')[15] be true, why should not all glossolalia spoken or sung, be regarded as 'mouth-music'? The best tongues are beautiful to hear, and their expression of worship, grief, ecstasy, repentance, love and regret are sometimes as poignant as poetry, especially when uttered unexpectedly by comparatively illiterate people. They need no vocabulary for their general tenor to be understood. To think of them as sound communicating as Bach rather than as Shakespeare does is their justification and their best defence. They are not everybody's form of worship, but can be a genuine one when allowed to develop in a right way – ugly glossolalia mentioned often by its critics probably arises from forced and hysterical utterance. Within the Christian Church there needs to be a tolerance on the side of the non-glossolalics that tongues are a legitimate expression of worship, although not theirs, and on the side of the speakers in tongues that glossolalia is not to be required of all believers as evidence that they are 'complete' Christians.

14

Debate and Discussion: The Psychology and Effects of Tongues

When in 1927 Cutten wrote what was then the definitive work on the psychology of speaking in tongues, glossolalics were categorized as illiterate, uncontrolled, neurotic, ruled by mob emotion, subject to auto-suggestion and self-hypnosis, suffering from disease or derangement of the nervous system, and classified with hysterics, cataleptics and schizophrenics. Women, who predominated in all forms of nervous instability (twenty to one in hysteria, for example) spoke in tongues more than men. Such observations may have been not unmerited in the salad days of Pentecostalism, but recent developments have opened the way to less dogmatic and more generous judgments.

Cutten, Davenport and other writers explained that in the less intelligent or educated, speech of some kind and even of considerable fluency is easier than thought. An example is the innocent use of a swear-word to fill hesitancies in speech where a better-educated man might say 'Er'. Slight emotion stimulates the speech centres; but if those who find even rudimentary thought difficult are impelled to continue speaking after thought is exhausted, a series of incoherent and meaningless syllables results, such as is expressed in the words, 'spluttering with rage'. Excitement or overpowering emotion may bring about such compulsion to utter. 'Brethren,' exclaimed a man at a New York camp meeting, 'I feel – I feel – I feel – I feel – I feel – I can't tell you how I feel but O, I feel! I feel!' Feeling is difficult for even a master of words to express and yet urgently needs to be communicated, and where an illiterate man has no words of any human tongue to describe his feelings he may, if sufficiently stimulated, break into glossolalia. The feelings inspired by revivalist gatherings are often of the most primitive and powerful kind – an overwhelming sense of sin, terror of hell-fire, sudden release due to a conviction of forgiveness resulting in excessive joy, an outpouring of a flood of love towards God and mankind – and these are sometimes accentuated by contrast. There is first despair as the sinner realizes the enormity of his guilt, the depth of his depravity and the hopelessness of his position in God's eyes; then comes the release as light and conviction that God's in his heaven, all's right with the world, flood in upon him and he is swept into ecstasy. The sudden conversion in the twinkling of an eye may be so cataclysmic that it seems to the convert like a miracle rather than a natural process; and, indeed, even when he knows the 'natural' explanation of it, he continues to see in it the finger of God using the processes of nature to make all things new for him, and himself a new creature in Christ Jesus. As the process results from a conscious surrender of the will, its results seem like the possession of the personality by a higher power. In extreme cases, voices are sometimes heard, lights or visions seen and automatic motor phenomena occur.

In the illiterate and ignorant the lower brain centres and spinal ganglia are relatively strong and the rational and volitional powers residing in the higher mental centres comparatively weak and untrained. The stimuli caused by great emotional excitement never reach the higher centres – they are like a flood of water trying under pressure to escape through a bottleneck, the pressure causing it to be forced through another vent, as it were, directly to the muscles. This discharge is more frequent and less difficult, and the same process inhibits thought. The state has been called one of personal disintegration. The verbo-motive centres of the subject can be obedient to subconscious impulse in two ways, resulting either in glossolalia or in automatic writing, perhaps in a foreign language, if this is known to the subject.

The suggestions that glossolalics are to be classified with certain types of mental illness may be denied. The schizophrenic, for example, withdraws from the real world into a dream, where he may speak irrationally. But the speaker in tongues tries to relate his experience to the world of daily living, to improve the quality of his personal relationships and the moral tone of his day by day dealings. Hysteria may call forth remarkable subconscious powers but is a sickness which disturbs and may partially or completely inhibit sensory or motor functions. The religious glossolalic, on the other hand, follows an ideal of becoming a more complete personality than before.

It is true that a glossolalic may put himself into a passive condition not unlike a hypnotic trance, narrowing consciousness to the smallest possible point and making his desire to speak in tongues central in his thought. But in hypnosis there is rapport with the hypnotist whereas the glossolalic withdraws into a state where is he alone with God. Auto-suggestion also, akin to self-hypnosis, is unable to bring about a sudden transforming religious experience, though it may, by discipline and training over a long period of time, improve the character.

Some religious experiences are undoubtedly pathological in origin and character, and alienists may find tongues in general abnormal states more frequently than in religious ecstasy. The number of genuine schizophrenics and psychotics in 'possession' religions is, however, small

> compared with the mass of ordinary 'normally' neurotic
> people who find some relief from anxiety and some resolution
> of everyday conflicts and problems in such religious activity.
> These are people who, in Christian theological language,
> know that they are sinners in need of 'getting right with
> God'.[1]

Other psychologists have seen significance in the fact that some of their patients who experienced motor-automata in religion had also usually experienced them in non-religious

201

situations, while those who did not have them outside religion were unlikely to undergo them at conversion, however greatly they desired them. This proved, the contention ran, that tongues therefore had no religious value. All it in fact proves is that people with different temperaments react in different ways. One might as well argue that the singing of sacred solos in church was irrelevant because the soloist had a good enough voice to sing at secular concerts during the week; and that therefore the only valuable way to worship was by spoken prayer or normal, that is to say, average to bad, congregational singing.

'Ruled by mob emotion' is itself an emotive expression, implying that all crowd psychology has poor, if not downright evil effects. The reluctance of a rational individual to surrender to the irrationality of a mob is a true instinct, and the more powerful the individual's rationality, the greater his reluctance. But if all communal activities involving emotion were to be censured, there would have to be condemned all congregational worship, public concerts and theatre-going, to say nothing of political meetings and public inquiries. Crowd emotion can be good or bad and directed towards worthy or evil goals, and it is by the intentions of the speakers, the immediate effects upon their audience and the wider effects upon the community at large that the quality of the emotion must be judged. So if a speaker out of a sincere love for God and man rouses a congregation who agree with him to pray for the conversion of visitors among them or a 'second blessing' on those of their number who have not received it, and if he does this convinced that the result will be lives of joy and fulfilment in both converts and believers, which will also benefit the community in which they live, his use of emotion is not to be condemned even if his theology is mistaken. A detached rational observer may find such a preacher's methods offensive and lacking in taste, but this is because he is one kind of man and the preacher another.

Yet it must be acknowledged that emotion is always wrongly used if it batters down a man's free will and directs him into ways, even paths of righteousness, in which he is really fundamentally unwilling to go. Such converts are likely to become psychological and spiritual casualties.

A crowd comprises individuals whose characteristics are imitation and suggestibility. These are caused partly by the tendency of every mental contact which grasps the attention to work itself out in voluntary muscular action, partly by the willingness of the mind to accept as true every uncontradicted idea presented to it. Social suggestion greatly influences all minds, but in more intelligent and educated individuals no one idea or motor impulse remains long without rivals for their attention. Conflicting ideas may inhibit each other and either prevent action or give time for consideration of all relevant issues before action is taken or adherence given to belief. More primitive minds largely lack this inhibitive power and accept any idea that comes from a source of prestige or power. The crowd increases suggestibility by weakening inhibiting tendencies and reinforcing the idea or impulse dominating its attention at the time. Thus a whole churchful of worshippers concentrating on tongues will exlude any other subject from the attention of an unsophisticated mind, strengthen its emotion and imagination, and render its already weak critical judgment weaker still. If there is an initial scepticism or a delayed 'break-through', habitual attendance at 'waiting meetings' will tend to overcome them.

There is no mystery in the way crowd psychology works. A number of people united by a common conviction, especially one with a divine or equally strong sanction, will reinforce an individual's personal suggestibility by the sum of their own convictions, expressed in cries, prayers, slogans or the hypnotic repetition of songs or choruses euphoric, rousing or sentimental. Merely as sensory objects moving and making sounds, they will excite him and dominate his attention. If he cannot escape from or move much physically in a crowd, even if he at first wants to, he may give up and allow himself to go with it, and physical contact may reinforce growing mental contagion. Since man is gregarious by nature, he may find pleasure in the company of those round him and discover a group identity often lacking in the anonymity of modern society. He will also have a feeling of security in performing actions which shyness or fear of ridicule might inhibit him from doing by himself or in a less appreciative gathering. The excitement and emotionalism of a fervent company, together with the feeling that many people agreeing in the same belief and sharing the same experience cannot be wrong, will further weaken any critical faculty he has. He will be released from monotony and routine through his fresh experiences. Hesitations, cares, responsibilities, will vanish in a pleasurable surge of elevation, freedom and becoming 'one with the universe'. Since man believes instinctively that he ought to be happy, he will look upon such euphoria as a sign that the common cause is right or that God is in the experience and that it is good. If he is placed physically with a crowd so organized that its attention is fixed on a common object in a common direction, such as an orator in a pulpit or on a platform, the common focus will rivet his attention with theirs and make him one with them. If he is at first an outsider, his initial resistance will be broken down by the expectation and insistence that a certain thing (such as glossolalia) is desirable or necessary and by the ability which religious gatherings particularly have of reproducing conditions which reinforce expectation and of repeating attitudes and circumstances.

He may also find himself the focus of flattering and beneficent attention. The crowd yearns for him to join them, demanding that he 'yield himself' ('surrendering oneself to Christ', 'letting go', with the opposite suggestions that those who do not are self-willed, stubborn, stiff-necked resisters of the divine grace or the Holy Spirit, are commonplaces of revivalist thought and vocabulary). There can be a complete opening of the individual to suggestibility by which his higher, deliberative, rational, analytical, conscious personality gives place to the lower, reflexive, impulsive, irrational, emotional, uncritical and unconscious self. Encouraged then to break through into the inner group who have achieved the common object, he will not only have an increased sense of power but a flattering gain in prestige. If the common object is a specified phenomen like tongues, regarded as an essential sign that the believer has achieved his goal and, unlike inner states of spiritual attainment, openly manifest to the senses of his companions, then sooner or later he will speak in tongues. The period of incubation of the idea may vary from a day to a month to years, and some, like Edward Irving, perhaps too intelligent or unfitted by temperament, though not without a longing to manifest the gifts of the Spirit, never receive them. Yet, however long the period of incubation, there is a spontaneity when they do happen which gives an impression that 'the dayspring from on high hath visited' the recipient.

Crowd psychology is always suspect, though seemingly on the increase to judge from the repetitive and mindless shouting of slogans by demonstrators seen almost daily on the television news. It is the more so in the twentieth century when the older generation remembers the results of the mass psychosis induced by the Nuremberg rallies and similar gatherings. Demagogues rousing crowds and revivalist preachers use the same methods, distasteful to objective analysers of the truth of their messages, of affirmation, repetition and contagion. The first must be free from all reasoning and proof, its truth being assumed, such as, 'The Bible, which is the Word of God, teaches that. . . .' The second can take the form of repeated appeals to sinners to repent while emotional choruses are sung to stir them, or prayer after prayer to the Holy Spirit to manifest himself with signs following. Contagion forces upon individuals not only the opinions held by those around them but their very feelings.

Such methods are often distasteful to men of scholarship and reserved temperament. Henri M. Yaker, a Christian minister and consulting psychologist, writing of the tongues movement in the mainline denominations of the United States, says,

Our time is spiritually defunct and sees tremendous need for group identity, and thus a group psychopathology can offer security on a level slightly less than chronic mental illness. . . . In the need of present conformity the new cultural schizophrenia has occurred in the pentecostal

205

experience – and in some ways has little actual connection with the Pentecostal Churches . . . we are not witnessing a valid biblical experience of God encountering men in history . . . but a group psychopathology.[2]

Yaker sees tongues as Satanic, others, notably Freudian psychologists, as childish. They find evidence for this view in the development of glossolalia – first, inarticulate sounds, then articulate, finally coined words, such as children invent. Even the longing to join the inner circle of believers is childish in its 'I'm better than you' mentality. William James wrote that 'automatisms . . . have no essential spiritual significance . . . involuntary vocal utterance . . . must be simply ascribed to the subject's having a large subliminal region, involving nervous instability'.[3] Clark states that sects in revolt, heretical parties and fanatics have always held that perfectionism is attained by an abnormal effusion of the Holy Spirit upon elect souls and says dogmatically (and inaccurately) that 'it is an experimental and emotional process entirely, careful ordering of conduct having little or no influence in the process of attainment'.[4] The late Episcopalian Bishop Pike saw tongues as 'either a possible sign of psychological instability or abnormality or, at the best, nothing more than a meaningless psychological mechanism'.[5] Dr Welmers is a more hostile critic.

> When Christians publicize, propagate and endeavour to perpetuate an apparent manifestation of psychological instability and an obvious blasphemy [he is referring to a 'presumption' to add to the inspired Word of God, the Holy Scriptures, or even to reinforce it with a new Spirit-breathed message in the shape of an interpretation of tongues] as a special 'gift of the Holy Spirit' . . . I can only conclude, with all the sympathetic Scripture-centred scholarship I know how to apply, that modern glossolalia is a sad deception. Even if I am wrong, we had best all heed Paul's admonition not to play it up but to control it most carefully.[6]

Another source of debate is the relative merits of the

conscious and subconscious parts of the human mind. Coe warns that 'the subconscious is not a fact of observation but wholly of inference'[7] and lists three types of theory of the subconscious. They are:

(1) *Neural*. All deliverances called subconscious are due to restimulation of brain tracts that have been organized in a particular way through previous experiences of the individual.

(2) *Dissociation*. The field of an individual's attention includes a penumbra as well as a focus; penumbral items of experience can be combined and elaborated while remaining within the penumbra, and thus, when the focus of attention shifts to them, can appear as ready made.

(3) *Detached Unconsciousness*. Each of us has a 'double' or secondary self, or an understratum of psychic existence, possessed of powers and characteristics of its own that outrun and are separated from the ordinary.

Facts exist which support all these types of theory, and perhaps a combination of them (they are not necessarily exclusive) should be held. If a choice has to be made, the emergence of secondary personalities and the production of complete mental artefacts seem to demonstrate the truth of the third type, for such personalities and systems seem to point to more than mere restimulation of brain tracts or arrangement of penumbral observations.

Some writers assume that the subconscious mind is inferior to the conscious. Drummond says emotively that it is difficult to believe that the Holy Spirit deliberately chooses 'the slime of the subliminal' while avoiding 'the sunlit hills of full rational consciousness' and quotes Dean Inge as writing that 'the wish to empty ourselves of our own personality, to empty ourselves that God may fill the void, is a mistake. It is when we are most ourselves that we are nearest God.'[8]

Yet mystical experiences, in which men are caught out of themselves, are an almost essential part of the character of religious leaders. 'Saint Paul . . . the Bernards, the Loyolas, the Luthers, the Foxes, the Wesleys, had their visions, voices, rapt conditions, guiding impressions, and ''openings''.'[9] Since many of such religious leaders, whatever their faults or extravagances, have inspired men to higher ideals of morals and living, the possibility must not be discounted of there being a Power greater than themselves with which they may be in touch through their mystical experiences. A. Lewis Humphries says,

> There may be sympathetic *rapports* of human nature with the greater nature around, and of man's mind with the moral mind of the universe, which gives results by unconscious processes; and if there be such faculties and relations, then we may assume that they would also enter into prophecy[10]

(of which glossolalia has been regarded as a department).

The theologian who writes thus is not entirely opposed by every school of psychology. Jung believed that there were non-physical forces which influenced human life. He compares the sphere of consciousness to an island in the midst of the ocean. The ocean is the unconscious. Directly below its surface and nearest to consciousness is the 'personal unconscious' which consists of 'what has been forgotten or repressed and of subliminary perceptions, thoughts or feelings of every sort. Beneath the personal unconscious lies the 'collective unconscious' which consists of the inheritance of the psychic experience of mankind which, Jung maintains, lies deep within the psyche. He arrived at his conclusion because dispositions to form certain symbols are found uniformly all over the world

> and that similar symbols emerge in dreams, in day-dreams, in the phenomena of 'second sight', in religious and magical figures and emblems, in myth and fairy-stories, in gnostic visions, in alchemy, and in automatic and 'inspired' designs and utterances. Everywhere this 'collective unconscious' displays, in the main essentials of its manifestations, a similar structure and pattern of behaviour, and appears to obey similar laws of its own.[11]

Speaking in tongues was one evidence of a breakthrough of this objective psyche on a deep collective level of the unconscious, a level not necessarily 'sub' in the sense of inferior. Experience springing from this level of the human psyche may be more than personal and actually transcend space and time. Jung saw elements in the unconscious which lead men forward and are superior to human consciousness. In addition to the subconscious there could also be

> layers lying *above* consciousness. . . . In my experience the conscious mind can only claim a relatively central position and must put up with the fact that the unconscious psyche transcends and as it were surrounds it on all sides. Unconscious contents connect it *backwards* with physiological states on the one hand and archetypal data on the other. But it is extended *forward* by intuitions which are conditioned partly by archetypes and partly by subliminal perceptions depending on the relativity of time and space in the unconscious.[12]

In this 'forward' extension could be an operation of the Holy Spirit and, if Jung's collective unconscious theory is accepted, glossolalia can be received as an experience of the Spirit and as prime evidence of the reality of religious experience.

One psychologically sophisticated tongue-speaker has summarized the value of glossolalia thus.

> If the Jungian approach to the collective unconscious is followed, it can be accepted that a numinous supra-personal quality does enter the life of one who speaks in tongues. This phenomenon is not, therefore, pathological nor infantile. Instead it can relate the conscious mind to the ground of its existence in the collective unconscious. It can free the conscious mind from its extreme rationalism. It can allow the emotional side of the psyche not only a means of expression but also a method of nurture. Speaking with tongues can be a most concrete means of expressing joy and praise to God. It is one evidence of the Spirit of God working in the unconscious

and bringing one to a new wholeness, a new integration of the total psyche, a process which the Church has traditionally called sanctification.[13]

Yet Jung also recognized a negative aspect of tongues. In *A Psychological Approach to the Trinity*, quoting the passage on tongues from the *Rituale Romanum* in a footnote, he admitted the possibility of what is called in religious terms 'devil-possession' – 'the more the unconscious is split off, the more formidable the shape in which it appears to the conscious mind – if not in divine form, then in the more unfavourable form of obsession and outbursts of affect'.[14] For those who admit the existence of a spiritual realm the dangers are that malignant spiritual reality may invade the human personality exposing itself to supernatural influences.

Not every psychologist accepts the existence of the collective unconscious, nor that the empiricism which allegedly bears it out is incapable of other explanations. A far greater body of evidence needs to exist before the general acceptance of one view or the other. Other psychologists question the value of tongues on the grounds that a not fully understood experience cannot have a positive effect upon the individual's conscious development. This doubt has been countered by the suggestion that dreams (to which some glossolalia is similar), likewise not fully understood, can make an impact on the personality. Some glossolalics have had their first experience of tongues in dreams or have been known to talk in tongues in their sleep, and Whyte mentions the case of a Göttingen professor who composed Greek verses while asleep and found them written down next morning without any memory of the dream in which he composed them or the act of recording them.[15] A most remarkable case was that of Madame Hannah Elias Aghaby who lived in Amman, Jordan, and who for two months in 1933 spoke and sang messages of a deeply religious character in Hebrew, German, French, Greek and Italian, languages unknown to her in her conscious state. She translated these, sometimes sentence by sentence, into Arabic. She remembered nothing, however, when awake, except for a dream the night before her speaking began when she was in a green place with others who were praying in a Germanic tongue.[16]

If the collective unconscious exists, it is possible that 'linguistic patterns belonging to the past, to some other part of the present, or to some other level of being, take possession of the individual and are expressed by him'.[17] Their moral and psychological effect may be good or bad according to the effect of the experience upon the individual – if any effect of a dream-experience is anything but transitory. Kelsey mentions the 'numinous power to change lives'[18] of dreams and visions and the possibility that such expressions can take the forms of glossolalia, but it can be questioned whether the dream changes the individual or the individual rationalizes a change that has already taken place in his personality in a dream. St Paul's experience on the Damascus road can be explained as a bringing to his conscious mind in the form of a vision a conviction reached by his subconscious, and perhaps inspired in it earlier by the courage and sincerity of the martyr Stephen, that the Christians were right and he wrong in persecuting them. In short, it was the conviction that expressed itself in the vision, not the vision that brought about the conviction. One would expect such an experience to be rational, and it is difficult to see how, and almost impossible to prove that, speaking in tongues *in itself* possesses the numinous power to change lives.

It has been suggested that speaking in tongues, like electric-shock therapy, contains a critical inhibition which breaks up the prior conditioning of the individual and frees him to develop new patterns of living. Again it may be asked, however, whether tongues are the cause or the symptom of the new life, and if they are of psychological value. Certain it is that lives have been changed without glossolalia – not Augustine nor Francis of Assisi nor a thousand other Christian saints and heroes that could be named spoke in tongues.

The most that psychology can do for the believer in tongues is to give the support of Jung's theories (rejected by other psychologists as famous as he) to the possibility that individuals may have direct contact with spiritual reality and that tongues may be a conceivable phenomenon. Jung gives a possible reason for the expression of this direct contact with the spiritual in tongues. In a personal letter to a clinical psychologist, Dr Tenney, written in 1955, he said,

> Speaking with tongues . . . is observed in cases of ekstasis (lowering of the mental level, predominance of the unconscious). It is probable that the strangeness of the unconscious contents not yet integrated in consciousness demands an equally strange language. As it does demand strange pictures of an unheard of character, it is also a traditional expectation that the spiritual demonic inspiration manifests itself either in hieratic or otherwise incomprehensible language. That is also the reason why primitive and civilized people still use archaic forms of language at ritual occasions (Sanskrit in India, old Coptic in the Coptic church, old Slavonic in the Greek-Orthodox Church, Latin in the Catholic Church and the mediaeval German or English in the Protestant church).[19]

The earlier writers on the psychology of glossolalics almost all stressed the ignorance, illiteracy and starved emotional nature of those who spoke in tongues and the abnormality of their surroundings. Tongues were inspired by extreme excitement, such as that of revivals, seldom if ever in solitude, and never as a result of solitary contemplation or individual preparation. Or they came about under intense nervous strain following persecution or at other periods of general insecurity. The viewpoint of these early writers seems to be borne out by results summarized in an unpublished M.D. dissertation on glossolalia by Dr Van Eetveldt Vivier, quoted by a number of authorities.[20] Dr Vivier gave a number of psychological tests to three groups of similar educational and vocational standing, one of Pentecostals who had spoken in tongues, a second of Pentecostals who had not, and a third of Reformed Church members whose pastor believed tongues had ended with apostolic times. Psychologically the third group ranked highest, followed by the non-glossolalic Pentecostals. The glossolalics were discovered to have had, psychologically, a poor beginning in life, characterized by insecurity, conflict and tension. This led them to turn from the orthodox and traditional to 'an environment of sensitiveness for emotional feeling and a group of people . . . clinging to each other for support toward the goal of being freed from themselves'.[21]

In recent years, however, glossolalia has been found increasingly in church circles anything but unsophisticated, among people far from unlettered and among surroundings anything but emotional. (It may be remembered that Paul, who 'spoke in tongues more than you all'[22] was an intellectual, better educated than most of his contemporaries.) Kelsey gives example after example of literate and professional people speaking in tongues, maintaining that 'they can occur in a quiet devotional atmosphere, a truth which cannot be emphasized enough'.[23] They have even occurred without frenzy before television cameras, thus confirming the view that speaking in tongues can be controlled and that, once the gift has been received spontaneously, the speaker can open himself to the experience at will and without stimulus or emotional effect. I have myself recorded tongues, which the speaker seemed capable of turning on like a tap, in the completely calm and normal atmosphere of a sitting-room in a London apartment. It is indeed claimed that nowadays extroverted people are the most likely to speak.

The reasons for this may be that many intelligent Christians may have an emotional hostility to the 'snare of the intellect' which seems to be leading mankind into more and more trouble rather than towards the golden age of which our grandfathers dreamed. Or they may realize that the latest developments in science seem more in tune with a spiritual conception of the universe than the confident materialistic view of yesterday. They have a renewed assurance that although many of the phenomena that excited the marvel of the early Church may now be psychologically explained, the new source of power which it received and described as the gift of the Holy Spirit and which enabled it to spread as it did against all the efforts of opposition and persecution to suppress it, cannot be explained merely in terms of psychology. Believing that the same Power can be drawn upon today, some of them find the experience of glossolalia (whatever the linguists and psychologists may say about pseudo-languages and personality problems) a legitimate source of Holy Spirit inspiration for themselves. It may be also that in an age of apparently little faith and clearly uncertainty among theologians and Bible scholars, whose findings seem so often to undermine the foundations of orthodox belief, Christians, collectively and without knowing it consciously, reach out towards manifestations of the Spirit to compensate for the lack of inspiration and dullness of routine only too apparent in most church services, and try to prove to themselves that Christ has not lost his ancient power.

Not all Christians approve of these views. Tongues and similar gifts, hostile critics maintain, are a return to the elementary and childish. Worse, the desire for signs and miracles and a belief in them, far from being symptoms of a more spiritual faith, are in fact a degradation of spiritual religion to materialism.

Whether speakers in tongues win or lose the theological, psychological or linguistic debates, they have one final line of defence – the empirical. Tongues, they claim, like detergents in television advertisements, 'really work', and this is their justification. They are, first, an expression of the best kind of religious euphoria, which can have a therapeutic effect in the integration of the personality and the healing of the body. From the earliest days of Pentecostal groups there has been as much interest in the physical, mental and moral healings that have taken place as in the phenomena of tongues itself, and many notable miracles are reported, from the recovery of sight and curing of paralysis to the removal of a stammer. Jung's case-histories include several in which the experience of glossolalia gave his patients the means of victory and led them to integrate their lives and achieve psychological maturity.

Charismatic Christians sometimes seem to confuse euphoria

with 'a continuous sense of joy'. Joy, in the sense of 'that peace which the world cannot give', which a man of supreme faith might have even in Dachau or Auschwitz, is not the same as euphoria, which can be misleading – otherwise every engaged couple could be sure of an ecstatic married life. Euphoria is, however, not to be despised. Life would be wretched without its moments of ecstasy, and these can be inspiring at the time and, as 'emotion recollected in tranquillity', of therapeutic value throughout one's whole life afterwards. A personal experience – the nearest I have attained to a speaking in tongues (a gift for which I have no desire for myself) – bears this out. When I was about nine years old, a sudden storm of wind and rain on a late summer evening, followed by the bursting forth of the sun shining through the raindrops bespangling the leaves of a poplar tree outside my bedroom window, filled me with such ecstasy that I have never forgotten it. I shouted aloud praise to God in snatches of psalms, canticles, Bible texts, any scrap of language with a religious content that came to mind. Ordinary language was quite inadequate to express the glory of ecstasy which filled me, but I could not have bottled up the feeling by using no language at all – I should have burst or suffocated. Nor ought I to have tried to refrain from expressing the inexpressible, for, whether God exists or no, and whatever kind' of being he is, such felt moments of oneness with creation have to be acknowledged with *Te Deum*. There are other experiences to which silence is the only possible and right response, but not this; and if glossolalia had been at my tongue's tip instead of the Psalms and Magnificat, the experience and the expression of praise would have been no less valid. My whole life has been enriched by this childhood experience, and over half a century later the recalling of it to mind at times of stress and doubt still brings peace and confidence.

Spontaneous euphoria is one thing; that which is artificially induced by a worshipper is another. His fantasy self then becomes the ideal he strives to recreate, failing to recognize that true revelation is to be found in growth, not euphoria. When in ecstasy, he stands aside and watches himself being used, as it were, by some outside power. Everything becomes easy, nothing is hard or obscure, he wonders what the fuss of living is about. The clarity of his inner light blinds him to the need for humility and the checking of his personal experience by the wisdom of his church or of humanity at large. Pratt sums up the danger well in his words on mysticism.

> This confidence in its own all-sufficing inner light and the intense joy of the experience have been the two great dangers of excessive mysticism, when not balanced by a suitable respect for the inherited wisdom of the race and never inhibited by the restraining hand of a cool and sober reason. The mystic inevitably and rightly trusts his own experience. But when he ceases to criticize it and ceases to trust to anything else, his mysticism becomes the most misleading form of subjectivism and superstition. And when this inner joyous experience is nourished and coaxed for its own sake exclusively, the mystic becomes little better than the sensualist. This has been the case . . . sometimes . . . among the neurotic ecstatics of Christendom. When this happens exaggerated mysticism becomes a psychological method of self-gratification and no longer an attitude towards the larger Beyond. Hence it too ceases to be in any real sense religious. [24]

The tendency to equate Christian experience with feelings and any psychological phenomena accompanying them is also mistaken. People can speak with tongues in any religion and it is the content of experience, not its intensity of feeling which, however pleasant, is irrelevant, that matters. If the experience is not a valid one and euphoria is generated for its own sake, the worshipper becomes introverted, his will is weakened and his mental sensuality may lead to a weakening of his whole moral character.

A further danger is that evangelists also like to 'catch 'em young' and that Pentecostalism still appeals to undeveloped personalities even if it has won the allegiance of some of the more mature. The danger 'may well lie in having the experience at any age before one is aware of his own conflicts, so that tongues become a way to suppress inner problems rather than resolving them'.[25] Licence or moral rigidity and perfectionism, a spiritual cul-de-sac in which all further progress comes to an end (as too much rich manure can stunt or even kill a plant), idolatry mistaking the gift for the giver and a neglect of virtues and truths far more vital, may all follow the experience of tongues in a child or an immature character.

The only test is the long-term result. An emotional experience accompanied by tongues may result in a well-ordered, morally healthy life. Opponents of the charismatic movement may be misled because negative results are easier to see than positive ones. Neurosis and insanity are more spectacular than the quiet good life and Pratt can point to three cases of temporary insanity in one week and many others in the southern USA 'especially from the sect which seeks to bring about the "second blessing"'[26] without feeling any obligation to find out how many had been given the ability to revolutionize their lives positively.

Tongues are clearly not for everybody, and charismatics who demand them as an essential sign of Holy Spirit baptism for every Christian are answered by instances such as the following, contained in a private letter to me. It concerned a nineteen-year-old college student, slightly above average intelligence, who spoke in tongues for two years. The gift came to her with dramatic suddenness one night after she had been praying for some time. She continued speaking in tongues with mounting intensity, at any time of the day and night, often for an hour on end. 'One might add,' continues the letter, 'without drawing breath, as the garbled sound is made on the "in-breath" as well as when in expelling air, as in normal speech.' The girl became utterly miserable, ruining her health, losing her looks, coming to the edge of a nervous breakdown with severe insomnia and seriously contemplating suicide. On giving up Pentecostalism, she gradually returned to normal health and pursuits,

but a basic emotional instability is still there, which was apparent before she started to speak in tongues and is even more obvious now. She herself looks back with nothing but horror on these two years, and one cannot see that anything came of it but evil.

Pentecostalists could argue that this unhappy experience arose from the basic emotional instability, but it does prove that tongues are not a panacea – if they were, the girl would have been cured of this. A Pentecostal minister who left the movement after nine years wrote, 'I do not believe tongues have any value as a devotional exercise, for I have proved this in my own life, for my devotion is more spiritual since I refrained from speaking in tongues.' But he adds, 'The many hours of honestly seeking the Lord, however, brought much blessing . . . the emphasis on prayer has brought a warmness of faith and Christian experience to the Pentecostal people which is many times lacking in our churches'.[27] And 'it has never been proved that [charismatic] converts are more persevering or fertile in good works than those whose change of heart has had less violent accompaniments'.[28]

Against this statement by James, Pentecostalists maintain that tongues lead to a deeper love for God, Christ and their fellow men. Sherrill emphasizes this in his experience of an outward-turning emotion of love to God and man resulting from tongues.

At the actual moment of the Baptism in the Holy Spirit, there was an overwhelming impression; I was bathed in, surrounded by, washed through with love. I don't know why more hadn't been made of this in the things I had read on the subject.[29]

'One word is too often profaned'[30] – but if tongues can lead to Paul's 'more excellent way', this is sufficient justification of them for the glossolalics who experience it.

Baptism with the Holy Spirit, say Pentecostalists, gives increased zeal for Bible study. Critics point to the dearth of Pentecostal Biblical scholarship and the contempt of the movement for 'worldly' wisdom which ensures a one-sided and often incorrect exegesis that emphasizes experience at the cost of exposition. The truth of their interpretation of the Scriptures, reply the Pentecostalists, needs no further evidence than that their experience confirms it.

Spirit-baptism makes the ordinary church member a power for God by emphasizing the importance of witnessing and the need for evangelizing and giving him consecration to live the good life and greater efficiency in soul-winning. These are often accompanied by greater physical power and resiliency in everyday life. Nominal Christians are transformed to vital believers. Opponents ask if Pentecostals seriously have the arrogance (which often leads to unloving divisiveness) to affirm that there have been no vital believers and 'full' Christians between AD 100 and 1900. Is Johnny Pentecostalist the only one in step?

Johnny's reply is fivefold. First, tongues did not disappear but were kept alive by sects on the periphery of Christianity, usually condemned as heretical by the orthodox. Second, if mainline Protestantism can affirm that error very early crept into the Church and was not seen to be error for some fourteen hundred years until the Reformation cleared away some of its mists, why should not the full truth have to wait a further four hundred until men should have recovered the spiritual maturity to accept it? Third, the Bible teaches that there is to be a great outpouring of the Spirit just before the Second Coming of Christ and that since all the signs indicate that we are living in days immediately prior to his return, the recovery of the gifts of the Spirit is exactly what is to be expected. Fourth, God's people lost the charismata because they failed to believe all his promises and the love of the many waxed cold during the long centuries of ignorance of the contents of the written Word of God. And, fifth, in the past individuals like Luther in his fight against indulgences have been the only ones in step.

Many in the past, however – comes the riposte – whose love was ardent and lives patently superior to those of many modern Pentecostalists were not glossolalics – such notable saints as Francis of Assisi and Protestants of the quality of Calvin, Knox,

Wesley, Booth, Moody and Spurgeon. Neither are some today, such as Billy Graham, in an age when they cannot be unaware of tongues. A reason for the disappearance of tongues which could be quoted, according to its emphasis, on either side, is Edward Irving's opinion, 'The true reason why the gift of tongues hath ceased to be in the Church is the exaltation of the natural means of teaching above or into copartnering with, the teaching of the Holy Ghost.'[31]

Charismatics use tongues to praise God and speak supernaturally to him. If a man prays in ordinary language, his own thoughts may mingle too easily with the words he is using and distract him. Robert V. Morris writes,

> For me the gift of tongues turned out to be the gift of praise. As I used the unknown language which God had given me I felt rising in me the love, the awe, the adoration pure and uncontingent, that I had not been able to achieve in thought-out prayer. Praise and adoration are basically non-conceptual things and glossolalia is non-conceptual prayer. It releases us . . . into a direct awareness of God.[32]

Perhaps even more important, tongues help a man to pray when he has no idea what to pray for in a given situation. Sherrill[33] tells of a minister called to a girl so badly injured in an accident that even if she lived she might be only a vegetable. What should he pray for? Death, which might be more merciful, or life? He held the girl's arm and prayed for fifteen to twenty minutes, not with his mind, but with lips and tongue only, feeling that the more passive and yielding he was, the greater the degree to which he could become an effective channel for God. He felt 'a current of warmth flow through him' to the girl accompanied by a conviction that she would get well, which she did. This incident perhaps illustrates St Paul's meaning when he wrote of praying with the spirit while his understanding remained unfruitful.

Sherrill also quotes Lydia Maxam an Episcopalian glossolalic.

To me tongues are always prayer. A special kind of prayer,

too. I use them when I'm praying about a problem to which my own mind has no solution – usually a prayer for somebody else when I can't possibly know all the factors and complications. So if you want me to speak in tongues you'll have to let me pray about some real problem – preferably one that concerns you or someone close to you.

Sherrill provided her with such a problem, and her prayer was answered.[34]

Critics ask how Pentecostalists know that prayer not understood is superior to understood, or that it is prayer at all. The experience of the minister above would seem to be sufficient answer, and perhaps there is something in Pratt's story of a Buddhist monk in Mandalay who once said to him,

> Prayer repeated by one who does not understand any of it – for instance, a Pali prayer recited by one who knows no Pali – may have some value; for it keeps the man's mind from evil thoughts for the time being, and because the man at least *knows that he is praying* and *means* the unintelligible syllables as a prayer, and this puts him into the prayerful state of mind.[35]

Prayer is surely an attitude of mind rather than the repetition of words, and he would be a poor pray-er who had to rely on his vocabulary alone to open the way to God. Prayer not understood is not *in itself* superior to prayer understood; but the seeker will know first that it is prayer and, second, feel intuitively the quality of his prayer. The genuineness of so subjective an experience cannot be proved or disproved, any more than it can be known whether the critically injured girl in the story above would have recovered if an understood prayer or even no prayer at all had been said over her.

Tongues edify, that is, spiritually build up the individual and the church. Brumbach writes, 'It is almost incredible how quickly this praying with the Spirit dispels every bit of drowsiness and dullness, and enables us to discern spiritual realities.'[36] The church is edified because the interpretation of

221

tongues brings about direct communication of God to man – although the comment already made that the messages are seldom of value must trouble any honest Christian. As for the wonder of tongues, miraculous though they appear the first two or three times one hears them, one grows accustomed to them as to everything else. 'Waiting upon God' as a congregation, however, has blessings for which no mere church organization can be a substitute. Tongues also have the negative value given them by St Paul of being a judgment on unbelievers who hear them and yet will not believe.[37]

Tongues are a unique sign of the Holy Spirit's activity in that nothing like Christian glossolalia appeared in the two previous dispensations (pre-Flood and pre-Christian times). Gee states categorically that tongues are the only Biblical charisma which did not exist under the old covenant.[38] He may not be accurate if the existence of glossolalia is as widespread in world cultures as anthropological studies show; and the essential nature of the practice may be the same the world over. Against this Kelsey asserts that 'The Christian experience was one which was quite different both in kind and quality from other contemporary experiences to which it has been compared and this is the best knowledge we have, based on sound, scholarly work'.[39]

Neo-Pentecostalists in the old-established denominations uphold the practice of tongues in small groups meeting for Bible study, prayer and Christian fellowship, thus meeting the problem of increasingly de-personalized living. The critic replies that such meetings are possible without the practice of a doubtful and divisive activity.

The official Roman Catholic view that tongues are a standard sign of devil-possession is shared by some Protestants. Mrs Alma White, an ex-Pentecostalist, in her *Demons and Tongues*, sees the glossolalic experience as evil and demonic in inspiration. Its fruits are evil. When the willed desire to set aside the individual ego and consciousness open the personality to the intrusion of spiritual powers beyond itself, it is evil rather than divine powers that are ready to step in and take over.[40] Other critics assert what Pentecostalists deny (and, I think, rightly) that the state of their glossolalics can be linked to the spiritualistic trance in which some alien entity speaks through the individual. The reply to this charge is that if Bible tongues were due to the Holy Spirit and modern ones due to devils, why should this be in the case of believers seeking the *Holy* Spirit. Millions, literally, of Pentecostalists, cannot all be wrong.

> If we see that which builds up and transforms for good as the result of divine agency, and that which destroys and divides as coming from some other agency, then it would take at least several impractical objective studies to support the identification of tongue-speaking with totally evil results, and this has not been done. *Demonic* tongue-speaking is in most authors associated with trance states, violence, parapsychical phenomena, which do not occur in cases of Pentecostal tongues. Clear examples of demonic tongue-speech have to be hunted for, while the searcher can find glossolalia which purports to be of the Holy Spirit in any Assembly of God church any Sunday morning.[41]

Brumbach has a 'heads-I-win-tails-you-lose' argument. He acknowledges that some Pentecostalists, to the shame of the movement, have used 'psychic methods' to produce ecstatic speech. The supposed tongues were then mere fanatical gibberish – yet some worshippers have actually been Spirit-filled following the use of these and have truly spoken with tongues. God in his mercy saw the hungry heart of the seeker and the honest heart of the over-zealous worker and answered the heart-cry of both. 'It was not because of the unwise methods but in spite of them!'[42] But he answers more potently against the psychological critics that Pentecostalists do not allow themselves to be entirely quiescent. They are in control.

Tongues inspire pride, individual as well as corporate. Those who possess the gift feel themselves spiritually superior to those who do not. Two levels of Christians are created, an inner band of elite who have attained Spirit-baptism and the 'ordinary' who have not. Pentecostalists reply that membership of the inner band is open to and should in time be attained by every believer. There are advanced and immature believers in all churches, the difference between the Pentecostal and the orthodox being that between belief in a sudden leap some time after conversion and steady growth. Opponents observe that since glossolalics are sometimes, perhaps often, without the fruit of the Spirit, tongues are a wrong criterion by which the elite may be selected. The spiritual maturity claimed is self-evidently absent in many glossolalics, and this view is supported by St Paul's opinion that the emphasis on gifts is childish. There is condemnation of greater weight than his; for the apparent inability of some Christians to realize the presence of the Holy Spirit save through some arresting appeal to the senses, a legacy from the Old Testament, and a defect and sign of immaturity, puts them on a par with those whom Christ condemned when he said, 'Except ye see signs and wonders ye will not believe',[43] and 'an evil and adulterous generation seeketh after a sign'.[44]

Psychological and spiritual tensions are built up in those who do not receive the Spirit-baptism within a reasonable period after seeking it. There are alleged instances where people have become mentally ill through frustration. And those Christians who have broken through may think that they have 'arrived' spiritually and may make no further effort.

Opponents maintain that Pentecostalists subordinate Christ to the Holy Spirit. Even if true, this subordination does no more than balance the inferior position to be found in much popular Christian thought all down the ages of the Holy Spirit to the Father and Son. To this day, quite experienced Christians customarily refer to the Spirit as 'it' and not 'he' and, by the very nature of things, the doctrine of the Person and work of the Holy Spirit has not been treated as thoroughly as those of Christ. The Pentecostalists for their part retort that it is their very lack of emphasis on the Spirit that renders other modern churches so powerless.

Even if tongues cannot be completely ruled out, how can Pentecostalists and neo-Pentecostalists be sure that what is going on in tongue-speaking circles today is the same thing that happened in New Testament times? We do not know for certain what the glossolalia practised by the Corinthians was. There was a significance in events practised so long ago, but many feel that they were neither described nor interpreted quite accurately, and that the experience was different from that which appears to be described. Even with neo-Pentecostalists, the belief that tongue-speaking is *an* evidence that one has been filled with the Holy Spirit is open to serious question.

But does the experience have to be exactly the same? How can anyone but the Spirit-filled believer know that he has been filled, if the alleged sign is not accepted? Brumbach asks reasonably on what grounds critics may know that Pentecostal tongues are different from those of the New Testament. While acknowledging that some tongues may be gibberish because 'it is inevitable that all physical manifestations will be counter-feited and speaking with tongues is no exception', he argues that 'surely it is not a difficult thing for the Spirit of God, who knoweth all tongues, to cause Christian believers to speak in one of the lesser known tongues?'[45] In a note he mentions that

> Dr Agida Pirazzini, possibly one of the greatest philologists in America, having taught Hebrew, Greek and Oriental languages at the Biblical seminary for thirty years, has identified the utterances of some Pentecostal believers in Aramaic, the language which Jesus spoke! There is no foundation for a demand that the tongues should be always recognizable, and all that is required for the glossolalic to be stamped as genuine is that utterance be given by the believer in a language unknown to him. Trustworthy believers, both Pentecostal and non-Pentecostal, have identified some of the tongues supernaturally spoken by believers today, but the critics will not accept their testimony.[46]

Brumbach wrote before the days of tape-recorders; regretfully it has to be acknowledged that there appears to be no tape-recording in existence of any recognizable language spoken by a glossolalic which cannot be accounted for by cryptomnesia or some other such explanation. But hostile critics must

225

recognize the difficulty already mentioned that Hebrew, Aramaic or other unknown tongue will be spoken spontaneously without prior notice, if spoken at all, and the chances of a tape-recorder being present at the right moment are remote; yet it is only a well-attested recording of this kind, followed by a full investigation into the speaker's linguistic background that could convince a sceptic.

Tongues are the least important gift, being mentioned last in two lists. But, comes the reply, love, the greatest of the trio faith, hope and charity, is mentioned last, and, since the relative positions of the other gifts vary, there is no significance in the placing. The critic answers that, granting this, tongues were unimportant in the primitive Church and excited little attention. The Church laid stress on very different matters, and the Pentecostal emphasis on tongues is disproportionate. Paul's denigration of tongues in favour of intelligible prophecy[47] seems to suggest it would be far better if they were eliminated altogether, at least in public worship.

Pentecostals give the physical sign priority over the Spiritual infilling. This is hardly a fair objection if it is sincerely believed that the one is the inevitable and necessary result of the other – one might as well criticize the faith of a man who switches on a lamp because light appears. Nor can it be a serious argument that no one would speak in tongues if they were not taught that it was expected of them, for this is true of any Christian activity. No man would go to Holy Communion by the light of nature. Children would not brush their teeth if they were not taught to do so, and 'babes in Christ' have to be educated into maturity.

The anti-charismatics go beyond arguing against Pentecost-alists with positive reasons of their own to explain the disappearance of tongues. First, they were given only to get the Church established. The cautious young community, entirely Jewish and conservative in its Judaism, apt to look askance at Gentiles, even at proselytes and God-fearers, had to be convinced that the Spirit willed their inclusion in the new society. Tongues, a sharing of the experience which the apostles had been given at Pentecost, proved this beyond doubt.

Second, the Church grew up in a world which accepted and valued the irrational; but the need soon appeared for restraint, not expression, of this. The enthusiasm that went with tongues was (and still is) an embarrassment to the appeal of Christianity to the rational and intelligent section of mankind. In the days of persecution, the Church restrained noisy practices which drew attention to itself, and recognized that what was really needed was the less spectacular fruit of high ethical ideals raising the moral tone of the society around it.

Third, sections of believers misused the gift and the Church soon found that it had to throw out the baby of tongues with the bath-water of Montanism. This was a case of individual experience, valid enough, perhaps, in itself, clashing with ecclesiastical authority. The latter won, and, indeed, had to win in the circumstances of the time if Christianity were to survive.

Fourth, Protestant critics say that the early Church had no established canon of (New Testament) Scripture, but that, once the canon was established, the finality of Scripture made tongues unnecessary. Pentecostalists could reply that the existence of so many Christian sects, all claiming the authority of Scripture, indicates that no one agrees as to what the 'finality' is and that their interpretation is as valid as any other.

So the arguments can be bandied to and fro almost *ad infinitum*, until the protagonists become like Bishop Earle's 'the precise hypocrite', as he calls a fanatical Puritan woman of his day who was 'an everlasting argument and I am weary of her'.[48] The conclusion of the whole matter seems to be that the Christian Church has room within its fold for believers of every kind. Whether modern tongues are like those of Corinth or not, and whether conservative or Pentecostal theology is truer to the meaning and spirit of the New Testament are questions largely irrelevant and impossible to answer in the same way for everybody. That charismatic worship is embarrassing to believers of a certain type has been and always will be true. That it is actively dangerous to the neurotic and mentally unbalanced is also true; and that it has brought emotional and spiritual fulfilment resulting in victorious Christian living for myriads of, mostly, humble people, is not rhetorical cant but can be observed by any disinterested enquirer. In the final issue, the criteria are still those upon which the Old and New Testaments agree: 'What doth the Lord require of thee but to do justly and to love mercy, and to walk humbly with thy God?'[49] and 'By their fruits shall ye know them.'[50]

15

Debate and Discussion: Spiritualist Tongues

The same explanations can be given for some Spiritualist tongues as for Christian. They may be genuine languages having their sources in the cryptomnesia or cryptesthesia of the speaker. They may be pseudo-languages, spoken in trance or arising out of the euphoria caused by the conviction that the sensitive is in touch with the spirit world. These and other explanations given below are suggested by those students of tongues who do not accept the beliefs of Spiritualism. For Spiritualists there is no difficulty. They maintain that of the thousands (literally) of stories of foreign languages unknown to the medium and spoken through him or her to sitters who understood them, a substantial number are incontrovertible and prove that the spirits of the dead are indeed alive and able to communicate.

The same observations may be made of their claims as of those of Christian xenolalia. Among the many made there may have been some in the past which were genuine but they cannot be proved or disproved to a modern investigator. As there was no means of recording them, so there is no means of studying them. Their acceptance or rejection depends partly on the reputations for integrity of the narrator and participators in the alleged communication, partly on the bias of the student studying them. The advent of the tape-recorder now makes it possible to study them, but it is not as easy to obtain specimens of Spiritualist tongues as of Christian. Any Pentecostalist meeting may produce examples of the latter. Communications in Spiritualist churches are seldom, if ever, in tongues; and when foreign languages are allegedly spoken, it is usually in private circles or in interviews between a sensitive and one or two sitters. These interviews frequently deal with intimate and confidential matters and are understandably not open to public investigation.

The fact that all taped specimens of Christian tongues can be shown to be pseudo-languages or traceable to cryptomnesia makes no difference to the determined believer. He can still maintain that among the untaped examples there are some where miraculous xenolalia resulted in the conversion of unbelievers. A similar position can be taken by the Spiritualist. He can also affirm that communication from the spirit world is so sensitive a business that the presence of even a disinterested investigator or a recording apparatus inhibits it, while that of a sceptic will certainly ensure that no results are obtainable. So phenomena happen in a circle of believers which can by the nature of things never occur if one out-of-tune person joins it. It is a matter of vibrations. No proof or disproof can be offered of such a belief, and this is unsatisfactory for everyone. The argument is nevertheless reasonable, parallel to the contention of a physicist that traces of impurity in a conductor seriously impede or completely inhibit the flow of electricity; or of a chemist that a chemical reaction will take place only under certain conditions of temperature and pressure.

Theories of Spiritualist tongues can depend for their explanation first on the belief that human personalities are closed, in which case the phenomena indicating communication are merely the products of the individual mind. Second, communications with other living minds by means of telepathy and extra-sensory perception can be recognized. Third come those theories that accept the existence of a cosmic consciousness in various forms. Fourth, there is an explanation based on belief in reincarnation. Fifth, there are hypotheses of various kinds of spirit-possession. Sixth is the contention of the extreme sceptic that all alleged spiritual communication is an edifice of exaggerated misrepresentation of experience or fraud. In every human mind subconscious cerebration takes place. The process can be recognized by some individuals as taking place in themselves. They can go to sleep with an unsolved problem knowing that they will wake with the solution in their minds the next morning. Writers faced with an *impasse* in a novel suddenly have revealed to them a way of escape, and it is said that composers sometimes find an opus presented as a whole to their minds which they then have to break down into movements, motifs and individual phrases, chords and notes – a process which has almost certainly already happened in reverse in their subconscious. It seems incontrovertible that Hélène Smith's Martian was the result of subconscious cerebration. Since some Egyptologists denied that Rosemary's language was Egyptian at all, it is possible that her language was also an incubated one, inspired by her belief that she was a reincarnation of a temple dancer. And as tongues can be spoken in dreams and the mind continues to work out in sleep experiences which it has had in waking, those who practise speaking in tongues in Pentecostalist churches or Spiritualist circles will continue to work at their gift subconsciously and astonish themselves by sudden outbursts of fluency apparently inspired by a source outside themselves.

Abnormal psychology recognizes the existence of secondary subconscious personalities as systematized fractions of the subject's psychological disassociation. There are case-histories of such personalities so bizarre that they would be incredible if they had not been the clinical reports by detached medical observers that they are, and one may safely say that they are more extraordinary than almost any miracle or spirit-communication claimed by believers in this or that creed. Hélène Smith's Espenal, Mrs Curran's Patience Worth and Rosemary's Nona could all have been secondary personalities incubated along with the languages they spoke – although, since subconscious cerebration must have material to work up, it is impossible to see any source of Mrs Curran's knowledge, and, if Rosemary's tongue were proved in truth to be ancient Egyptian, the theory could not be applied to her.

A variation on the subconscious personality theme is that there may be a subconscious 'listening' to a secondary personality. Some sensitives claim that they clairaudiently hear communications which they repeat. If foreign languages which they do not understand are given them in this way, they repeat them phonetically. Since, according to the closed personality theory, nothing can come out of the mind except that which has gone into it, this theory is unsatisfactory if it can be proved that clairaudient sensitives speak languages they can never have known or heard.

A somewhat bizarre variety of the subconscious personality hypothesis is that sitters with direct-voice mediums enter into conversation with their own exteriorized personalities. Against this theory Bozzano argues that to exteriorize or vitalize their own doubles, the sitters would have themselves to be mediums of high power who would inevitably fall into trance to achieve such results (he does not say on what grounds he asserts this). There have been numerous cases, he claims, where this did not happen. In addition, direct voices have in some cases spoken languages unknown to both mediums and sitters, occasioning the invitation of linguists to later séances to understand them. [1]

The externalized personalities could be those of the medium rather than the sitters. But this would entail a far larger number of subconscious personalities than could be imagined to exist in a single personality without its disintegration and a fluent knowledge of many languages somehow absorbed by them. Even if the theory were tenable it would have to explain the sources of the linguistic knowledge.

There could be, even within a closed personality, ancestral memory handed down from forebears with other mental and physical characteristics. Whereas in the normal individual this could be of a certain average quality and quantity, in some exceptional characters it could be of the nature of genius, a gift corresponding to the talents of a Shakespeare or Michelangelo.

Such a person might be able to reproduce the language of an ancestor. It has been suggested that Patience Worth's language could have arisen from Mrs Curran's ancestral memory. But even if this theory, for the truth of which on such a scale there is no convincing evidence, were found acceptable, there would still be needed an explanation of how and why so otherwise ordinary a woman as Mrs Curran should have developed it so strangely and so strongly.

There are other arguments against ancestral memory. Spiritualists, like Bozzano, allege that some languages spoken are of extreme antiquity, that some sensitives speak a great variety of tongues, not all of which can have been spoken by their ancestors, and that European mediums or Americans of very recent European stock, have spoken Red Indian languages. It is difficult to see, too, why ancestral memory should pick on, say, Ancient Egyptian, when many more recent languages should be available. Xenoglossic conversations are also alleged to be about topics of the moment, not with memories; although if so extraordinary a feat as the ancestral memory of a whole language be admitted, it is no very wonderful an extension of it to include the ability to adapt the tongue to the discussion of contemporary affairs.

For those who accept the evidence of telepathy, extra-sensory perception, clairvoyance and travelling clairvoyance, which includes the ability to read closed books in distant libraries, explanation of xenolalia is easier. It may be asked who would telepathize Patience Worth's English so long, so consistently and so anonymously, or how the vowels of Ancient Egyptian could be communicated when no living mind knows them. Given the unconscious communication of minds and the existence of subconscious personalities and cerebration, it is not impossible that Mrs Curran could have 'picked up' Patience Worth and her language from the mind of some scholar of archaic English and that Rosemary was in tune with a student of ancient Egyptian who communicated to her his own clear subconscious theory as to how the language was pronounced. The normality of the two women is irrelevant – all that would be needed would be for them to be on the same mental wave-length as their unconscious mentors. Just as every human being is different from every other in some physical detail and yet there are some, such as identical twins and doubles that are indistinguishable, so there may be 'identical minds'. The theory is far-fetched and full of difficulties. It does not explain Patience Worth's originality in composing verses and aphorisms on subjects hurled at her at random by an audience, nor the speed and fluency with which Nona communicated. Some will, however, feel that it is not as far-fetched as the idea of communication from spirits or that of reincarnation.

The special case of communication between hypnotist and subject may be mentioned. Some subjects, it is alleged, can answer in their own language questions put to them in a tongue they have never learned. One far-fetched explanation is that they 'borrow' all the memories of the hypnotist. A more likely one is that the subject does not understand the words addressed to him but by that empathy which must exist between him and the hypnotist reads in the latter's brain the thought expressed by the words. The stuff of thought is identical in all thinking subjects apart from the words in which it is expressed, so that thought expressed in one language can be understood and answered in another.

Mrs Laura Finch's experience with Greek from a recognized printed book is explicable on the surface by clairvoyance of some kind. The physical laws governing mirages are understood. It may be that every material object can appear as a 'mental' mirage to individual minds because of physico-mental conditions and laws not yet understood; though why Mrs Finch should 'tune in' to a particular book in such a way is impossible to surmise. All that can be said is that the evidence points to her 'reading' a projected image of the book with some understanding of the meaning of the extracts she quoted.

Several thinkers have suggested various theories of group or collective consciousness. Group self-consciousness may have preceded individual in human mental evolution, and there may still exist in the subconscious or superconscious of the individual links with the collective subconscious either of societies within humanity or with humanity as a whole. Hegel suggested 'an all-inclusive world-consciousness of which the individual consciousness of each man is somehow but a constituent element or fragmentary manifestation'.[2] Frederick Myers, one of the founders of the Society for Psychical Research, put forward the theory that there exists in man a subliminal consciousness far more comprehensive than his conscious self, furnished with supernormal faculties and intellectual capacities, the sporadic emergence of which gives rise to the inspiration of genius.[3] Jung's theory of the cosmic subconscious underlying the individual subconscious and the possible superconscious overlying it extends Myers's conception to embrace much wider possibilities; for these realms could include categories of information and abilities unknown to the individual, including the speaking of foreign languages. Varieties of the theory include that of Mr Henry Holt, a publisher, who, faced by the Patience Worth phenomenon, postulated an inflow from the 'cosmic soul' – 'personalities – strings of them – postcarnate ones, if there are such'.[4] Or the cosmic consciousness could exist in the sense conceived by William James of a cosmic reservoir of individual memories to which sensitives have free access 'and from which they draw all they require for the mystification of wretched mortals'.[5] Hartmann speculated that the Cosmic Consciousness might be a real and actual attribute of the Absolute, that is, God, 'in which case,' Bozzano observes, supporting James's view, 'one would have to admit that the subconscious of mediums enters into direct rapport with the Supreme Being, and that for the noble end of deceiving their fellows.'[6] To these theories of a kind of celestial dustbin the objection can be made that they do not take into account the problem of the selection of facts, in that information suggesting a unity of personal experience is presented falsely. Does the individual subconscious, presented with access to all the contents of the dustbin, select only those items which constitute a preconceived personality of its own? Is it limited or inhibited in its choice and, if so, why, and by what factors? Nona, communicating through Rosemary, commented, not inaptly,

> There *is* a Cosmic Mind, I suppose, but no one can tap any source of knowledge just by wishing. Every mind can receive only that which it has trained itself to comprehend. There is no such thing as acquiring knowledge at will here, any more than on your side.[7]

Believers in reincarnation have some evidence to support the doctrine that human spirits live a succession of lives on this earth, and there is even a method by which further evidence may be empirically gathered. This method is that of regression into past lives under hypnosis. An early, probably the first, case of this kind was that of 'Bridie Murphy', in which an American girl was, under hypnosis, taken back into her childhood and then regressed further than was intended to an earlier life which she had lived in Ireland about a century before. There was some interesting evidence in her revelations but not enough to be convincing. In 1958 D. Arnall Bloxham wrote *Who was Ann Ockenden?*, a book in which he claimed to have regressed Miss Ockenden under hypnosis into a series of past lives, some of which she had lived as a man, some as a woman. In reply to a letter I wrote to Mr Bloxham in November, 1969, he said,

> A subject may certainly, in some circumstances, be regressed to a state where a foreign tongue or dialect is spoken. It so happened that I have obtained dialect and accent and have consistently had names in authentic foreign pronunciation, together with some foreign phrases, when the subject was at a loss to explain in English. You will appreciate that were a subject to break into foreign speech, I could not understand and therefore could not continue the interview. It is customary for thought to be expressed in the language of the day – for instance, when asked about one's childhood one does not reply in baby talk or in, say, Hindustani, if early childhood has been spent in India, but from time to time phrases may be used. . . . Names, I find, are invariably in the original tongue. . . . Obsolete words are sometimes used.

J. Stearn, another reincarnationist, goes a little further than this, claiming that

> There are many subconscious channels into the past, under hypnosis . . . with the mind-expanding drugs, in psychic trance, sometimes in spontaneous recollections. Thus, many recalled fragments of previous existence, speaking languages they know nothing about consciously and recalling people and events indelibly engraved on their subconscious.[8]

He mentions Joanne McIver, aged fourteen, who regressed under hypnosis to a French life and 'spoke with a strong accent'[9] but as she was a Canadian, presumably acquainted with French-speaking Canadians, this could well have been subconscious play-acting. Dennis Campbell, a young serviceman, went back to mediaeval France and then to Atlantis, and spoke colloquial French under hypnosis.[10] Did he speak *mediaeval* colloquial French? And I must confess that the mention of Atlantis raises my sceptic's hackles.

Certainly the most remarkable instance of alleged reincarnation is that described by Dr Ian Stevenson in his thoroughly researched study of the Jensen Jacoby case mentioned on page 137. As this cautious and scholarly writer admits, the facts seem to indicate either reincarnation or possession.

If possession is an explanation of some spirit communications, it may be by discarnate entities who were once human beings. These may be 'earth-bound' – unhappy creatures unable to adjust to the conditions of existence beyond the grave, some not realizing that they are dead and therefore instinctively seeking to express themselves through still-living humans who open themselves to their influence in certain conditions such as trance. They may be non-human entities masquerading as spirits of deceased humans out of mischief or devilry with an intent to deceive and lead astray. They and we, according to a theory of quantitative monism, may be aspects of one Absolute Self. Given the right conditions, one aspect of the Self can influence another, or a finite self may draw upon the store of all-knowledge possessed by the Absolute Self and rationalized as communication from another self. Or, as the Spiritualist hypothesis is, they may be genuinely what they claim to be, spirits of those who have been 'loved and lost awhile'[11] and who express their love and concern for those still on this side of life by temporarily taking possession of the bodily organism of a sensitive and communicating through it.

Fraud is the final explanation, sometimes a blanket condemnation covering all psychic phenomena given by determined sceptics. It must be admitted that the history of psychical research is riddled with instances of discovered fraud, a fact which suggests that there could be many more of undiscovered. Dr Wood, historian of the Rosemary communications, writes, 'It would be ridiculous to suggest that Nona, Vola, Rosemary and myself are all liars, engaged in a conspiracy to deceive mankind. The sceptic must think out a better argument than that.'[12] In fact, the sceptic need not. There is nothing to prevent a group of practical jokers who think their time, energy and ingenuity worth spending in such a way, from building up and publishing a body of evidence calculated to deceive their readers. This may be done from motives of profit or sheer fun, to answer some kind of challenge, to win a bet, to confirm a feeling of superiority in themselves, to prove the gullibility of mankind or to score a victory for one point of view and against another – as the fabricators of the Piltdown skull could have been fundamentalists who wished to prove the theory of evolution wrong and the scientists who upheld it gullible.

There is also an instinct which warns the psychical researcher against evidence that appears to be too good. An example of an above-average interview with a good sensitive is that of Dr van Eeden with Mrs Thompson (pages 113–15). The non-Spiritualist will see in this an example of parapsychological ability on the part of the sensitive in taking information from the sitter's mind and feeding it back to him. The believer in genuine spirit-communication will recognize its vagueness and incompleteness as typical of the difficulties which those 'on the other side of life' constantly complain of in their attempts to break through to this world. It is not therefore unfair to suspect cases in which the communications seem to be too good to be true. Of this kind are some of the exploits of George Valiantine, a direct-voice medium, later allegedly guilty of fraud in the production of physical phenomena (which were outside his province). Whymant, Bradley (who nevertheless acknowledges his attempt at fraud) and Geraldine Hack all wrote books in which he features as communicating with a large number of spirit personalities in at least thirteen foreign tongues. These communications are so explicit, so fluent and of so much higher a quality than the Thompson–van Eeden interviews that the reader feels, 'None of the "genuine" spirit communications recorded by psychical researchers are of this kind or quality – these must be fraudulent, even if I cannot see how.' The same is true of the de Reuter messages. They are of too high a quality.

Yet it is not beyond the bounds of possibility that there are psychic geniuses, men and women whose ability to act as channels of spirit communication is as great in their sphere as Dante's was in poetry and da Vinci's in art. This seems to be borne out by the cases of Rosemary and Patience Worth. The former's claims to have communicated with ancient Egypt and recovered the pronunciation of its language met with a mixed reception from Egyptian scholars. The significant fact is that the reception *was* mixed; one would have expected a downright fraud or a mere mental aberration to have been rejected instantly and unanimously. Patience Worth has so marked a personality and her communications are of so outstanding a quality by any criterion that the only conclusion that fits the facts is that an entity or intelligence of some kind quite independent of the medium seems to be speaking.

In the final issue, the quality and quantity of acceptable evidence is debatable. Some individual experiences such as that of Mijatovitch, claiming to have talked via mediums with his mother and his former master, King Alexander, are, on the surface, convincing; but there is always the doubt in the researcher's mind that, honest and sincere though ambassadors are expected to be in their private lives (even though, publicly, they are sent 'to lie abroad on behalf of their countries'),[13] they are not above exaggeration and the gullibility of ordinary men in the matter of their personal beliefs. Yet, when all allowances have been made for misreporting, exaggeration, self-deception, gullibility and fraud, there is a residue of phenomena which is either inexplicable except on the hypothesis that a spiritual dimension exists, or needs knowledge to explain it that we do not yet have.

The investigator has to recognize that normality is always extending its boundaries and that much of what was believed supernatural the day before yesterday and supernormal yesterday is accepted, because of greater knowledge, as normal today. When faced with apparently incontrovertible facts, he must trust no one, not even himself, recognizing his own fallibility and recognizing that even apparently irrefutable evidence may one day be refuted. Yet there can be no final answer this side of the grave, and by its nature the debate can never end.

16

Summary and Conclusion

In the end, acceptance or rejection of phenomena classified as supernatural or paranormal is a matter of personal belief. Many of the best-attested stories of past happenings rest on the testimony and personal integrity of witnesses whose creeds and convictions make them *personae non gratae* with sceptics and whose deaths, often decades ago, make a proper investigation impossible. That parapsychologists and many psychologists accept as normal faculties of the human mind such as telepathy, cryptomnesia, telemnesia, telesthesia and other abilities which may come under the general heading of extra-sensory perception, undermines any spiritual interpretation of the universe for many thinkers. Words 'heard' are a common delusion of madness and are frequently terrifying in their intensity; if not due to madness, they may be internal auditions proceeding from the subliminal self, externalized so as to give an impression of physical hearing; or, again, they may be drawn by extra-sensory perception from the mind of a sitter who speaks the foreign language heard, or even from the cosmic consciousness, the existence of which may be as physical as the vibrations of a tuning-fork grown too faint to be heard by human ear yet capable of being picked up by an amplifier. Automatic writing of foreign tongues or writing by appliances like the planchette could also be an expression of extra-sensory

241

perception or drawn from the universal subconscious. If the existence of the latter could be demonstrated for certain, it would be the answer to the evidence for reincarnation and to most, if not all, of that for the survival of individual spirits. Ancestral memory may be more of a factor in paranormal phenomena than is commonly thought, although few authorities give it much weight on the present evidence. The spirit controls of mediums can all be explained as subconscious personifications or dissociated personalities combined with extra-sensory ability in some instances. Although examples of Christian xenolalia may have happened, none has as yet been recorded on tape.

In spite of the enormous mass of evidence, there is little that can be quoted confidently as proof of any position, positive or negative. On balance the sceptic is justified rather than the believer, but always he is given pause by such phenomena as those of Patience Worth. There is room for experiment. Are there sufficient devoted psychical researchers to repeat the Nepenthes experiments under the far stricter test conditions which could be imposed today? That is to say, men and women, a number of whom would have to be sceptics, who would discipline themselves strictly according to whatever ascetic principles were judged fitting to prepare for a possibly prolonged series of séances in the hope that a xenolalic spirit would materialize as Nepenthes is alleged to have done (perhaps, as a timeless spirit, she would manifest herself again and confirm her previous appearance). Series of sittings with direct voice or clairaudient mediums could be held and recorded, in which groups of foreigners, their nationalities unknown to the sensitives, would sit; if there is anything in spirit communication one would expect something to come through in languages unknown to the medium but known to some of the sitters. Many more subjects could be regressed into 'previous lives' by competent hypnotists, asked to speak the languages they used in them and requested to converse with linguistic experts in the tongues they spoke. No doubt other experiments could be devised, though always one is faced by the problem already mentioned that the very presence of sceptics, or even of disinterested, open-minded students, and the very existence of the clinical atmosphere surrounding tests may inhibit the phenomena to be studied. Perhaps there is no answer to this. Only one thing is sure: much more has to be made certain before the whole truth can be known about the voices from the gods.

Appendix 1
Cases with Unusual Features

1 Gee reports that a Mrs Howard Carter heard a man at one of the Sunderland conventions give

> a peculiar cry and then shortly afterwards a message in tongues. Mrs. Crisp interpreted the message. It happened that in that convention there was a missionary from the Congo, Mrs. Alma Doering. She testified that the language spoken was that of the Kifioti tribe of the Congo. She said that in the Congo sentries were put at certain places and when an important message was to be sent from one tribe to another they would send out a warning note. It was a call to attention. This brother under the power of the Spirit had given the call to attention before the message came forth. She further stated that the interpretation embodied the message that he had given in the language of the Congo.[1]

The peculiar cry and its significance are interesting features which need an explanation beyond those usually given of glossolalia. The claims that the tongue was genuine and that the interpretation 'embodied' (a loose term) its message rest on the uncorroborated testimony of one witness, and the full circumstances are not known. Had the glossolalic, for example, ever been exposed to the customs or language of the Kifioti tribe? Had Mrs Doering ever talked about their practices in his hearing?

2 Kelsey mentions a friend of his who, on 17 August 1932, went to Bethel Temple, Los Angeles, looking for spiritual sustenance to help her in her teaching religion to adults. She did not want to speak in tongues, but was willing to do so if this were God's will.

Almost immediately, out of my mouth began to pour sentence after sentence in a strange language. I spoke more fluently than I could ever have done in English and with a beautiful cadence. It seemed to come from down in the Center, and not from my mind. With it at first was such indescribable joy, such a sense of power from beyond, and such an unquestioning assurance that this was God doing His work. After a time the emotional overtone changed from one of joy to cries of grief which wrenched my entire physical being. I did not know what any of the individual words meant but I did sense that the first speaking was praise and that the latter was the cries of grief of our Lord for the whole world for its suffering. Tears streamed down my cheeks and my dress was soaking wet where the tears fell for, I suppose, something over an hour. But the Voice which used my lips was so different from my own. It was so gentle, full of kindness and compassion and love. [2]

The speaker who, with her husband, had been a post-Second World War rehabilitation missionary in the Philippines, 1947–8, remembered a number of the words she had spoken and learned from Moro students that the words she recalled from her 1932 glossolalia were Moro (southern Philippine Muslim). One would like to know if the lady had visited the Philippines before 1932. If not, cryptomnesia is unlikely to be the explanation here, and, in any case, it is a far-fetched explanation of a speech of over an hour's length. The experience, with its unusual change of mood from praise to sorrow, seems to have been a genuinely mystical one, with its coming from 'down in the Center', and is unusual in that the speaker spoke, as a medium can do, with a voice not her own. Glossolalics normally feel that the power comes from without, but their voices remain theirs, even though imbued with supernormal fluency. On the face of it, this would seem a genuine infilling with at least a good 'entity' and, for the Christian believer, with the Holy Spirit. An interesting feature of the experience is that a Christian missionary spoke in tongues in a Muslim dialect.

Sherrill records at second hand the experience of nine Filipino marines who heard an American woman whom they knew give a message in an obscure Filipino dialect, and they agreed in the sense of what they had heard. She did not speak Filipino at all, much less the strange dialect from a region rarely visited by Westerners. Is this a doublet of the story told above? If it is, the 'students' have become 'marines' and the woman who, as a rehabilitation missionary to the Philippines would presumably have learned some of the language, 'did not speak Filipino at all'. These may have been two separate experiences, but the stories read like two versions of the same one.[3]

3 Clifford Tonnensen of New Jersey spoke at a revival meeting in Michigan in fluent and beautiful High German, recognized as such by a lady present. But he was a deaf-mute, whose hearing had been destroyed by illness when he was two months old.[4]

If this story were proved to be factually correct beyond all doubt (and it is not the only one of its kind), it is beyond any of the usual explanations.

4 'A Christian friend, intelligent in the highest degree, and perfectly reliable to me as my right hand, who was present at a rather private gathering assembled to pray, relates that after one of the brethren had been speaking in a strain of discouraging self-accusation, another present shortly arose, with a strangely beaming look, and, fixing his eye on the confessing brother, broke out into a discourse of sounds, wholly unintelligible, though apparently a true language, accompanying the utterance

with a very strange and peculiarly expressive gesture, such as he never made at any other time; coming finally to a kind of pause, and commencing again, as if at the same point, to go over again in English, with exactly the same gestures, what had just been said. It appeared to be an interpretation, and the matter of it was a beautifully emphatic utterance of the principle of self-renunciation.

'There had been no conversation respecting gifts of any kind, and no reference to their possibility.' The circle were put out by the demonstration, 'not knowing what to make of it. . . . The instinct of prudence threw them on observing a general silence.'[5]

This case, although too far removed from the original to be remotely capable of confirmation, has a ring of truth about it. It is interesting for the fact that the same speaker gave the tongue and its interpretation.

Appendix 2
Development of a Tradition

Following are examples of how differences of tradition can arise about genuine experiences and of the difficulties facing a researcher into psychic and spiritual matters even when he can consult an individual who had the experience described.

According to Kelsey, the Reverend Harald Bredesen wrote of his receiving the gift of tongues as follows.

> At the time he was public relations secretary of the World Council of Christian Education. And he had just been offered a bigger job. One evening as he was walking down the sidewalks of New York, worrying over his doubts about accepting it and listening to an inner voice, a man stepped up behind him with the words, 'You are a Christian!' His face was glowing, and telling Bredesen that God had shown him a need to speak, he went on, 'God will open a door for you that no man can open.' Then for two hours they talked. And some three weeks later Pastor Bredesen, with expectation, attended a Pentecostal camp meeting at Green Lane, Pennsylvania. There he received the gift of tongues, and a new joyful ministry opened up to him, a ministry which later sparked the outbreak of tongues at Yale.[1]

Sherrill's account runs thus. Harald Bredesen, Pastor of the First Reformed Church, Mount Vernon, New York, dissatisfied with the quality of his spiritual life, became convinced from his Bible that the early Churches received their vitality from the Holy Spirit and especially from an experience called 'the Baptism of the Holy Spirit'. Retreating to a cabin in the Allegheny Mountains, he kept up a prayer vigil day after day until he should reach 'a new level of communication with God'. One day, as he was outside the cabin, praying aloud, a stillness seemed to settle over the hills.

[He tensed] as if his whole being were centering into a new plane of awareness. He stopped speaking for a moment. And when he began again, out of his mouth came . . . 'the most beautiful outpouring of vowels and consonants and also some strange guttural syllables. I could not recognize any of it. It was as though I was listening to a foreign language, except that it was coming out of my own mouth.' Bredesen ran down the mountain, still talking aloud in the tongue, and came to the edge of a small community. A man answered him in a language he did not know. When it became obvious that they were not communicating, the man asked in English, 'How can you speak Polish but not understand it?' '*I* was speaking in Polish?' The man laughed, thinking that Bredesen was joking. 'Of course it was Polish,' he said. But so far as he knew Bredesen had never before heard the language.[2]

Bredesen may well have had both experiences, but only one can have been his initial speaking in tongues.

I have read three accounts of another experience of Bredesen's. In 1965 he was talking about religion to a young Egyptian woman, daughter of an Egyptologist who was a dealer in Egyptian antiquities, in the lobby of a New York hotel. He told her about tongues and, reassuring her that he would not embarrass her, volunteered to pray in tongues there and then. Bowing his head he prayed silently for a short time and then began to speak words unintelligible to him. The sounds were clipped and full of 'p's and 'k's. The young woman, who spoke several modern Arabian languages and had studied archaic

Arabic, was white with astonishment. She had understood him, and told him that he had praised God in a very old form of Arabic, quickly writing down about forty words in the strange dialect which Bredesen had used. She told him that he had pronounced the words perfectly without a trace of accent and that language scholars, even after years of study, could not speak that ancient tongue without a clumsy accent. 'You sound just like an old Bedouin saying his prayers on his prayer-rug,' she said.[3]

William E. Walmers, Professor of African languages, University of California at Los Angeles, comments on this:

> Farrell refers to a minister who claims to have witnessed to foreigners in their own languages. Polish is mentioned; fine, I hope he did. Also mentioned is Coptic Egyptian. The latter must have been in a spiritualistic séance, because there have been no native speakers of Coptic Egyptian for a good many years. I fear this is typical of the mistaken, although perhaps sincere, claims of modern glossolalics.[4]

(The reader may well feel that the transformation of 'a very old form of Arabic' into 'Coptic Egyptian' is 'typical of the mistaken, although perhaps sincere' misrepresentations by critics of what they are criticizing.)

There is another side to the story. This experience, which is not a decade old at the time of writing, seemed so capable of confirmation that I wrote to Sherrill and asked him for the name and address of the young Egyptian woman so that I could confirm the story from her. He suggested I wrote to Bredesen who replied, not with the name of the Egyptian, but with a copy of a letter from Abraham Vereide, founder of the Presidential Prayer Breakfast which a number of Presidents and other government leaders have attended. Vereide wrote,

> I am happy to say that I was one of three men who came on the scene while you were witnessing to an Egyptian. Though I do not speak in tongues myself, I do recognize the incident as a demonstration of the occurance [*sic*] of a known language in

the glossolalic phenomenon. The two men with me were Ernest Williams, a member of the Archbishop of Canterbury's Commission on Evangelism, and Christian Oftsdahl, a member of the Nobel Peace Prize Committee.

This is confirmation of a kind, but, legally, it is 'hearsay evidence' coming from a man who came on the scene towards the end of the experience, perhaps after the tongue had been spoken, and who presumably could not have recognized it as archaic Arabic even if he did hear it. One wonders why there is so much coyness about revealing who the Egyptian lady was, for so much is known about her that she can scarcely have been anonymous.

Bredesen in the correspondence with me mentioned a case confirmed by a Mrs Milke Na Pier which happened to him as he was laying hands on candidates at the Living Waters Tabernacle prayer group on 21 February 1970, on 'the very day your enquiry arrived'. Born in Montenegro, Mrs Na Pier spoke Serbian as a child. She wrote,

> As you [Bredesen] were praying in tongues over each person desiring the Baptism of the Holy Spirit, I began to discern words spoken in my native tongue. It was astonishing and distracting to my devotion and I promptly stopped praying to listen.
>
> You kept saying 'Sada Boze Daj' which in the Serbian-Croatian language, means 'Now, Lord, give!' Of course one must imply (sic) the command to refer to the Baptism of the Holy Spirit for which you were specifically praying.

A short phrase is not so evidential of a true language as a longer discourse, for it is open to the explanation that in any collection of glossolalic syllables which can be shown by analysis not to be a genuine language, there are bound to be some which belong to one of the tongues of the world. On the other hand, the repetition of the phrase is evidential.

It may be noted that Bredesen spoke Polish when a Pole was

close by, archaic Arabic to a girl knowledgeable of it, and Serbo-Croat when a Serbian-speaking woman was in his congregation. Mrs Na Pier herself could well have been praying in her own language, and a possible explanation is that of telepathic communication. There is no reason why a Christian sensitive should lose the psychic abilities he possesses because he is a Christian – Bredesen may well be a sensitive and may therefore have the faculty of 'receiving' his languages from those who speak them. This need make them none the less of God, for what he has received in two cases of the three is prayer and no information is given as to what he said when he spoke Polish.

Appendix 3
A Television Experience

Since this book was completed I have had an experience which, I believe, should be included as a commentary upon its contents.

In September, 1977, I received a letter from Dr William J. Samarin to the effect that he had given my name to the Italian Radio-Television Corporation, which was preparing a series of programmes on glossolalia. As a result of this I was asked to bring together three speakers in tongues for a programme to be recorded on 20 December. I invited Mr T. D. Morgan, whom I had met twice previously and whose tongues I had recorded and sent to Dr Samarin (his verdict was that they were pseudo-languages), and Mr Robert Nokes and Mrs Louise Smith, put into touch with me by members of the Society for Psychical Research. I had received cassettes of their tongues but had not met them. None of the three had met each other before; so, when we came together with Professor Paolo Fabbri of the University of Urbino and two or three of his technical colleagues on 19 December for a preliminary discussion about the programme and its contents, we had only the sketchiest knowledge of each other. We discussed for about a couple of hours in preparation for the recording on the 20th, Professor Fabbri, the only Italian who could speak English, taking notes from which to prepare questions and comments for the programme.

253

The recording was in four parts; first, an interview between Professor Fabbri and each tongue-speaker in turn; then a general discussion by the three together and myself, the object of which was to enlarge upon the philosophies held by each glossolalist and to clarify points raised in the separate interviews; next, a conversation between the three speakers, each talking in his or her own tongue or tongues; and, finally, an interview between Professor Fabbri and myself in which we discussed the theory of tongue-speaking and the recordings which had been made. There was also what might be described as an epilogue, when Mr Morgan sang twice in tongues.

The three speakers hold different philosophies. Mrs Smith is a healer whose tongues developed a year after she discovered her healing ability. She has no set creed and belongs to no church or organization. She wants her tongues to be used to bring happiness to the listeners and, as she phrases it, 'for the healing of the nations'. She is a down-to-earth Lancastrian with a happy and extrovert nature in spite of much distress in her life. Mr Nokes, also a healer, is a Spiritualist, with a quiet, reserved, sincere and attractive personality which later revealed considerable humour. Mr Morgan's philosophy is somewhat syncretistic and he would probably best be described as a Christian reincarnationist. He remains convinced, in spite of Dr Samarin's findings to the contrary, that his languages are tongues spoken by him in previous incarnations. His personality is a blend of the practical and the mystical, and if initiative was required at any point in the programme, he was able to provide it. As for me, I am a convinced though somewhat unorthodox Christian. In spite of the differences between us, we turned out to be a team; and I do not believe, had I had a thousand tongue-speakers to choose from and all the time in the world to choose them, that I could have found a happier combination. Perhaps this was a factor in the making of what we all felt was an exhilarating and valuable programme.

The individual speeches in tongues showed that *listening* to tapes provides only half of any communication that is made. One needs to see the speakers. For their personalities develop and their gestures change and, as men of different nationalities tend to use different types of gesture in communicating with their hands and bodies, so do glossolalists. Mr Nokes's personality, for example, became more forceful, that of a lecturer or demonstrator, and he used his hands vigorously to make his points in a manner quite unlike his normal behaviour. Mr Morgan became more mystical, reflecting aloud, as it were, with gentle, delicate gestures conveying an impression of a Buddhist philosophizing (I have never seen one, so this is an entirely subjective interpretation). The most remarkable communication was achieved by Mrs Smith. The other two speakers, an Italian girl and I were watching her in the viewing-room, and to all of us she communicated a feeling of joy which expressed itself for me as a bubble of delight rising from my solar plexus and bursting in laughter of happiness and pleasure. I tried while feeling this also to observe my three companions objectively and saw that they, too, were all laughing and obviously moved with the same pleasure that I was experiencing.

All three glossolalists spoke in tongues immediately they were asked to do so without the slightest hesitation and without any suggestion of trance or any altered state of consciousness.

More remarkable than the individual speeches was the conversation in tongues. Mr Morgan began the conversation after which, without hesitation and with complete spontaneity, it continued like an animated discussion between three old friends entirely at ease with each other. What was impressive were the changes in mood, now humorous (the camera crew, I was told, joining in the gaiety when Mr Nokes appeared to be cracking jokes about them and his surroundings), now serious and weighty, now purely conversational. There were marked changes of mood which the speakers picked up and responded to instantly – there was no looking from one to the other to see what was going to happen next, no awkward pause, no interruption or false start by two speakers beginning at the same moment and checking. The changes in mood came across clearly to the watchers in the viewing and control rooms. Each of the speakers spoke a variety of tongues and used different ones at different times.

The communication, however, remained in my opinion closer to that of music than of language. I was reminded of a trio of instrumentalists speaking to and replying to each other, the violin addressing the cello, the cello replying, the piano commenting on them both. Coleridge Taylor composed a once popular piece of music entitled 'Demande et Réponse', a phrase which exactly conveys what happened here.

Whether the tongues communicate mood in themselves or act as a vehicle for some kind of telepathic communication it is difficult to say. The feeling of joy inspired in me by Mrs Smith's tongue did not come through the sound of the language, which was not particularly joyful in itself and which had inspired no such feeling in me when I heard it on tape. It came across because she was communicating it in person. There is communication in language, but this sometimes hides the speaker's meaning and can be misunderstood. There is communication by music, but this is of a different kind. There can be communication in silence between people who are in close sympathy with one another. Some psychical researchers hold that there is telepathic communication. Perhaps tongues convey yet another kind of communication, partly musical, partly telepathic. This could account for the feeling that so many religious glossolalists have that they have genuinely prayed to or worshipped God in the Spirit and that He has answered their prayer or accepted their worship even when they have no idea of what has been communicated. The result is that they are at peace. Agnostic psychologists may feel that the peace comes from some release of tension in the subliminal mind brought about by the experience of glossolalia. I can record only that there was communication between a number of individuals on the occasion of this telecast and that the participants and observers were the happier for having experienced it.

Notes

1 Tongues in Non-Christian Cultures

1 J. Hastings (ed.), *Encyclopedia of Religion and Ethics,* Edinburgh, Clark, 1910, vol. III, p. 371.
2 Aristophanes, *The Frogs*, 1, 357.
3 E. R. Dodds, *Pagan and Christian in an Age of Anxiety*, Cambridge University Press, 1965, p. 55 (note).
4 Lines 235–44. Tn. F. Storr, *Sophocles*, Loeb Library, London, Heinemann; Cambridge, Mass., Harvard University Press, 1951, 25–7.
5 Herodotus, *History*, 8, 135.
6 Clement of Alexandria, *Miscellanies*, bk I, p. 443, quoted by J. L. Nevius, *Demon Possession*, New York, Revell, 1894, p. 192.
7 *Institutionis Oratoriae*, bk I, Section 35.
8 Dio Chrysostom, *Works*, Loeb Library, vol. I, London, Heinemann, and New York, Putnam, 1932, pp. 434–7.
9 Lucian, *Alexander the False Prophet*, Loeb Library, vol. IV, pp. 192–3.
10 Irenaeus, *Against Heresies*, Ante-Nicene Christian Library, Edinburgh, Clark, 1868, vol. V, p. 53.
11 L. Carlyle May, 'A Survey of Glossolalia and Related Phenomena in Non-Christian Religions', *American Anthropologist*, Washington, City of Washington Anthropological Society, LVIII, February 1956, pp. 75–96.
12 F. M. Davenport, *Primitive Traits in Religious Revivals*, London, Macmillan, 1905, p. 237.
13 T. K. Oesterreich, *Possession Demoniacal and Other*, London, Kegan Paul, 1930, pp. 359–60.
14 Van der Goltz, 'Zauberei und Hexenkunde in China', *Ges fur Natur und Volkerkunde Ostasiene*, vol. VI, 1893–7, pp. 17–19, 21.

257

15 J. Beattie and J. Middleton (eds), London, Routledge & Kegan Paul, 1969.
16 N. K. Chadwick, *Poetry and Prophecy*, Cambridge, 1942, pp. 37–38.
17 Oesterreich, op. cit. pp. 230–5, and T. M. Lewis, *Ecstatic Religion*, Harmondsworth, Penguin, 1971, *passim*.
18 E. Dermengham, *Muhammed and the Islamic Tradition*, New York, Harper, 1958, p. 168.

2 The First Whitsun

1 T. & K. Reilly, article on 'Tongues, Gift of', *Catholic Encyclopedia*, London, Caxton, and New York, Appleton, 1912, vol. XIV, pp. 776–7.
2 Acts 2:1–13.
3 Ibid. 2:33.
4 1:4.
5 2:2–3.
6 Verses 3–4.
7 Quoted by C. Clemens in an article, 'The "Speaking with Tongues" of the Early Christians', *Expository Times*, Edinburgh, May 1899, vol. 10, pp. 344–52.
8 Philo, *On the Decalogue*, Loeb Library, vol. VII, London, Heinemann, and Cambridge, Massachusetts, Harvard University Press, Sections 33–5.
9 St John's Gospel 3:8.

3 From Jerusalem to Corinth

1 I Thessalonians 5:19–22; II Thessalonians 2:2; II Corinthians 12:3–4; Colossians 3:16; Romans 8:26–7; Hebrews 6:4–5; Ephesians, 5:18–19; Acts 4:31; I John 4:1; St Mark's Gospel 16:17.
2 Acts 10:46.
3 Ibid. 11:15.
4 Ibid. 19:6.
5 I Corinthians 14:31.
6 Ibid. 12:3.

4 Tongues before the Reformation

1 The Reverend P. T. Weller, (tr. and ed.), *The Roman Ritual*, vol. II, Milwaukee, The Bruce Publishing Co, 1952, p. 169.
2 Quoted in article, 'Speaking with Tongues', *The New Schaff-Hertzog Encyclopedia of Religious Knowledge*, New York & London, Funk & Wagnalls, 1911, vol. XI, pp. 36ff.
3 The Rt Reverend Richard Laurence (tr.), London, Kegan Paul, Trench & Co., 1883, ch. 70, v. 14.

4 G. H. Box (tr.), London, S.P.C.K., and New York, Macmillan, 1918, ch. 17.

5 R. H. Charles (tr.), London, Adam & Charles Black, 1900, ch. 8, v. 17.

6 M. R. James, *Texts and Studies. Apocrypha Anecdotes* II, Cambridge University Press, 1893–97, ch. 28, pp. 104ff.

7 Quoted by the Reverend J. L. Nevius, *Demon Possession and Allied Themes*, Chicago, New York, Toronto, Revell, 1894, p. 193.

8 Lucian, *Works*, Loeb Library, vol. IV, London, Heinemann, and New York, Putnam, 1925, pp. 192–3.

9 Irenaeus, *Against Heresies*, V, ch. VI, 1, Ante-Nicene Christian Library, Edinburgh, Clark, 1868, vol. V, p. 68.

10 Epiphanius, *Historia Ecclesiae*, XVI, 7f.

11 Tertullian, *Against Marcion*, Book V, ch. VIII.

12 Tertullian, *Concerning the Soul*, ch. IX.

13 Origen, *Contra Celsum*, VII, ix.

14 Eusebius, *Ecclesiastical History*, V, 17.

15 H. Wace and P. Schaff (eds), *The Ecclesiastical History of Sozomen*, A Select Library of Nicene and Post-Nicene Fathers, Oxford, Parker, 1890–1900, New 2nd Series, vol. II, bk III, ch. 14. Gennadius, *Lives of Illustrious Men*, A Select Library of Nicene and Post-Nicene Fathers, Oxford, Parker, 1890–1900, vol. III, ch. VII, p. 387.

16 Gregory Nazianzen, *Oration 41, On Pentecost*, A Select Library of Nicene and Post-Nicene Fathers, Oxford, Parker, 1890–1900, New Series, vol. VII, p. 384.

17 Chrysostom, *Homily IV on Acts, 2, and XXIX on Paul to the Corinthians*, A Select Library of Nicene and Post-Nicene Fathers, Oxford, Parker, 1890–1900, First Series, vol. XII.

18 P. Schaff (ed.), Augustine, *De Civitate Dei*, Bk XVII, Sermo CCLXVII, and *De Verbis Apostolorum*, CLXXV, Sermo IX, New York, Christian Literature Co., 1887–92.

19 F. C. Conybeare, review of *Le Langage Martien*, *Hibbert Journal*, vol. I, 1902–3.

5 From the Reformation to 1800

1 Anon., *La Véritable Histoire des Diables de Loudon . . . par un Témoin* (des Niau), Poitiers, 1634; translated and edited by Edmund Goldsmid, London, 1887, pp. 27–8.

2 The Reverend M. T. Kelsey, *Tongue Speaking*, New York, Doubleday, 1964, pp. 27–8.

3 Souer, *History of the Christian Church*, vol. III, quoted by Kelsey, op. cit.

4 G. B. Cutten, *Speaking with Tongues*, New Haven, Yale University Press, and London, Oxford University Press, 1927, pp. 84–5.

5 Ibid., p. 59.
6 T. J. M. McCrossan, *Speaking with Other Tongues, Sign or Gift – Which?* Harrisburg, Pa, Christian Publications, n.d., p. 8.
7 F. M. Davenport, *Primitive Traits in Religious Revivals*, New York, Macmillan, 1905, p. 218.
8 E. D. Andrews, *The People Called Shakers*, New York, Oxford University Press, 1953, pp. 144–5.
9 D. R. Lamson, *Two Years Experience among the Shakers*, Lamson & Boyston, 1848, p. 80.
10 R. A. Knox, *Enthusiasm*, Oxford, Clarendon Press, 1950; quoting Dwight, *Travels*, 1783, p. 564.
11 E. D. Andrews, op. cit., pp. 144–5.
12 D. R. Lamson, op. cit., p. 80.

6 The Nineteenth Century

1 R. A. Knox, *Enthusiasm*, Oxford, Clarendon Press, 1950, pp. 553–4.
2 A. L. Drummond, *Edward Irving and His Circle*, London, Clarke, 1937, p. 160.
3 S. Hawthornthwaite, *Mr. Hawthornthwaite's Adventures Among the Mormons*, Manchester, the Author, 1857, pp. 92–3.
4 T. Brevior, *The Two Worlds. The Natural and the Spiritual*, London, Pitman, 1864, pp. 296–7.

7 Nineteenth-century Spiritualism

1 S. B. Brittan and B. W. Richmond, *A Discussion of the Facts and Philosophy of Ancient and Modern Spiritualism*, New York, Partridge and Brittan, 1853, p. 179.
2 Ibid., pp. 186–7.
3 Campbell Holms, *The Facts of Psychic Science and Philosophy*, London, Kegan Paul, 1925, p. 179.
4 E. Hardinge, *American Spirtualism*, New York, the Author, 1870, p. 425.
5 Judge Worth Edmonds, *Spiritual Tracts, No. 6*, quoted in, for example, Eugene Crowell, *Primitive Christianity and Modern Spiritualism*, New York, the Author, 1875, pp. 249–52.
6 Bozzano, *Polyglot Mediumship*, London, Rider, 1932, p. 15.
7 F. G. Fairfield, *Ten Years with Spirit Mediums*, New York, the Author. 1875, pp. 53–4.
8 G. B. Cutten, *Psychological Phenomena of Christianity*, London, Hodder & Stoughton, 1909, p. 56.
9 De Verne, *Annales des sciences psychiques*, June, 1907.
10 R. Warcollier, *Annales des sciences psychiques*, August, 1907.

11 Bozzano, op. cit., p. 16.
12 F. Podmore, *Modern Spiritualism*, London, Methuen, 1902, pp. 260–2.
13 E. Hardinge, op. cit., p. 16.
14 Campbell Holms, op. cit., pp. 219–20.
15 E. Hardinge, op. cit., p. 101.
16 N. B. Wolfe, *Startling Facts in Modern Spiritualism*, Cincinnati, 1874, pp. 247–8.
17 J. S. Farmer, *Twixt Two Worlds*, London, The Psychological Press, 1886, p. 48.
18 J. C. F. Zöllner, *Transcendental Physics*, London, Harrison, 1882, p. 36.
19 Ibid., p. 222.
20 Ibid., p. 230.
21 Campbell Holms, op. cit., p. 172.
22 Bozzano, op. cit., pp. 171–8.
23 Albert Le Baron, 'A Case of Psychic Automatism including "Speaking with Tongues"', London, *Proceedings of the Society for Psychical Research*, vol. XII, pp. 277ff.

8 The Twentieth Century: Christian Tongues

1 N. Bloch-Hoell, *The Pentecostal Movement*, Oslo, Bergen, Universitets-forlaget, 1964, p. 38, quoting S. H. Frodsham, *With Signs Following*, Springfield, Mo., Gospel Publishing House, 1946.
2 St John's Gospel 3:8.
3 J. L. Sherrill, *They Speak with Other Tongues*, London, Hodder & Stoughton, 1965, pp. 41–2.
4 Ibid., pp. 98–100.
5 G. B. Cutten, *Speaking with Tongues*, New Haven, Yale University Press, 1927, p. 121.
6 A. Kempmeier, 'Recent Parallels to the Miracle of Pentecost', *Open Court*, 22, 1908, p. 492.
7 D. J. Bennett, 'Pentecost; When Episcopalians Start Speaking in Tongues', *The Living Church*, vol. 142, no. 1, 1 Jan. 1961, p. 12.

9 Tongues in Twentieth-century Spiritualism

1 June, 1905, pp. 318–53. More available to English readers is the identical account in the *Proceedings of the Society for Psychical Research*, vol. XIX, 1905–7, pp. 80ff.
2 *Proceedings of the Society for Psychical Research*, vol. XIX, 1905–7, pp. 201–3.
3 Ibid., p. 240.
4 Ibid., pp. 253ff.

5 Bozzano, *Polyglot Mediumship*, London, Rider, 1932, pp. 24–6.

6 Vol. XVIII, 1901–3, pp. 82ff.

7 Ibid., vol. IX, pp. 124–7; quoting *The Holy Truth*, pp. 64–7.

8 Quoted by Bozzano, op. cit., pp. 64–7.

9 Ibid., pp. 67–70.

10 Ibid., pp. 35–8.

11 Ibid., pp. 134–6, quoting Usborne Moore, *The Voices*, London, Watts, 1913, pp. 3–8.

12 Bozzano, *Polyglot Mediumship*, London, Rider, 1932, pp. 67–70.

13 W. F. Prince, *The Case of Patience Worth*, New York, University Books, 1964, p. 210.

14 Campbell Holms, *The Facts of Psychic Science and Philosophy*, London, Kegan Paul, 1925, p. 146.

15 Bozzano, op. cit., pp. 140–1; quoting H. D. Bradley, *Towards the Stars*, London, T. Werner Laurie, 1924, p. 210.

16 H. D. Bradley, *Towards the Stars*, London, T. Werner Laurie, 1924, pp. 32–3.

17 Bozzano, op. cit., pp. 139–40.

18 Bradley, op. cit., pp. 32–3.

19 N. Whymant, *Psychic Adventures in New York*, London, Morley & Mitchell Kennerley, 1931.

20 Bozzano, op. cit., pp. 39–44.

21 L. Fairfield, 'Thérèse Neumann', *Journal of the Society for Psychical Research*, vol. 39, 1957–8, pp. 164–73.

22 F. H. Wood, *This Egyptian Miracle*, London, Rider, 1955 (2nd edn), p. 19.

23 Ibid., pp. 170–1.

24 Ibid., p. 181.

25 Ibid., p. 182. For Dr Wood's other books, see Bibliography.

26 I. Stevenson, *Xenoglossy*, The University Press of Virginia and Bristol, John Wright & Sons, 1974.

27 M. Manning, *The Link*, Colin Smythe, Gerrards Cross, 1974; Corgi (paperback), 1975.

10 The Charismatic Movement

1 Fountain Trust leaflet.

2 W. J. Hollenweger, 'Charismatic Movements Today', article in *Faith and Freedom*, vol. 30, part 2, Spring 1977, p. 95.

3 Ibid., p. 96.

4 Isaiah 11:9 (A.V.).

11 **Psychological and Medical Glossolalia**

1 A. Moll, *Hypnotism*, Walter Scott, London, 1890, p. 126.

2 J. Abercrombie, *Inquiries Concerning the Intellectual Powers and the Investigation of Truth*, London, John Murray, 1838 (9th edn), p. 141.

3 Ibid., p. 155.

4 Ibid., p. 142.

5 Ibid., pp. 141–2.

6 Ibid., p. 144.

7 Ibid., p. 142.

8 Ibid., p. 142.

9 H. Freeborn and C. A. Mercier, 'Temporary Reminiscence of a Long-forgotten Language during Delirium', *Journal of the Society for Psychical Research* and *The Lancet*, 1902, pp. 279–83.

10 Abercrombie, op. cit., p. 143.

11 F. W. H. Myers, *Human Personality and the Survival of Bodily Death*, London, Longmans, Green, reprinted 1939, vol. I, pp. 305–6.

12 T. K. Oesterreich, *Possession Demoniacal and Other*, London, Kegan Paul, 1930, p. 367.

13 Abercrombie, op. cit., p. 304.

14 Everyman Edition, London, Dent, pp. 58–60.

15 G. A. Coe, *The Psychology of Religion*, University of Chicago Press, 1925, (7th edn), pp. 203–4.

16 A. D. White, *Warfare of Science with Theology, in Christendom*, New York, Appleton, 1896, vol. 2, pp. 160–1.

17 W. A. Hammond, *Spiritualism and Allied Causes and Conditions of Nervous Derangement*, London, H. K. Lewis, and New York, Putnam, 1876, pp. 292–3.

18 'A Divided Self', in *Journal of Abnormal Psychology*, 1919, pp. 281–5.

19 F. W. H. Myers, op. cit., pp. 53–4.

20 A. Maeder, 'La Langue d'un aliéné, analyse d'un cas de glossolalie', *Archives de psychologie*, March, 1910.

21 'Automatic Phenomena in a Case of Hysteria', *Journal of the Society for Psychical Research*, vol. IX, 1899–1900, S.P.R., London, pp. 333–9.

22 L. Hahn, 'Phénomènes remarquables observés dans un cas d'hystérie', *Annales des science psychiques*, 1901, pp. 148–59.

12 **Debate and Discussion: Christian Tongues I**

1 Humbert Wolfe, *Requiem* (dedicatory poem), London, Benn, 1927.

2 J. J. M. McCrossan, *Speaking with Other Tongues: Sign or Gift*, quoted by G. Jeffreys, *Pentecostal Rays*, London and Worthing, Henry E. Walter, 1954 (2nd edn), pp. 98–9.

3 *Apology for the Gift of Tongues*, Greenock, W. Johnston, 1831, pp. 6–9, 12.

4 Ibid., p. 13.

5 *Mysterious Psychic Forces*, Boston, 1907, p. 57.

6 'The Gift of Tongues and Related Phenomena at the Present Day', *The American Journal of Theology*, vol. XII, no. 2, April 1909.

7 Quoted by G. B. Cutten, *Speaking with Tongues*, New Haven, Yale University Press, pp. 178–9.

8 N. Block-Hoell, *The Pentecostal Movement*, Oslo, Universitetsforlaget, 1964, p. 144.

9 J. L. Sherrill, *They Speak with Other Tongues*, London, Hodder & Stoughton, 1965, ch. 9.

10 W. E. Welmers, correspondence following an article by F. Farrell, 'Outburst of Tongues: The New Pentecostalism', *Christianity Today*, vol. VII, no. 24, 13 Sept. 1963.

11 Bloch-Hoell, op. cit., p. 226, note.

12 Ibid., p. 145. The grammar is J. Philgaard, *Selikum saj sih, tungotal med uttydningar*, 1916.

13 Quoted by G. S. Hall, *Jesus in the Light of Psychology*, London, G. Allen & Unwin, 1921, vol. II, p. 690, from Pfister, *Die Psychologische Enträtselung Der Relig. Glossolalie.*

14 Sherrill, op. cit., p. 113.

15 See Bibliography.

16 W. J. Samarin, 'The Linguisticality of Glossolalia', *The Hartford Quarterly*, vol. 8 (4), p. 55.

17 Ibid., p. 53.

18 W. J. Samarin, 'The Forms and Functions of Nonsense Language', *Linguistics*, no. 50, The Hague, Mouton, July 1969, p. 73.

19 'The Linguisticality of Glossolalia', p. 68.

20 W. J. Samarin, 'Glossolalia as Learned Behaviour', *Canadian Journal of Theology*, no. 15, 1969, p. 60.

21 'The Linguisticality of Glossolalia', p. 54.

22 Ibid., p. 56.

23 Ibid., p. 55.

24 Ibid., pp. 54–5.

25 J. R. Jaquith, 'Toward a Typology of Formal Communicative Behaviour', *Anthropological Linguistics*, vol. 9, no. 8, Nov. 1967, p. 6.

26 Ibid., p. 2.

27 E. Lombard, *De La Glossolalie chez les premiers chrètiens et des phénomènes similaires*, Lausanne, Bridel, 1910, p. 177.

28 'The Linguisticality of Glossolalia', p. 57.

29 W. J. Samarin, 'Glossolalia as Regressive Speech', paper given at the

summer meeting of the Linguistic Society of America, Columbus, Ohio, 1970.

30 'Glossolalia as Regressive Speech'. Paper given at the summer meeting of the Linguistic Society of America, Columbus, Ohio, July, 1970.

31 'The Linguisticality of Glossolalia', p. 52.

32 'Glossolalia as Regressive Speech', p. 13.

33 Glossolalia as Learned Behaviour', pp. 61, 64.

34 Jaquith, op. cit., p. 6.

35 'The Linguisticality of Glossolalia', p. 60.

36 'Glossolalia as Learned Behaviour', p. 62.

37 Ibid., p. 62–3.

38 'Glossolalia as Regressive Speech', p. 2.

39 Ibid., p. 16.

40 Ibid., p. 13.

41 Donald Gee, *The Pentecostal Movement, Including the Story of the War Years 1940–7*, London, Elim Publishing Co., 1949, p. 15.

42 G. B. Cutten, op. cit., pp. 127–8.

43 Ibid., p. 126.

44 E. B. Tyler, *Primitive Culture*, London, John Murray, 1929, vol. I, p. 156.

13 Debate and Discussion: Christian Tongues II

1 G. B. Cutten, *Speaking with Tongues*, New Haven, Yale University Press, 1927, p. 129.

2 St Matthew's Gospel 3:11 (AV).

3 A. A. Hoekema, *What About Tongue Speaking?* London, Paternoster Press, 1966, pp. 53–4.

4 C. Brumbach, *What Meaneth This?* London, Elim Publishing Co., 1949, p. 66.

5 Acts 10:46 (AV).

6 Ibid., 19:6.

7 Ibid., 19:2.

8 Brumbach, op. cit., p. 266.

9 Cutten, op. cit., p. 183, quoting Lombard.

10 N. Bloch-Hoell, *The Pentecostal Movement*, Oslo, Bergen, Universitetsforlaget, 1964, p. 146.

11 W. J. Macmillan, *The Reluctant Healer*, London, Gollancz, 1952, pp. 134–5.

12 J. L. Sherrill, *They Speak with Other Tongues*, London, Hodder & Stoughton, 1965, ch. 8.

13 Block-Hoell, op. cit., p. 146.

14 D. Gee, *Concerning Spiritual Gifts*, Springfield, Mo., Gospel Publishing House, 1947, pp. 37, 94.

15 From an African student's essay on church music, told me by the Rt Reverend J. V. Taylor, Bishop of Winchester, formerly General Secretary of the CMS.

14 Debate and Discussion: The Psychology and Effects of Tongues

1 M. Lewis, *Ecstatic Religion*, Harmondsworth, Penguin Books, 1971, p. 186.
2 H. M. Yaker, in a letter re F. Farrell's article, 'Outburst of Tongues: The New Pentecostalism', *Christianity Today*, vol. VII, no. 24, 13 Sept 1963.
3 William James, *Varieties of Religious Experience*, London, Longmans Green, 1902, pp. 250–1.
4 Elmer T. Clark, *The Small Sects in America*, New York, Abingdon-Cokesbury Press, 1937 (revised edn), p. 53.
5 Quoted by M. T. Kelsey, *Tongue Speaking*, New York, Doubleday, 1964, p. 206.
6 W. E. Welmers in a letter re F. Farrell's article 'Outburst of Tongues: The New Pentecostalism', *Christianity Today*, vol. VII, no. 24, 13 Sept. 1963.
7 G. A. Coe, *The Psychology of Religion*, Chicago (7th edn), pp. 202–3.
8 A. L. Drummond, *Edward Irving and His Circle*, London, Clarke, 1937, pp. 268–70.
9 *Varieties of Religious Experience*, p. 478.
10 *The Holy Spirit in Faith and Experience*, London, S.C.M. Press, 1917, p. 49.
11 Quoted by Victor White, O.P., *God and the Unconscious*, New York, The World Publishing Co. (Meridian Books), 1961, pp. 248–9.
12 C. G. Jung, *Collected Works*, vol. 12, New York, Pantheon Books, Bollinger Foundation, p. 132.
13 M. T. Kelsey, op. cit., pp. 221–2.
14 C. G. Jung, *A Psychological Approach to the Trinity*, 1948, quoted by Kelsey, op. cit., pp. 198–9.
15 L. L. Whyte, *The Unconscious Before Freud*, New York, Basic Books, 1960, p. 120.
16 Kelsey, op. cit., p. 213–14, quoting *Signs and Wonders in Rabbath-Amman*, Milwaukee, Word and Witness Publishing Co., 1934.
17 Ibid., p. 216.
18 Ibid., p. 217.
19 Ibid., p. 197.
20 E.g. Kelsey, Hoekema, Farrell, Samarin.
21 Quoted by F. Farrell, 'Outburst of Tongues: the New Pentecostalism', article in *Christianity Today*, vol. VII, no. 24, 13 September 1963.
22 I Corinthians 14:18 (A.V.).

23 Kelsey, op. cit., p. 13.
24 J. B. Pratt, *The Religious Consciousness*, New York, Macmillan, 1920, p. 19.
25 Kelsey, op. cit., p. 222.
26 J. B. Pratt, *The Psychology of Religious Belief*, New York, Macmillan, 1907, pp. 221–2.
27 A. A. Hoekema, *What About Tongue Speaking?* London, Paternoster Press, 1966, pp. 134–5.
28 James, op. cit., pp. 250–1.
29 J. L. Sherrill, *They Speak With Other Tongues*, London, Hodder & Stoughton, 1965, p. 149.
30 P. B. Shelley, *Posthumous Poems, 1824*, 'To——'.
31 Quoted by C. Brumbach, *What Meaneth This?* London, Elim Publishing Co., 1949, p. 85.
32 J. L. Sherrill, op. cit., p. 88.
33 Ibid., pp. 93–4.
34 Ibid., pp. 74–7.
35 J. B. Pratt, *Religious Consciousness*, p. 316.
36 Brumbach, op. cit., p. 297.
37 I Corinthians 14:22.
38 *Concerning Spiritual Gifts*, Springfield, Mo., Gospel Publishing House, 1937, rev. edn., pp. 62f, quoted by N. Bloch-Hoell, *The Pentecostal Movement*, Oslo, Bergen, Universitetsforlaget, 1964, p. 142.
39 Kelsey, op. cit., pp. 142–3.
40 Quoted in Kelsey, op. cit., p. 147.
41 Kelsey, op. cit., p. 148.
42 Brumbach, op. cit., ch. 17.
42 St John's Gospel, 4:48.
44 St Matthew's Gospel 12:39.
45 Brumbach, op. cit., ch. 7.
46 Ibid.
47 I Corinthians 14:6–24.
48 J. Earle, *Microcosmography*, Bristol, W. Crofton Hemmons, and London, Simpkin, Marshall, Hamilton, Kent & Co., 1897 (reprint of 1811 edn), p. 88.
49 Micah 6:8.
50 St Matthew's Gospel 7:20.

15 Debate and Discussion: Spiritualist Tongues

1 E. Bozzano, *Polyglot Mediumship*, London, Rider, 1932, pp. 185–6.
2 Quoted by W. McDougall, *The Group Mind*, Cambridge, 1921, p. 30.

3 F. H. W. Myers, *Human Personality*, London, New York and Bombay, Longmans Green, 1903, vol. I, pp. 70ff.
4 W. F. Prince, *The Case of Patience Worth*, Boston, Boston Society for Psychical Research, 1927; New York, University Books, 1964, p. 65.
5 Bozzano, op. cit., p. 80.
6 Ibid.
7 F. H. Wood, *After Thirty Centuries*, London, Rider, 1935, p. 79.
8 J. Stearn, *The Second Life of Susan Garnier*, London, Leslie Frewin, 1969, p. 14.
9 Ibid., pp. 18-19.
10 Ibid., pp. 20-1.
11 From the hymn, 'Lead Kindly Light', by Cardinal Newman..
12 F. H. Wood, *Ancient Egypt Speaks*, London, Rider, 1937, pp. 99-100.
13 An alleged saying of Sir Thomas Wootton, an ambassador in the reign of Queen Elizabeth I.

Appendix 1 Cases with Unusual Features

1 N. Bloch-Hoell, *The Pentecostal Movement*, London, Oslo, Bergen Universtetsforlaget, 1964, pp. 43-4.
2 M. T. Kelsey, *Tongue Speaking*, New York, Doubleday, 1964, pp. 153-7.
3 J. L. Sherrill, *They Speak With Other Tongues*, London, Hodder & Stoughton, 1965, ch. 9.
4 Ibid., ch. 9.
5 A. L. Drummond, *Edward Irving and His Circle*, London, Clarke, 1937, p. 291; quoting Bushnell, *Nature and the Supernatural*, Edinburgh, Strahan, 1862, p. 376.

Appendix 2 Development of a Tradition

1 M. T. Kelsey, *Tongue Speaking*, New York, Doubleday, 1964, pp. 111-12.
2 J. L. Sherrill, *They Speak With Other Tongues*, London, Hodder & Stoughton, 1965, pp. 13-14.
3 Ibid., pp. 14-15.
4 W. E. Walmers, in a letter re F. Farrell's article, 'Outburst of Tongues: The New Pentecostalism', *Christianity Today*, vol. VII, no. 24, 13 Sept. 1963.

Select Bibliography

(Note: A comprehensive study of glossolalia needs to cull information, often in small details found in a mass of irrelevant information, from literally hundreds of books and articles in the fields of theology, parapsychology, psychical research, anthropology and linguistics. The following list of books, most of which themselves contain bibliographies, together with publications referred to in the notes in this volume, should carry the interested reader as far as he wants to go.)

Baird, A. T., *One Hundred Cases of Survival after Death*, London, Werner Laurie, 1943.

Baxter, R., *Extracts from a Narrative of Facts Characterizing the Supernatural Manifestation in . . . Mr. Irving's congregation*, London, T. P. Dixon, 1833.

Beattie, J. and Middleton, J. (eds), *Spirit Mediumship and Society in Africa*, London, Routledge & Kegan Paul, 1969.

Bloch-Hoell, N., *The Pentecostal Movement: Its origin, development and distinctive character*, Oslo and Bergen, Universitetsforlaget, 1964.

Bozzano, E., *Polyglot Mediumship*, London, Rider, 1932.

Bradley, H. D., *The Wisdom of the Gods*, London, Werner Laurie, 1925.

Britten, E. H. (sometimes catalogued under Hardinge, E.), *Modern American Spiritualism*, New York, the author, 1870.

Cutten, G. B., *Speaking with Tongues: Historically and Psychologically Considered*, New Haven, Yale University Press, 1927.

Davenport, F. M., *Primitive Traits in Religious Revivals*, London, Macmillan, 1905.

Drummond, A. L., *Edward Irving and His Circle*, London, Clarke, 1937.

269

Select Bibliography

Edmonds, J. W., *Letters and Tracts on Spiritualism*, London, the author, 1875.

Frodsham, S. H., *With Signs Following*, Springfield, Missouri, Gospel Publishing House, rev. edn, 1946.

Gee, D., *The Pentecostal Movement, Including the Story of the War Years, 1940–47*, London, Elim Publishing Co., 1949.

Hoekema, A. A., *What About Tongue Speaking?* London, Paternoster Press, 1966.

Kelsey, M. T., *Tongue Speaking. An Experiment in Spiritual Experience*, New York, Doubleday, 1964.

Knox, R. A., *Enthusiasm*, Oxford, Clarendon Press, 1950.

Litvag, I., *Singer in the Shadows*, New York, Popular Library, 1972.

Lombard, E., *De la Glossolalie chez les premiers chrétiens et des phénomènes similaires*, Lausanne, Bridel, 1910.

May, L. Carlyle, 'A Survey of Glossolalia and Related Phenomena in non-Christian Religions', Washington, City of Washington Anthropological Society, *American Anthropologist*, Feb. 1956.

Oesterreich, T. K., *Possession, Demoniacal and Other*, London, Kegan Paul, 1930.

Prince, W. F., *The Case of Patience Worth*, New York, University Books, 1964.

de Reuter (or von Reuter), F., *Psychical Experiences of a Musician*, London, Simpkin Marshall, 1928.

Samarin, W. J., 'The Linguisticality of Glossolalia', Connecticut, Hartford Seminary Foundation, *The Hartford Quarterly*, vol. VIII, no. 4, 1968.

Samarin, W. J., 'The Forms and Functions of Nonsense Language', The Hague, Mouton, *Linguistics*, no. 50, July 1969.

Samarin, W. J., 'Glossolalia as Learned Behaviour', *Canadian Journal of Theology*, no. 15, 1969.

Samarin, W. J., 'Glossolalia as Regressive Speech', paper given at the summer meeting of the Linguistic Society of America, Columbus, Ohio, 1970.

Samarin, W. J., *Tongues of Men and Angels*, New York, Macmillan; London, Collier-Macmillan, 1972.

Sherrill, J. L., *They Speak with Other Tongues*, London, Hodder & Stoughton, 1965.

Whymant, A. N. J., *Psychic Adventures in New York*, London, Morley & Mitchell Kennerley, 1931.

Wood, F. H., *After Thirty Centuries*, London, Rider, 1935.

Wood, F. H., *Ancient Egypt Speaks*, London, Rider, 1937.

Wood, F. H., *This Egyptian Miracle*, London, Rider (2nd edn), 1955.

Index

Index

Index

Index

Hydesville, 68
Hymn to Apollo, 2
Hypnosis, 112, 158, 162–3, 201, 234, 236–7, 242

Identical minds, 234
Ideograms, 56
Individual subconscious, 235
Inge, Dean, 207
'Inspirational speakers', 193
International Church of the Foursquare Gospel, 104
International Pentecostalist Conference, 102
Interpretation of tongues *see under* Tongues
Irenaeus, 3, 35
Irving, Edward, 55–9, 91, 205, 220
Irvingites, 54, 91, 167
Isaiah, 1, 169, 186
Islam, 12
Italian Radio-Television Corporation, 253

Jacob, 62
James, Epistle of St, 187
James, William, 206, 218, 235
Jansen, Cornelius, 44
Jansenists, 45
Jean of St Francis, 43
Jeanne (Camisard), 48
Jeanne of the Cross, 43
Jeffries, Pastor George, 103
'Jensen Jacoby', 137, 181, 237
Jerusalem, 14–23
Jesuits, 44, 143
Jesus Christ, 1, 16, 17, 18, 19, 23, 31, 35, 45, 54, 100, 124, 142
'Jesus-prayer', 46
Joel, 186–7
John the Baptist, St, 187
Johnson, Miss Alice, 112–13
Journal of the Society for Psychical

Research, 135, 159
Jung, C. G., 155, 208–14 *passim*, 235
Jürgenson, Friedrich, 135–7
Justin Martyr, 35

Kara Kala, 65
Kelsey, Reverend Morton T., 106, 149, 211, 213, 222, 245, 248
Keswick Convention, 92
Kifioti tribe, 244
Kleeberg, Herr, 79
Knox, Monsignor Ronald, 56
Kurt, Christian, 148

Lacey, John, 50, 51, 56
Laing, George, 138
Languages, of animals, 4; of divinity, 185; of spirits, 4, 140; sacerdotal, 4, 11; *see also* Tongues
La Réalite des esprits et le phénomène merveilleux de leur écriture directe, 71
Latourette, James, 91
Latter Rain Movement, 92
Le Baron, Albert, 86–90, 176
Lee, Ann, 51–2, 54
Lee, William, 52
Lexa, Professor, 133
Light, 116, 117, 118, 136
Link, The, 138
'Little Prophets of the Cevennes, The', 48
Living Church, The, 106
Lodge, Sir Oliver, 112
London Christian, The, 66
Loudun, 43–4
Lourdes, 62
Lordelot, Mademoiselle, 45
Lucian, 3, 35
Lücken, widow, 46
Lucretius, 3

Index

Index

materialization of, 69, 141;
possession by, 1–13 *passim*, 52,
138, 164, 231, 237
Spiritual Telegraph, The, 78
Spiritual Tracts, 72
Spiritualism, 70, 152, 229, 238
Spiritualist tongues, 68–90,
109–41; theories of, 230–1; view
of, 165–6
Spurlings, 92, 100
Stearn, J., 237
Stephen, St, 43, 211
Stevens, F., 78
Stevenson, Dr Ian, 137–8, 181, 237
Stoic thought, 3
*Story of a Case of Hysteria with
Spontaneous Somnambulism,
The*, 159
Subconscious mind, 21, 23, 25, 71,
83, 84–5, 167, 231, 234, 241;
theories of the, 207, 235
Subliminal *see* Subconscious
Sufi, 10
Sunderland Conventions, 94, 98,
99, 100
Superconsciousness, 234, 235
Surrey Demoniack, The, 47

Telepathy, 23, 52, 71, 75, 127,
230, 233, 241, 252, 256
Telesthesia, 241
Telika Venturi, 129
Tenney, Dr, 212
Tenth Discourse on Servants, 3
Tertullian, 36
Testament of Job, The, 35
Thévenet, widow, 45
Thompson, Mrs, 113, 238–9
Tomlinson, A. J., 100
Tongues: of angels, 28, 30, 39; and
Bible study, 218–9, and devil-
possession, 222; and frustration,
224; as least of gifts, 226; and

ignorance, 220; interpretation
of, 5, 31, 32, 175, 176, 193–7,
247; and love, 218; materialist
view of, 164–6; as music, 256;
and power for God, 219; and
praise of God, 220; and pride,
223; and spiritual maturity, 224
Tonnenson, Clifford, 246
Topeka, 92–3, 100
Tribal glossolalia *see under*
Glossolalia
*True and Faithful Relation of What
Passed for Many Years between
Dr. John Dee and Some Spirits,
A*, 63
Truter, Maggie, 100
Tugwell, Simon, 151, 152
Twigg, Mrs Ena, 139
Tyler, 183

Ultramartian language, 84
Unconscious, collective, 208–10,
234, 235; personal, 208
Ungern-Sternberg, Madame d', 84
United Society of Believers in
Christ's Second Appearing
(Shakers), 51
Unknown Tongue, The, 38
*Unknown Tongues, Discovered to
be English, Spanish and Latin,
The*, 58
Uranian language, 84

Valiantine, George, 122, 123, 239
Vango, Mrs, 117, 118
Ventriloquism, 63
Vereide, Abraham, 250
Verne, De, 74
Verrall, Mrs, 112
Victory of the Cross, 100
Vincent, Isabel, 47
Visual phenomena, 186, 200
Vivier, Dr Van Eetveldt, 212

279

Index